PLACE NAMES of the OUTER BANKS

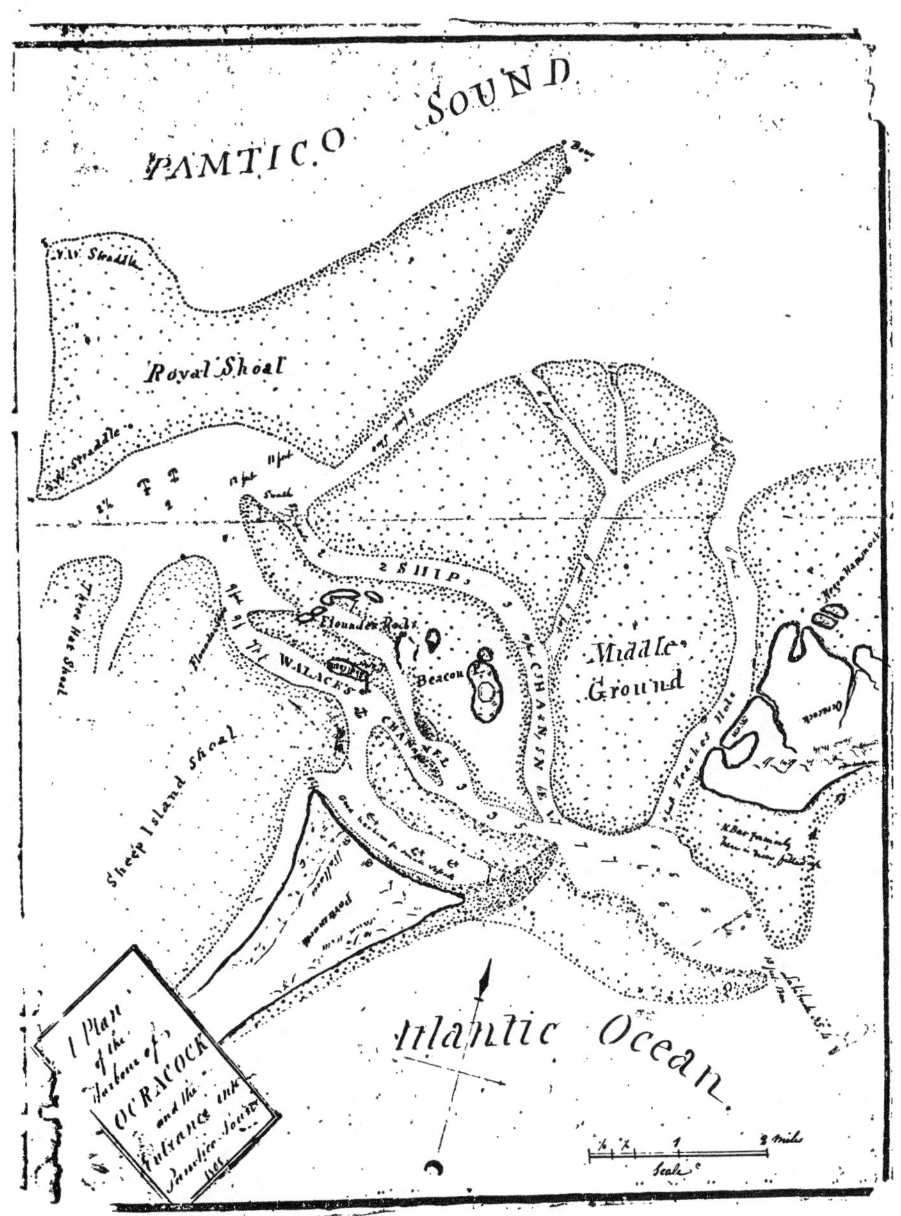
PAMTICO SOUND
Royal Shoal
Middle Ground
SHIP CHANNEL
WALACE'S CHANNEL
Flounder Rocks
Beacon
Sheep Island Shoal
Teaches Hole
Atlantic Ocean
Scale
Plan of the
OCRACOCK
and the

PLACE NAMES of the OUTER BANKS

by Roger L. Payne

with illustrations by
Ronald A. Crowson

For James Berry
with regards
Roger L. Payne

Thomas A. Williams, *Publisher*
Washington, North Carolina

LC 84-052496
ISBN 0-932707-01-4

This book is dedicated to
Irvin L. Payne,
my father,
who first introduced me to the Outer Banks
and
to the memory of
Gladys Binkley Payne,
my mother.

Acknowledgements

A study of geographic place names requires assistance from many and varied people. First and foremost are those people who have spent much time answering questions about specific location and name origins. Fortunately, "Bankers" are congenial people and take great pride in the Outer Banks, which has made field work a good deal easier. It is with the deepest appreciation that I extend thanks to all those (too numerous to name) who assisted me in this study by agreeing to interviews and spending time answering questions.

I especially appreciate the work of Ronald A. Crowson, who compiled the maps and drawings for the publication. He also provided suggestions and guidance where needed, and his expertise is greatly appreciated.

My deep thanks too, to Carolyn M. Asby, who typed the entire manuscript, edited as she typed, and altered the format several times to accomodate changes. I relied heavily on her patience and perseverence.

A special recognition and appreciation is extended to Sally, my wife, and Jennifer, my daughter, for their constructive comments and their patience.

Roger L. Payne

Contents

Introduction 12
Place Names 12
Outer Banks Defined 13
Sounds and Inlets 14
Indian Names 16
User's Guide 17
Glossary 20
Place Names of the Outer Banks 25

List of Tables

Table 1 List of U.S. Geological Survey Topographic maps 22
Table 2 A Listing of Townships by County 23
Table 3 Grouping of Names on the Outer Banks According to Type of Name 23

Illustrations

1807 Chart of Ocracoke Inlet ..... Frontispiece
Ashbee Harbor 26
Bodie Island 39
Burnside Headquarters 44
Cape Kenrick and Wimble Shoals 48
Crab Claw Spit 62
Diamond Shoals 68
Dunes of Dare 74
Etheridges Point and Blockade Shoal 77
Location of Existing and Historic Inlets 101
Present Towns and Villages of the Outer Banks 102
Historical Villages of the Outer Banks 103
Topographic Maps of the Outer Banks 104
No Ache and Pains Bay 134
Roanoke Marshes 160
Shallowbag Bay and Ballast Point 170
Teaches Hole and Teaches Hole Channel 181
Vera Cruz Shoal 189

Preface

WORK ON THIS VOLUME BEGAN SOME YEARS AGO WITH MY first trip to the Outer Banks. While waiting for the ferry at Oregon Inlet (before the bridge), I asked my Dad "why is this inlet called Oregon Inlet?" He hesitated, thought for a while, and responded, "That's a good question." It seemed a very unlikely name to be located on the Outer Banks of North Carolina. After all, what does Oregon have to do with North Carolina? Thus began my interest in geographic names of the Outer Banks and in geographic names in general. On this trip and subsequent ones, I began to keep records of unusual names on the Outer Banks. Later, while attending East Carolina University, I continued my interest in the Outer Banks and its place names.

About five years ago I began to organize my accumulated notes and began a serious systematic study of the place names of the Outer Banks. The work was done sporadically, in my spare time, until about two years ago when I decided to publish the results of my efforts. Since that time, a concerted effort toward this book has been made.

I hope that those interested in names and name origins find this work as interesting, informative and enjoyable to read as I did to compile. The study of Outer Banks place names is dynamic and should be expanded and updated periodically. The process is continuous and any name contributions will be appreciated and researched accordingly. Please direct all suggestions, questions, and other reference materials to Roger L. Payne, P.O. Box 3356, Reston, Virginia 22090.

Roger L. Payne
Fairfax County, Virginia
1984

Introduction

THE OUTER BANKS OF NORTH CAROLINA HAVE BEEN studied by researchers in almost every discipline. There are books on Outer Banks history, geography, geology, land use, and folklore, but a toponymic study - the study of place names - has been lacking. Incomplete or highly localized lists have appeared in magazines, but until now there has been no complete, systematic study of the named features of the Outer Banks.

Place Names

Originally, the term "place names" referred only to populated places such as cities, towns, villages, etc., while "geographical names" or "feature names" was used for physical features. Today the use of place names has expanded to include all named features, and that is the way I use it in this book.

Place names are "the language of maps" because they convey images of features and define specific locations. To test the importance of place names, try to use a map without any names, try to give directions without using a place name, or try to change the established name of a feature. Place names are landmarks in the development of our "sense of place" or our identification with a place which seems to be important in our overall development. A sense of place represents one's emotional identification with a mentally defined area, including the physical landmarks and the names of places within this area. Place names then become the means by which one describes the landscape. Generally, place names refer to specific places and convey information about how people categorize phenomena. A study of place names provides insight into how people view their environment. Local usage of a proper name for a feature generally establishes it as a reference.

Place names by nature are proper names that usually are made up of two parts. The first part is specific and relates the portion of the place name bestowed by the person naming the feature. The second part represents the type or category of feature and is referred to as the generic. This part is more general and establishes the kind of feature. It may have the same attributes or elements of meaning over a wide range, or the generic may be highly localized. For example, in the name Ashbee Harbor, Ashbee is the specific part and refers to a family name, while Harbor is the generic part and, in this case, describes an activity as well as conjuring a mental image or a perception of the feature being described. Also, the attributes of the generic "harbor" are likely to be similar throughout the United States. However, the use of the generic "hill' on the Outer Banks expresses different attributes and images from the use of the same generic in the North Carolina mountains. In a similar manner, the use of the generic "creek" on the Outer Banks usually retains the original English meaning of a small tidal inlet or cove, while in the mountains of North Carolina the word "creek" denotes a swift flowing stream.

The use of generics, then, may be somewhat universal, localized, or represent any range in between. For example, a large group of names on the Outer Banks is indicative of the former practice of grazing animals on the Banks. For conservation reasons, all grazing had been stopped by the early 1950s, but names such as Horsepen Point and Sheep Pen Point indicate the long history of livestock grazing. Another group of names represents communities and former communities. Some of the community names were of Indian origin and were difficult to pronounce and others were duplicated on the mainland. Since the Post office Department required unique names that were not confusing when post offices were established, the Post Office Department did not accept the existing community name but assigned, in many cases, an arbitrary name for postal use. After a short time it was only natural that the community idenified with the post office name. The original community name usually fell into disuse. Unfortunately, there are few postal records from the late nineteenth century and the reason for the choice of many of the names, such as Rodanthe, Buxton and Corolla, is unknown.

Place names are important for a variety of reasons, including environmental perception, study of settlement patterns, urban and regional planning, product marketing, site selection and analysis, emergency preparedness, and as a general reference system.

Outer Banks Defined

The Outer Banks have been delineated by many authors many different ways, and oftentimes the particular delineation suited the nature of the study. For purposes of this study, the Outer Banks includes the barrier complex of North Carolina that extends from the North Carolina-Virginia boundary in Currituck County, generally southward to Cape Lookout, then westward to Bogue Inlet in Carteret County. This delineation is believed to be logical, both physically and culturally. Beyond Bogue Inlet the barriers cease to be true barriers and are often attached to the mainland at low tide, or are a series of many broken marsh islands just off the mainland. Cultural differences are apparent beyond Bogue Inlet, while cultural activities in the study area are generally similar. In addition, four large islands and many smaller islands located in the system of sounds or lagoons have been included because they are culturally part of the Outer Banks. These are Knotts Island, Colington Island, Roanoke Island, and Harkers Island.

Physically, the Outer Banks are a complex barrier system known as a barrier chain. This barrier system is narrow, varying from as little as 1/4 of a mile (2/5 of a kilometer) on Core Banks to over 3 miles (4.8 kilometers) in the Kitty Hawk area. There has been much debate over the years as to how barriers form. It has been suggested that a multiplicity of causes is at work in barrier formation, and this seems to be the case on the Outer Banks.

Barriers can develop as long as transported material is available and the shore has a low offshore gradient or slope. A composite of the Outer Banks barrier system includes barrier islands, barrier beaches, and barrier spits. All barriers characteristically are linear, with one or more sand ridges, and they separate the open sea from an enclosed lagoon. The lagoon and the sea are connected by one or more water passages (called inlets) through the barriers. A barrier island is a complex barrier composed of multiple sand ridges, multiple dune formations, overwash fans (deposition in the sound from waves washing over), and tidal marshes. A barrier beach is a more simple formation, consisting only of a single sand ridge with possibly some overwash fans and tidal marshes. A barrier spit may be either simple or complex, but is always connected on one end to the mainland. From False Cape in Virginia to Oregon Inlet, the formation is that of a barrier spit, while from Oregon Inlet to Ocracoke Inlet is an area of barrier islands. From Ocracoke Inlet south to Barden Inlet, the barriers are the more simplified barrier beaches, and from Barden Inlet west to Bogue Inlet, the formation consists of a series of short barrier islands.

Sounds and Inlets

Characteristics of any barrier system are the lagoons (locally called sounds) and the inlets. The sound system of the Outer Banks is extensive and includes Pamlico Sound, the largest inland body of water on the east coast of the United States. From north to south, the sounds are Currituck, Albemarle, Croatan, Roanoke, Pamlico, Core, Back, and Bogue.

Currituck Sound is oriented north-south and separates Currituck Banks from the mainland. It has become a fresh water sound since New Currituck Inlet closed in 1828. Periodically, the inlet has water during storms but has remained closed. Albemarle Sound is also a fresh water sound, is oriented east-west, and is physically an estuary or drowned river mouth. Most of its area is inland from the Outer Banks, and historically Albemarle Sound served as a transportation route for northeastern North Carolina.

Croatan Sound separates Roanoke Island from the mainland, and Roanoke Sound separates Roanoke Island from Bodie Island (no longer an island). Both of these features are straits that connect Albemarle Sound to Pamlico Sound.

Historically, Croatan Sound was partially blocked at the southern end by Roanoke Marshes, an area of tidal flats and marsh islands, because Albemarle Sound drained through Roanoke Inlet and Currituck Sound drained through New Currituck Inlet. When these inlets closed in the early nineteenth century, Roanoke Marshes was inundated as water drained southward to other open inlets.

Pamlico Sound is the widest sound (more than 25 miles, or 40 kilometers, in some places) and encompasses the area south of Roanoke Island to Ocracoke Inlet. Core Sound separates Portsmouth Island and Core Banks from the mainland, is oriented northeast-southwest, and is only a few miles wide. Back Sound is oriented east-west and separates Shackleford Banks from Harkers Island and the mainland. Bogue

Sound is oriented east-west and separates Bogue Banks from the mainland in the vicinity of Morehead City. All of these sounds are quite shallow. They are only three or four feet in most places. The deepest part is in Pamlico Sound at about fifteen feet. The lack of depth poses hazards to navigation.

Inlets might more correctly be referred to as "outlets" because their purpose is to provide drainage outlets for the sounds, which are catchment areas for some of the major river systems in North Carolina and southern Virginia. New inlets may open during storms and may remain open only a short time. A naming practice on the Outer Banks has been to refer to a newly opened inlet as New Inlet for a time - even as long as a year. If it remained open, the inlet would acquire a name, often that of a nearby closed inlet while retaining the adjective "new".

Wave action from the sea can push water over the dunes, but the energy of a frontal wave attack is usually dispersed quickly and not likely to establish a channel. Wave overwash instead, deposits material in the sound (called an overwash fan because it fans out) which soon establishes itself as a salt marsh. This process tends to provide a means of self-perpetuation for the barriers. When man interupts the process, as he has in the Cape Hatteras National Seashore, problems result.

Inlets are more likely to occur with surges from the sounds. The most violent surges of sound water can occur as a tropical storm moves northward along the coast. When the storm approaches, the winds are onshore causing high water and frontal wave attack on the sea side, but low water on the sound side of the barrier, where the high sound water is "piled up" against the mainland shore. As the center of the storm passes, there is a rapid reversal to an offshore wind. This causes low water at the beach while the high water in the sound at the mainland is "pushed" toward the sound side of the barrier. The larger the sound, the greater the volume of water pushed against the barrier. Unlike overwash, which dissipates in the tidal flats of the lagoon, the sound surge is often channeled and moves with force down the dunes to the open sea, where water has been displaced by the passing storm. This is one method by which inlets can occur.

There are other variables to consider. While inlets have existed just about everywhere on the Outer Banks at one time or another, the major inlets have occupied the same general area at different specific sites. For example, there have been a number of inlets in the Oregon Inlet area occupying slightly different sites. Evidence of stable zones of inlets are Beaufort, Ocracoke, and Bogue Inlets, which have been in existence since the first maps were made in 1585. As with all barrier features, inlets are dynamic or they tend to migrate. Generally, material is deposited on the north side and eroded from the south side, causing the inlet to eventually change its orientation from east-west to northeast-southwest. Eventually, this process may cause a temporary closure, but the new material is likely to be breached again.

Inlets play a vital role in the barrier process and create a controversey for man. Should inlets be maintained at all costs or should the natural opening and closing of inlets occur with no human intervention?

Indian Names

Indian names are part of the history and toponymic evolution of the Outer Banks, Unfortunately, the earliest adventurers and colonists kept very infrequent records. Little is known about the Indians of the area and especially their place names. By the middle of the eighteenth century, when the first accurate maps of the area appeared, the Indian influence had become minimal.

It is not known for sure whether the Banks themselves were ever permanently inhabited by Indians. There were certainly no large villages on the "Banks." More than likely, the Indians used the islands as temporary campsites with semi-permanent villages at what is now Ocracoke and Hatteras with a more permanent satellite village of the mainland on Roanoke Island.

There was a loose but complex confederation among the various tribes. The classification of these Indian groups is usually a linguistic classification and most of the Indians on the Outer Banks area were of the Algonkian group, which inhabited most of the coastal area from New England south to northeastern North Carolina. Other parts of North Carolina contained linguistically different groups. An exception is the Coree Indians from whom Core Banks and Core Sound received their names. Little is known of this group except that they were quite war-like with the Europeans and other Indian tribes. They left practically no place names since they had become extinct by the mid-seventeenth century, little more than fifty years after the arrival of the Europeans.

The population of Indians in the Outer Banks area was never very significant. Wars and exposure to European diseases, for which they had no immunity, soon reduced their numbers to insignificance. By the beginning of the eighteenth century, the Indians had disappeared from the Outer Banks and Roanoke Island.

Many Indian place names were lost because of inadequate mapping and records prior to the disappearance of the Indians: only about seven percent of the Outer Banks place names are of Indian origin. However, this percentage includes some of the most colorful and interesting ones.

No Indian place names exist in their original form, but have become Anglicized through various phases of evolution. Many possibilities exist, but records are incomplete and true origins may never be known. For example, the root "accomic" may be seen in the place names of Maryland, Delaware, Virginia, and on the Outer Banks (Chicamacomico), and probably refers to a dwelling or campsite. "Kitt" is found to mean big, and "hakki" to mean land. Not much imagination is needed to obtain Kitty Hawk.

Another possibility is "moskitu-auke", meaning grassland. This could evolve etymologically (the study of the origin and history of the meaning and form of words) to mosquito hawk to Kitty Hawk. These are only possibilities and caution should be used when studying the origin and etymology of place names.

User's Guide to Place Names of the Outer Banks

Names are arranged alphabetically. All entries in the "other names" category also appear in proper alphabetical sequence and are cross-referenced to the appropriate main entry. The format and order of information in each entry is the same throughout, although in some entries some types of information may not be applicable or, in a few cases, available.

Consider the following as a sample entry:

ASHBEE HARBOR A harbor, 0.1 mi. (0.2 km) wide, in Dare County, Nags Head Township at 35°52′42″N 75°40′14″W and located on the Manteo map. The harbor is in Croatan Sound at Roanoke Island just west of Skyco 2.1 mi. (3.4 km) south of Manteo. **Other names** Ashbys Harbor and Old Dominion Docks **Historical note** The name Ashbee or Ashby was formerly a prominent name in this area of Roanoke Island, but today is of historical significance only. During the late nineteenth and early twentieth centuries, the harbor was a stop along the Old Dominion Steamship Company route to Norfolk and, therefore, was sometimes referred to as Old Dominion Docks. The nearby village of Skyco (q.v.) was originally known as Ashbees Harbor, but the Post Office Department used the name Skyco when a post office was opened in 1892.

The format of each entry is narrative to facilitate ease of reading and the order of the information is constant to allow quick referencing. Entries are divided into three main divisions that provide available information on location, other names and historical notes.

The locative elements generally are contained in a two-sentence structure. The first part describes the site or the specific location of the feature. The proper name of a feature or place is listed and followed by the kind or type of feature (see the Glossary for a list of feature types and their definitions). Names appearing *in italics* are historical features no longer in existence. The next category, if present, is an appositive that describes the size or extent of the feature. The measurement is in miles (mi.) or portions of miles with kilometers (km.) in parentheses. The population is included, if necessary, and the elevation or altitude in feet (ft.) with meters (m.) in parentheses is present if the feature is of significant relief in relation to its surroundings. This is followed by the name of the county and township in which the feature is located. If the feature is located in more than one county or township, each is listed accordingly and in some cases, counties and townships outside the Outer Banks are included (see Table 2). The county and township are followed by the precise location by geographic coordinates listed to degrees, minutes, and seconds. *This affords location accurate to within about 200 feet on the ground.*

Geographic coordinates are measured from an artificial grid system applied to the earth's surface. It is one of many types of grid systems used for precisely locating points on the earth's surface, and is used in this study because geographic coordinates or latitude and longitude are the most widely known and understood of any of these grid systems. The coordinates are presented as two distinct sets of numbers. The first set is always the latitude which is used to measure distances north and south of the equator (0 degrees latitude) and are represented by imaginary parallel lines drawn in an east-west direction. The distance between each degree of latitude is approximately 69 miles (110.4 km) anywhere on the earth's surface. The latitude numbers are followed by the letter "N" which is the standard abbreviation for North and indicates that all points and places on the Outer Banks are located north of the equator.

The set of numbers that follow the latitude represents the longitude or a specific distance from 0 degrees longitude. Lines of longitude measure distances east and west and represent imaginary lines drawn in a north-south direction. Unlike lines of latitude, lines of longitude "converge" as one moves from the equator poleward; therefore, the distance between a degree of longitude varies according to one's position on the earth's surface. In the Outer Banks area, the distance between degrees of longitude is about 57.7 mi. (92 km) in the southern part of the Outer Banks to about 55.5 mi. (88.8 km) in the northern part. In the late nineteenth century, 0 degrees longitude was established by international agreement to be the line of longitude or meridian that passes through the town of Greenwich near London, England, in the United Kingdom and is known as the Prime Meridian. The meridian opposite the Prime Meridian is at 180 degrees (one-half of 360 degrees - the number of degrees in a circle). It is located in the Pacific Ocean and is the basis for the International Date Line. The set of numbers representing the longitude is followed by the letter "W" which is the standard abbreviation for West and indicates that all points and places on the Outer Banks are west of the Prime Meridian.

Information is portrayed on a map basically as point, line and area data. The coordinates of point features such as sand dunes, points of land, etc., were taken precisely at the map symbol portraying the point. The coordinates of linear features were taken at each end and in the center to indicate the extent of the feature. In the few cases of true fresh water streams on the Outer Banks, coordinates were taken at the mouth where the stream empties into a larger body of water and at the source or where the stream begins. The coordinates of areal features (such as bays, coves, inlets, populated places, etc.) were taken at the approximate center of the feature as determined by the feature's size.

The geographic coordinates are followed by a reference to the topographic map published by the U. S. Geological Survey on which the feature is located (see Table 1). A topographic map portrays horizontal and vertical positions on a specific part of the earth's surface determined by geographic coordinates and specifically portrays elevation or altitude by isohypse or lines connecting points of equal elevation which are called contour lines. These topographic maps are large scale maps or maps that show considerable detail which is why they were used as a basis for all compilation. Features not named on these maps could then be located and identified for purposes of precise location. The scale of each map is 1:24,000 or one inch on the map equals 2,000 feet on the earth's surface. Many features are named on the topographic map, but one value of this study is the identification of features not named on the topographic maps. If the feature is not named or not shown (because it no longer exists) on the topographic map, it is so stated in the map reference (see Table 1 for a list of U. S. Geological Survey topographic maps that cover the Outer Banks). In a few instances some named features lie outside the bounds of a topographic map, in which case a reference is made to the number of the National Ocean Service Chart on which the feature is located.

The second part of the locative elements describes the situation or the location of the feature in relationship to other named features. The feature is first generally located and associated with a major known feature and then related to nearby features according to distance. The named feature is further described by one or more precise "straight line" distances from a town or village. In some cases, isolation necessitates the distance reference to be from a village or town on the mainland and is so indicated. Distances are given in miles with kilometers in parentheses.

The second division of information is entitled "other names." Included here are other known names or forms or spellings of the name in current usage. Generally, this refers to names used historically but may include names in use today of less widespread acceptance. If more than one name is found, these other names are arranged alphabetically. These names may also be found in their proper alphabetical sequence in the body of this book, cross referenced to the appropriate entry.

The third main division of information is entitled "historical note." These notes include all known physical or cultural information concerning the named feature that I have been able to gather. Particular attention is given to presenting as much information as is available about the origin and evolution of the name.

Many possibilities exist concerning name origins and many variables contribute to the evolution of a name. All known legends and possible origins are given followed by what I believe to be the original meaning or reason for the name. Other named features are often mentioned here because they are related to the name origin or may provide insight into the naming process. These names are followed in parentheses by the reference q.v. which lets the reader know he or she should refer to that entry for additional information. Sometimes there may be only a reference in this category instructing the reader to refer to another entry for an explanation. This means that there is another name occurring alphabetically before the one in question where a reference is given that also applys to the name being studied. If no information is provided for this category, it means that the feature is obviously named for a person, it is obviously descriptive, or that no information of any kind could be discovered.

Glossary

The following list relates specifically to the Outer Banks and may not necessarily apply in the same way in other regions. The word "former" indicates a physical feature that no longer exists as described, while the word "historical" indicates cultural features that no longer exist.

anchorage a protected place, having little or no facilities, where ships can safely anchor. Generally used on the Outer Banks in an historical context.

area a term used to describe a feature with vague, poorly defined or implied boundaries.

barrier beach an offshore, single, elongated sand ridge rising above the high tide level with one or more inlets and separating an open body of water (such as the ocean) from an enclosed body of water (such as a lagoon or sound).

barrier chain a series of barrier islands (q.v.), barrier beaches (q.v.), and barrier spits (q.v.).

barrier island a complex barrier formation composed of multiple sand ridges, dunes, washover fans and tidal marshes above the high tide level. Separates an open body of water from an enclosed body of water in the same manner as a barrier beach (q.v.).

barrier spit a barrier connected to the mainland at one end but otherwise conforming to the definition of either a barrier beach (q.v.) or a barrier island (q.v.).

bay an indentation of a body of water into the land (over 1 mile (1.6 km) wide). Wider than a cove but smaller than a bight or gulf.

beach the sloping accumulation of material along a body of water washed by waves or tides.

bight a wide, shallow curve or indentation of a body of water into the coast where the width is greater than the indentation.

breakers an area of violent, turbulent water created by waves from deep water passing over shoals or shallows.

camp a temporary place used for a variety of commercial, recreational or military activities.

canal an artificial water course constructed for purposes of navigation by water craft. Used on the Outer Banks previously in an historical context.

cape a prominent projection of land into a body of water, usually the open sea.

channel the linear deep part of a body of water, either natural or dredged, through which the main volume of water flows. Used for navigation by water craft in the characteristically shallow or shoal waters of the area.

civil division a political division or subdivision formed for administrative purposes.

cove a small indentation of a body of water into the land (less than 1 mile (1.6 km) wide).

estuary a drowned river mouth or valley where the tide ebbs and floods. Normally created by a general rise in the level of the sea.

flat a relatively level place within an area of greater relief. Generally refers to flat expanses of sand within areas of high sand dunes (q.v.) or hummocks (q.v.).

fort an enclosed or fortified place displaying some barrier of defense. Usually equipped with guns.

harbor a protected area of water where ships and boats can dock. Usually has shipping or boating facilities.

hill an elevation rising steeply from the surrounding area. Refers to areas or sand dunes that have generally become stabilized by vegetation.

hummock an area of drier land rising slightly above a surrounding swamp or marsh. May oftentimes refer to a marsh island in a body of water. The usage on the Outer banks is usually **hammock** instead of **hummock.**

Indian village a permanent or temporary place of residence for a tribe or portion of a tribe of Indians. In this book the term is used totally in the historical sense because the Indians of the Outer Banks and neighboring mainland were decreased to only a few mainland villages by the middle of the eighteenth century and were extinct by the beginning of the nineteenth century.

island an area of dry or relatively dry land completely surrounded by water or wetlands.

lagoon a body of water, either brackish or fresh, separated from a larger body of water (such as the open sea) by barrier islands (q.v.) and barrier beaches (q.v.).

lake a body of water completely surrounded by land but frequently with a stream (q.v.) as an outlet. On the Outer Banks features classified as lake usually contain fresh water.

landing originally the term referred to the place where a ship or boat was loaded or unloaded, but now also includes other activities. Generally the built up area around the dock.

marsh wet, low areas with standing water that may be fresh but is usually salt and contains a variety of grasses. Extensive marsh areas on the Outer Banks are often the result of deposition from overwash fans created during storm surges from the ocean.

ocean current a distinct large stream of ocean water moving continuously and generally in the same path, usually with a marked difference in temperature and color from the surrounding water.

park a place or area set aside for recreation or preservation of a cultural or natural resource and under some form of government administration.

peninsula a projection of land surrounded on three sides by water but connected on one side to land.

point of land any protuberance of land into a body of water. Less prominant than a cape.

populated place a place or area with any number of permanent human inhabitants.

region any defined unit on the earth's surface, differentiated by one or more similar characteristics or activities.

rock a mass of rock or rocks exposed or submerged in the water but usually visible at low tide.

sand dune a general term for a dynamic or changing ridge or hill of sand piled up by wind action.

sand dunes a series or complex of sand dunes referred to collectively or as a unit.

sea a general term that refers to any large open body of salt water.

shoal the accumulation of sand, mud, and other materials in a body of water that creates a shallow area surrounded by deeper areas.

strait a narrow body of water of some magnitude representing a major feature and connecting two larger bodies of water.

stream a linear flowing body of water on the earth's surface and on the Outer Banks is used infrequently because it refers to fresh water features.

swamp a general term applied to poorly drained wetland, fresh or saltwater, and its associated vegetation.

tidal flat an area of mud and sand covered by water at high tide but exposed at low tide.

tidal stream a linear feature that ebbs and floods with the tide, that originates in the interior of a marsh, swamp or similar feature and gradually opens or trends toward a larger body of water.

water passage a relatively small waterway that ebbs and floods with the tide and connects larger bodies of water or other waterways.

woods a small area covered with a dense growth of trees in contrast to a lack of trees in the surrounding area.

TABLE 1
List of U.S. Geological Survey Topographic Maps Covering the Outer Banks

The following is an alphabetical list of the U. S. Geological Survey topographic maps used as the base maps series for this study:

Atlantic
Barco
Beaufort
Buxton
Cape Hatteras
Cape Lookout
Corolla
Davis
Green Island
Harkers Island
Hatteras
Horsepen Point
Howard Reef
Jarvisburg
Kitty Hawk
Knotts Island
Little Kinnekeet
Mansfield
Manteo
Martin Point
Mossey Islands
North Bay
Ocracoke
Oregon Inlet
Pea Island
Point Harbor
Portsmouth
Roanoke Island NE
Rodanthe
Salter Path
Styron Bay
Swansboro
Wainwright Island
Wanchese

TABLE 2

A Listing of Townships by County on the Outer Banks

Carteret:	*Currituck:*
Atlantic	Fruitville
Beaufort	Poplar Branch
Cedar Island	
Davis	*Dare:*
Harkers Island	Atlantic
Morehead	Croatan
Portsmouth	Hatteras
Sea Level	Kennekeet
Smyrna	Nags Head
Stacy	
White Oak	*Hyde:*
	Ocracoke

TABLE 3

Grouping of Names on the Outer Banks According to Type of Name

The following list displays the percentage of name types on the Outer Banks according to the eight categories established by H.L. Mencken in his voluminous work on American English. It is important to note that the list represents assignment to categories based upon a name's known or suspected meaning. Many names may have secondary classifications, but only the primary meaning was used in this classification.

Category	Total Names	Percentage
Personal Names	274	25.3
Transferred from England	25	2.3
Indian	72	6.6
Other Languages	0	0.0
Biblical and Mythological	7	.7
Descriptive	376	34.7
Flora, Fauna, and Geology	197	18.2
Fanciful	73	6.7
Unknown	60	5.5
Total	1,084	100.0

A

Abbots Island See Croatoan Island

Albacore Point See Power Squadron Spit

ALBEMARLE COUNTY A former civil division that included the northeast portion of the "new province" of Carolina and contained approximately 1600 square miles. **Historical note** This historical political division was established in 1664 and was divided into Chowan, Currituck, Pasquotank, and Perquimans Precincts in 1668. The civil division ceased to exist in 1689.

Albemarle River See Albemarle Sound

ALBEMARLE SOUND An estuary, 50 mi. (80 km) long and 15 mi. (24 km) wide, in Currituck, Dare, Camden, Pasquotank, Tyrrell, Perquimans, Bertie, and Washington counties at 35°58′00″N 75°45′00″W (east end), 35°59′00″N 76°41′00″W (west end), 35°58′30″N 76°13′00″W (center). The estuary is a non-tidal, body of fresh water into which the Chowan and Roanoke rivers flow. The sound then drains south through Roanoke and Croatan sounds into Pamlico Sound. The feature is named for Monck, Duke of Albemarle, who was one of the eight Lords Proprietors of Carolina. **Other names** Albemarle River, Bay of Albemarle, Carolina River, Chowane River, Chowan River, Occam River, Roanoke Sound, Sea of Rawnocke, Sound of Weapemeoc, Sound of Weapomeiock, Sound of Weapomeiok, and Sound of Weopemeiok. **Historical note** Since the earliest settlement, Albemarle Sound has provided an outlet for agricultural products of the Albemarle (q.v.). Today the sound is important for transportation, fishing and recreation.

Albemarle Sound See Pamlico Sound

ALLEN SLOUGH A cove, 0.2 mi. (0.3 km) wide, in Carteret County, Morehead Township at 34°42′08″N 76°43′10″W and located on the Beaufort Map. The cove is in Bogue Sound at the east end of Bogue Banks 1.4 mi. (2.2 km) south of the mainland town of Morehead City and 1.1 mi. (1.7 km) east of the town of Atlantic Beach.

ALLIGATOR GUT A tidal stream, 0.2 mi. (0.3 km) long, in Carteret County, Morehead Township at 34°41′44″N 76°50′30″W and located but not named on the Mansfield map. The tidal stream is at White Ash Swamp, 2.2 mi. (3.3 km) west of Hoop Pole Woods and 5.8 mi. (9.3 km) west of Atlantic Beach. **Historical note** The origin of the name is not verified, but since it appears on the earliest maps of the area it is possibly named for the alligators found there.

AMITY SHOAL A former shoal area in Carteret County, Portsmouth Township and Hyde County, Ocracoke Township and located but not shown on the Portsmouth map. The shoal was at the entrance to Ocracoke Inlet about 4 mi. (6.4 km) southwest of the village of Ocracoke. **Historical note** The exact location of this feature is not known and it may have been another name for a portion of Dry Sand Shoal (q.v.) or Shark Shoal (q.v.).

Angel Island See Baum Point Island

Annunciata See Outer Banks

Arabia See Outer Banks

ARCADIA An historical area. This name was applied to the general area of Nags Head and Kitty Hawk by early English explorers. As with many names applied during early visits, it was short-lived and is of historical significance only. **Historical note** See Outer Banks for an explanatory note.

Arcadia See Outer Banks

ARCHER CREEK A cove, 0.5 mi. (0.8 km) long, in Carteret County, White Oak Township at 34°40′22″N 77°01′00″W and located on the Swansboro Map. The cove is in Bogue Sound just south of Archer Point and 6.3 mi. (10.1 km) east southeast of the mainland town of Swansboro. **Other names** Piney Creek

ARCHER POINT A point of land in Carteret County, White Oak Township at 34°40′32″N 77°00′50″W and located on the Swansboro Map. The point is on west Bogue Banks and is the north point of Archer Creek, 6.5 mi. (8.8 km) east southeast of the mainland town of Swansboro. **Other names** Piney Point

Arundells Ile See Croatamung

Arundells Ile See Currituck Banks

ASHBEE HARBOR A harbor, 0.1 mi. (0.2 km) wide, in Dare County, Nags Head Township at 35°52′42″N 75°40′14″W and located on the Manteo Map. The harbor is in Croatan Sound at Roanoke Island just west of Skyco 2.1 mi. (3.4 km) south of Manteo. **Other names** Ashbys Harbor and Old Dominion Docks **Historical note** The name Ashbee or Ashby was formerly a prominent name in this area of Roanoke Island, but today is of historical significance only. During the late nineteenth and early twentieth centuries, the harbor was a stop along the Old Dominion Steamship Company route to Norfolk and, therefore, was sometimes referred to as Old Dominion Docks. The nearby village of Skyco (q.v.) was originally known as Ashbees Harbor, but the Post Office Department used the name Skyco when a post office was opened in 1892.

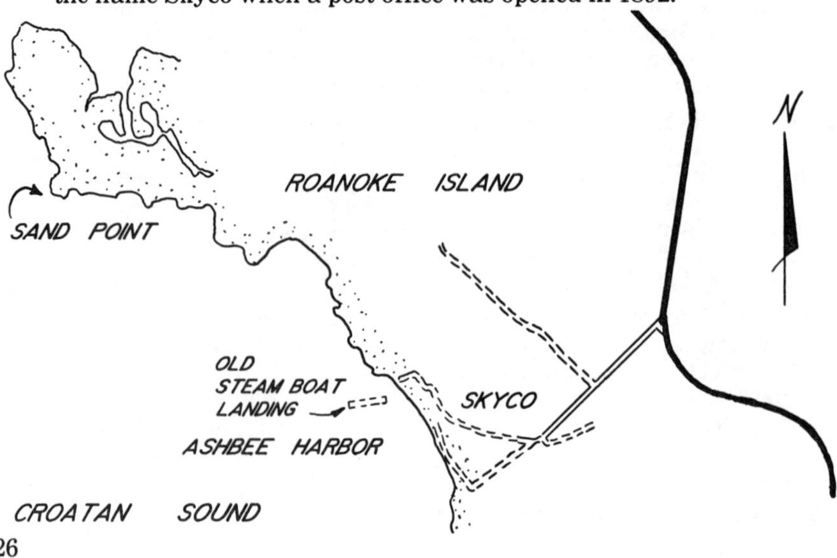

Ashbee Harbor See Skyco

Ashbees Harbor See Skyco

Ashby Harbor See Skyco

Ashbys Harbor See Ashbee Harbor

Ashbys Harbor See Skyco

ASKINS CREEK A tidal stream, 0.4 mi. (0.6 km) long and 0.1 mi. (0.2 km) wide, in Dare County, Kennekeet Township at 35°19′24″N 75°30′53″W and located on the Buxton map. The tidal stream is located in Pamlico Sound 5.2 mi. (8.4 km) north of Cape Hatteras and 1.9 mi. (3.1 km) south of Avon.

ATLANTIC BEACH A populated place, with a population of approximately 300, in Carteret County, Morehead Township at 34°41′54″N 76°44′21″W and located on the Beaufort Map. The town is located on the east end of Bogue Banks 1.6 mi. (2.6 km) south southwest of the mainland town of Morehead City. **Historical note** The community was chartered and incorporated in 1937 and is a major tourist area at the southern end of the Outer Banks.

ATLANTIC BEACH A beach, 1 mi. (1.6 km) long, in Carteret County, Morehead Township at 34°41′50″N 76°44′20″W and located but not named on the Beaufort map. The beach is on Bogue Banks at the town of Atlantic Beach, 1.9 mi. (3 km) south of the mainland town of Morehead City.

Atlantick Ocean See Atlantic Ocean

ATLANTIC OCEAN A sea in Currituck County, Fruitville township; Dare County, Atlantic, Nags Head, Kennekeet, and Hatteras townships; Hyde County, Ocracoke Township; and Carteret County, Portsmouth, Atlantic, Sea Level, Stacy, Davis, Smyrna, Harkers Island, Beaufort, Morehead, and White Oak Townships. The sea forms the North Carolina coast in a generally north-south direction for approximately 328 mi. (524.8 km). The Atlantic Ocean separates North America from Europe and separates South America from Africa. The ocean extends from the Arctic to the Antarctic and the equator divides the sea into the North Atlantic Ocean and the South Atlantic Ocean. **Other names** Atlantick Ocean and The Western Ocean **Historical note** The name is of Latin origin referring to Atlas and probably means "body of water west of the Atlas" a range of mountains in the northwest part of Africa.

AUNT PHOEBES MARSH A swamp, 0.2 mi. (0.3 km) wide, in Dare County, Kennekeet Township at 35°34′37″N 75°28′14″W and located on the Rodanthe Map. It is located 0.2 mi. (0.3 km) south of North Drain, 0.8 mi. (1.3 km) north of Waves and 1.2 mi. (1.9 km) south of Rodanthe.

AUSTIN CREEK A cove, 0.02 mi. (0.03 km) wide, in Dare County, Hatteras Township at 35°12′34″N 75°42′17″W and located on the Hatteras Map. The cove serves as a docking basin in Pamlico Sound for the Hatteras-Ocracoke Ferry and is located 1.1 mi. (1.8 km) southwest of the village of Hatteras. **Other names** Clubhouse Creek

AUSTIN REEF A shoal, 0.5 mi. (0.8 km) long, in Dare County, Hatteras Township at 35°13′20″N 75°44′54″W and located but not shown on the Hatteras Map. The shoal is in Pamlico Sound, 1.5 mi. (2.4 km) northeast of Pelican Shoal and 3.2 mi. (5.1 km) west of the village of Hatteras. **Other names** Austin Shoal, Austins Shoal and Cross Shoal

Austin Shoal See Austin Reef
Austins Shoal See Austin Reef

AVALON BEACH A populated place in Dare County, Nags Head Township at 36°02′45″N 75°40′50″W and located on the Kitty Hawk Map. The community is part of the village of Kill Devil Hills 5.3 mi. (8.5 km) north northwest of Nags Head. **Other names** Moores Shore **Historical note** Avalon Beach is a subdivision established in the 1950s that is now an integral part of the town of Kill Devil Hills.

AVALON BEACH A beach in Dare County, Atlantic Township at 36°02′49″N 75°40′37″W and located on the Kitty Hawk map. The beach is located in the town of Kill Devil Hills 2 mi. (3.2 km) southeast of Kitty Hawk and 6.8 mi. (10 km) northwest of Nags Head.

AVON A populated place, 3 ft. (1 m) high and with a population of approximately 350 (summer 1,000), in Dare County, Kennekeet Township at 35°21′07″N 75°30′38″W and located on the Buxton Map. The village is on Hatteras Island 7.1 mi. (11.5 km) north of Cape Hatteras and 4.2 mi. (5.1 km) south of Little Kinnakeet. **Other names** Big Kennakeet, Big Kinnakeet, Kennekut, Kinekeet and Kinnakeet **Historical note** A post office was established in 1873 and called Avon because of confusion over the spelling of Kinnakeet. The name of the village gradually changed from Kinnakeet to Avon. The name is thought to have been selected for the river of the same name in England, but the reason is unknown.

Avon Harbor See Peters Ditch

AYERS ROCK A rock in Hyde County, Ocracoke Township at 35°05′04″N 76°03′32″W and located on the Portsmouth Map. The rock is in Pamlico Sound just west of Wallace Channel 3.7 mi. (5.9 km) southwest of the village of Ocracoke.

B

Back Bay See Croatan Sound

BACK CREEK A cove, 0.4 mi. (0.6 km) wide, in Currituck County, Fruitville Township at 36°31′43″N 75°58′15″W and located on the Knotts Island Map. The cove is in North Landing River at Great Marsh just north of Mackay Island 2.6 mi. (4.2 km) west of the village of Knotts Island.

BACK OF THE BEACH An historical reference. The use of this term is a reference to the ocean side of the barrier island and is totally unknown today. It indicates that the original settlements and areas of concentration on the Banks were on the more protected sound side and generally in wooded areas for additional protection. There was little interest in the exposed beach until the tourist trade began in earnest in the 1920s with the construction of the first real roads. It is true that as early as revolutionary times, and especially in the late nineteenth century, mainland families and hunters came to the Banks to vacation, but the organized tourist industry did not really begin until the early twentieth century. Therefore, the term Back of the Beach is opposite in meaning from its modern implication.

BACK SOUND A lagoon, 8.2 mi. (13.1 km) long and 2 mi. (3.2 km) wide, in Carteret County, Harkers Island Township at 34°30′00″N 76°34′15″W and located on the Harkers Island Map. The lagoon is separated from the Atlantic Ocean by Shackleford Banks and trends northwest - southeast from Core Sound to Bogue Sound. **Other names** Back Sound Channel

Back Sound Channel See Back Sound

Bacon Island See Beacon Island

BALD BEACH A beach in Dare County, Kennekeet Township at 35°24′47″N 75°29′06″W and located but not named on the Little Kinnakeet map. This small section of beach is on upper Hatteras Island just north of Little Kinnakeet and 4.7 mi. (7.5 km) north of Avon.

BALD HILL A sand dune in Carteret County, Harkers Island Township at 34°40′02″N 76°35′15″W and located on the Harkers Island Map. The hill is on Shackleford Banks just west of Bald Hill Bay 2.5 mi. (4 km) south southwest of the village of Harkers Island and 4.2 mi. (6.7 km) northwest of Barden Inlet.

BALD HILL BAY A cove in Carteret County, Harkers Island Township at 34°40′04″N 76°34′37″W and located on the Harkers Island Map. The cove is in Back Sound just east of Bald Hill 2.2 mi. (3.5 km) south southwest of the village of Harkers Island and 3.9 mi. (6.2 km) northwest of Barden Inlet.

BALD POINT A point of land, less than 5 ft. (1.5 m) high, in Dare County, Hatteras Township at 35°16′40″N 75°31′29″W and located on the Manteo map. It is the north point of a marsh island in Pamlico Sound 0.5 mi. (0.8 km) north of Cape Creek, 1.1 mi. (1.8 km) northeast of Buxton and 2.2 mi. (3.5 km) north of Cape Hatteras.

BALLAST BAY A bay, 0.2 mi. (0.3 km) across, in Currituck County, Poplar Branch Township at 36°15′25″N 75°48′59″W and located on the Mossey Islands map. The bay is located in Currituck Sound just southeast of Indian Gap, 8.3 mi. (13.3 km) south of Corolla and 8.6 mi. (13.8 km) northwest of Duck.

BALLAST POINT A point of land, less than 5 ft. (1.5 m) high, in Dare County, Nags Head Township at 35°54′37″N 75°38′54″W and located on the Manteo map. The point is on Roanoke Island at the southeast entrance to Shallowbag Bay 1.3 mi. (2.1 km) east of Manteo. **Historical note** Ballast is any heavy substance that gives weight and stability to a ship in the water. The points at the entrance to Shallowbag Bay were often used as a place to leave ballast rocks and the rocks at this point have been found to be of foreign origin.

BANKS CHANNEL A channel, 0.7 mi. (1.1 km) long, in Carteret County, White Oak Township at 34°39′45″N 77°05′10″W and located on the Swansboro map. The channel is in Bogue Sound and trends east-west as a branch of Main Channel at the west end of Bogue Banks 2.3 mi. (3.7 km) southwest of the mainland town of Swansboro.

Barbage Island See Harbor Island

BARDEN INLET A water passage, 1.2 mi. (1.8 km) long, in Carteret County, Harkers Island Township at 34°37′50″N 76°31′35″W and located on the Harkers Island map. The water passage trends northeast-southwest and connects Lighthouse Bay, Back Sound, and Core Sound to the Atlantic Ocean and separates Core Banks from Shackleford Banks 5 mi. (8 km) south southeast of the village of Harkers Island. **Other names** Bardens Drain, Bardens Inlet, Borden Inlet, Bordens Inlet, Cape Inlet, Lookout Bight Channel, The Drain, and the Haulover **Historical note** The feature is named for Graham Arthur Barden, a former congressman from North Carolina. It was open from 1770 to 1860 and re-opened in 1933. The inlet is relatively unimportant because it is shallow and continues to "shoal up" or fill in with sediment and shifting sand. Locally and historically, the inlet is known simply as The Drain.

Bardens Drain See Barden Inlet

Bardens Inlet See Barden Inlet

BAREGRASS ISLAND An island, 0.2 mi. (0.3 km) long and less than 5 ft. (1.5 m) high, in Carteret County, Harkers Island Township at 34°39′17″N 76°32′19″W and located on the Harkers Island map. The island is in Back Sound 0.5 mi. (0.8 km) west of Sheep Island Slue, 3 mi. (4.8 km) south of the village of Harkers Island, and 1.7 mi. (2.7 km) north northwest of Barden Inlet.

BARE HILL A sand dune in Dare County, Hatteras Township at 35°13′04″N 75°39′55″W and located but not named on the Hatteras map. The dune is on lower Hatteras Island, 1.5 mi. (2.4 km) east of the village of Hatteras. **Other names** Blue Hill

BARNES MILL A former populated place in Dare County, Kennekeet Township at approximately 35°21′00″N 75°32′55″W and located but not shown on the Buxton map. The mill was located in Avon about 6 mi. (9.6 km) north of Buxton.

Barney Slue See Hatteras Inlet Channel

BARREL HEAD An area of beach in Dare County, Nags Head Township at approximately 35°48′00″N 75°32′30″W and located but not named on the Oregon Inlet map. The feature is part of the beach at the south end of Bodie Island about 1.5 mi. (2.4 km) north of Oregon Inlet and about 6 mi. (9.6 km) southeast of Wanchese. **Historical note** The name is historical and not generally known today.

Battery Clark See Fort Clark

BAUM BAY A cove, 0.2 mi. (0.3 km) wide, in Dare County, Atlantic Township at 36°00′22″N 75°40′53″W and located but not named on the Kitty Hawk map. The cove is just east of Colington Creek, 1 mi. (1.6 km) southwest of the Wright Brothers National Memorial and 3.9 mi. (6.2 km) northwest of Nags Head.

Baum Bay See Baum Creek

BAUM CREEK A cove, 0.4 mi. (0.6 km) long and 0.2 mi. (0.3 km) wide, in Dare County, Nags Head Township at 35°50′47″N 75°39′42″W and located on the Wanchese map. The cove is in Croatan Sound at the southwest part of Roanoke Island 0.5 mi. (0.8 km) west southwest of Baumtown and 1.4 mi. (2.2 km) west of Wanchese. **Other names** Baum Bay **Historical note** The name is an old established family name that predominates on this part of Roanoke Island.

BAUM POINT A point of land, less than 5 ft. (1.5 m) high, in Dare County, Nags Head Township at 35°55′10″N 75°39′35″W and located on the Manteo map. The point is on Roanoke Island at the northwest entrance to Shallowbag Bay 0.9 mi. (1.5 km) east northeast of Manteo. **Other names** Baums Point, Dolbys Point, Dollys Point, Duffys Point and Point of the Creek **Historical note** See Baum Creek for an explanatory note.

BAUM POINT A point of land in Dare County, Atlantic Township at

36°01'30"N 75°42'38"W and located but not named on the Kitty Hawk map. The point is the northwest point of Baum Point Island, 1.2 mi. (1.9 km) northwest of the village of Colington and 2.7 mi. (4.3 km) south of Kitty Hawk. **Historical note** See Baum Creek for an explanatory note.

BAUM POINT ISLAND An island, 0.9 mi. (1.4 km) long and 0.3 mi. (0.5 km) wide, in Dare County, Atlantic Township at 36°01'23"N 75°42'10"W and located on the Kitty Hawk map. The island is an irregularly shaped marsh island separating Kitty Hawk Bay and Blount Bay just west of Colington Creek, 2.8 mi. (4.5 km) south of Kitty Hawk, 6.5 mi. (10.4 km) northwest of Nags Head and 1.9 mi. (3.1 km) west northwest of the Wright Brothers National Memorial **Other names** Angel Island, Braum Point Island and Bum Point Island **Historical note** See Baum Creek for an explanatory note.

BAUMS CREEK A water passage, 0.8 mi. (1.3 km) long, in Currituck County, Poplar Branch Township at 36°15'23"N 75°47'38"W and located on the Mossey Islands map. This is a tidal area between unnamed tidal flats and marshes and Currituck Banks 7.3 mi. (11.7 km) north northwest of Duck and 8.5 mi. (13.6 km) south southeast of Corolla. **Other names** Baums Lead **Historical note** See Baum Creek for an explanatory note.

Baums Lead See Baum Creek

BAUMS MILL A former populated place in Currituck County, Poplar Branch Township at approximately 36°15'45"N 75°47'30"W and located but not shown on the Mossey Islands map. The mill was on Currituck Banks about 1 mi. (1.6 km) south of the former village of Poyners Hill and about 8 mi. (12.8 km) north northwest of Duck.

Baums Point See Baum Point (Dare County, Nags Head Township)

BAUMTOWN A populated place, 5 ft. (1.5 m) high, in Dare County, Nags Head Township at 35°51'02"N 75°39'15"W and located on the Wanchese map. The community is on southwest Roanoke Island 1 mi. (1.6 km) northwest of Wanchese. **Historical note** See Baum Creek for an explanatory note.

BAY MARSH A swamp in Carteret County, Portsmouth Township at 35°04'10"N 76°04'28"W and located but not named on the Portsmouth map. The swamp is part of Sheep Island 0.5 mi. (0.8 km) west of the village of Portsmouth and 6.8 mi. (10.9 km) southwest of the village of Ocracoke. **Other names** Baymarsh

Baymarsh See Bay Marsh

BAY MARSH BAY A cove, 0.1 mi. (0.2 km) wide, in Carteret County, Portsmouth Township at 35°03'58"N 76°04'25"W and located but not named on the Portsmouth map. The cove is just north of Casey Bay, 0.6 mi. (1 km) west southwest of the village of Portsmouth and 6.6 mi. (10.5 km) southwest of the village of Ocracoke.

BAYMARSH THOROFARE A water passage, 0.6 mi. (1 km) long, in Carteret County, Portsmouth Township at 35°04'04"N 76°04'14"W and located on the Portsmouth map. The water passage is in Pamlico Sound and separates Sheep Island from Portsmouth Island while it connects Casey Bay and Pamlico Sound 0.4 mi. (0.6 km) west of the village of Portsmouth and 6.3 mi. (10.2 km) southwest of the village of Ocracoke.

Bay of Albemarle See Albemarle Sound

Bay of Kitty Hawk See Kitty Hawk Bay

Bay of Muskito See Muskito Inlet

BAY POINT A peninsula, 0.4 mi. (0.6 km) long and 0.3 mi. (0.5 km) wide, in Currituck County, Fruitville Township at 36°29′20″N 75°54′22″W and located on the Barco map. The peninsula is the southeast part of Knotts Island, extending east into Knotts Island Bay 1.9 mi. (3.1 km) south of the village of Knotts Island and 8.4 mi. (13.4 km) southeast of Corolla.

BAY TREE An island, 0.1 mi. (0.2 km) across, in Currituck County, Poplar Branch Township at 36°17′26″N 75°51′05″W and located on the Mossey Islands map. The island is located in Currituck Sound at the west end of Big Narrows, 6.2 mi. (9.9 km) south southwest of Corolla and 11.5 mi. (10.4 km) northwest of Duck. **Other names** Bay Tree Island

Bay Tree Island See Bay Tree

BEACH CREEK A bay, 0.4 mi. (0.6 km) long and 0.1 mi. (0.2 km) wide, in Currituck County, Poplar Branch Township at 36°13′58″N 75°47′08″W and located on the Jarvisburg map. The bay is located in Currituck Sound 0.6 mi. (1 km) west of Currituck Banks, 0.8 mi. (1.3 km) south of Doxeys Salthouse, 5.2 mi. (8.3 km) northwest of Duck and 10.2 mi. (16.3 km) south of Corolla.

BEACH SLUE A cove, 0.7 mi. (1.1 km) long and 0.2 mi. (0.3 km) wide, in Dare County, Kennekeet Township at 35°40′10″N 75°29′25″W and located on the Pea Island map. The cove is a former water passage located just west of former New Inlet and trends east-west 5.4 mi. (8.7 km) north of Rodanthe. **Historical note** Between 1950 and 1970, the east end filled with sediment changing the tidal water passage to a cove.

BEACON ISLAND An island, less than 0.3 mi. (0.5 km) long and 5 ft. (1.5 m) high, in Carteret County, Portsmouth Township at 35°05′54″N 76°02′50″W and located on the Portsmouth map. The island is in Pamlico Sound at the west end of Ocracoke Inlet between Wallace Channel and Blair Channel, 2.2 mi. (3.5 km) north northeast of the village of Portsmouth and 3.8 mi. (6.1 km) west of the village of Ocracoke. **Other names** Bacon Island and Beacon Islands **Historical note** The name originated from two large beacons on the island used by pilots to guide ships through Ocracoke Inlet during the eighteenth and early nineteenth centuries.

BEACON ISLAND FORT A former fort in Carteret County, Portsmouth Township. The exact geographic coordinates are unknown but the former fort was allegedly located somewhere on Beacon Island in Ocracoke Inlet which would be on the Portsmouth map. No trace has been found on any map. **Other names** Fort Ocracoke **Historical note** In 1799 John Wallace and John Gray Blount, the owners of Beacon Island, sold the island to the federal government which was to build a fort there. There is some question as to whether the fort was ever built, but according to some historians there is evidence that indicates Beacon Island Fort was actually built. Additionally, a small fort was built on Beacon Island during the War Between the States and referred to as Fort Morgan (q.v.).

Beacon Island Road See Wallace Channel

BEACON ISLAND ROADS An historical anchorage in Carteret County, Portsmouth Township at 35°05′54″N 76°02′45″W and located but not named on the Portsmouth map. The anchorage was in Pamlico Sound at

Beacon Island 3.7 mi. (5.9 km) west of the village of Ocracoke. **Other names** Lower Roads and The Port of Beacon Island **Historical note** In the late eighteenth and early nineteenth centuries ships would ride at anchor here before delivering or obtaining cargo from the economic concerns that had been established on Beacon Island. Eventually the name Beacon Island Roads referred to the entire area in and around Ocracoke Inlet. Usage for this name disappeared during the early nineteenth century. Roads is a generic term used often in the seventeenth, eighteenth, and nineteenth centuries as a place where ships could anchor, but an area less enclosed than a harbor. While the term is not used as extensively today, some use can be identified such as that found in the Tidewater, Virginia area.

Beacon Island Roads See Ocracoke Inlet

Beacon Island Roads See Wallace Channel

Beacon Islands See Beacon Island

BEACON ISLAND SHOAL A shoal in Carteret County, Portsmouth Township at 35°05′37″N 76°03′23″W and located but not named on the Portsmouth map. The shoal is located in Pamlico Sound between Beacon Island and Wallace Channel, 0.7 mi. (1.1 km) west of Beacon Island and 4.4 mi. (7 km) west of the village of Ocracoke. **Historical note** The shoal was named for its nearby proximity to Beacon Island.

BEACON ISLAND SLUE A former channel, about 0.5 mi. (0.8 km) long, in Carteret County, Portsmouth Township at 35°05′35″N 76°03′00″W and located but not shown on the Portsmouth map. The channel was in Pamlico Sound just south of Beacon Island and it connected Wallace Channel and Blair Channel, 3.3 mi. (5.3 km) west southwest of the village of Ocracoke. **Historical note** Today there is no trace of the channel. See Shackeford Slue for an explanatory note about the generic slue.

BEAN ISLAND An island, less than 0.02 mi. (0.03 km) wide and 0.05 mi. (0.08 km) long and less than 5 ft. (1.5 m) high, in Carteret County, Davis Township at 34°45′59″N 76°24′40″W and located on the Davis map. The island is an elongated island in Core Sound 0.2 mi. (0.3 km) south of Great Island and 3.7 mi. (5.7 km) east southeast of the mainland town of Davis.

BEAN ISLAND An island, 0.2 mi. (0.3 km) long, in Carteret County, White Oak Township at 34°40′47″N 76°59′35″W and located on the Salter Path map. The island is located in Bogue Sound 6.9 mi. (11 km) west of Salter Path. **Other names** Piney Island and Wood Island

BEARHEAD An island, 0.4 mi. (0.6 km) long and 0.2 mi. (0.3 km) wide, in Currituck County, Poplar Branch Township at 36°17′50″N 75°50′58″W and located on the Mossey Islands map. The island is located in Currituck Sound just north of Lone Oak Channel, 3.8 mi. (9.3 km) south southwest of Corolla and 12 mi. (19.2 km) northwest of Duck.

BEAR ISLAND A former island, about 3 mi. (4.8 km) long, in Carteret County, White Oak Township and located but not shown on the Swansboro map. The elongated island was in Bogue Sound about 5 mi. (8 km) northeast of Bogue Inlet.

BEASLEY BAY A bay, 1.2 mi. (1.9 km) wide, in Currituck County, Poplar Branch Township at 36°16′45″N 75°48′28″W and located on the Mossey Islands map. The bay is in Currituck Sound just west of Currituck Banks, 6.7 mi. (10.8 km) south of Corolla and 9.1 mi. (14.6 km) north northwest of Duck. **Other names** Hicks Bay

Beaufort Channel See Beaufort Inlet Channel

Beaufort Entrance See Beaufort Inlet

Beaufort Harbor See Beaufort Inlet

BEAUFORT INLET A water passage in Carteret County, Beaufort and Morehead Townships at 34°41′45″N 76°40′05″W and located on the Beaufort map. The water passage connects Back Sound and Bogue Sound to Onslow Bay and the Atlantic Ocean, and separates Shackleford Banks from Bogue Banks, 1.8 mi. (2.9 km) south of the mainland town of Beaufort. **Other names** Beaufort Entrance, Beaufort Harbor, Core Sound, Core Sound Inlet, Gore Sound, Old Topsail Inlet, Port Beaufort, Port Beaufort Inlet and Topsail Inlet **Historical note** Beaufort Inlet, Bogue Inlet, and Ocracoke Inlet are the only three inlets known to be open continuously since 1585.

BEAUFORT INLET CHANNEL A channel, 1.3 mi. (2.1 km) long, in Carteret County, Beaufort Township at 34°41′30″N 76°40′06″W (north end), 34°39′30″N 76°40′25″W (south end), and 34°40′30″N 76°40′16″W (center) and located but not shown on the Beaufort map. The channel is in Onslow Bay at the entrance to Beaufort Inlet, 5.5 mi. (8.8 km) south of the mainland town of Beaufort and 7.5 mi. (12.1 km) southeast of the mainland town of Morehead City. **Other names** Beaufort Channel **Historical note** This is the main approach channel for shipping to Beaufort Inlet, the entrance to the port of Morehead City, which has large docks for processing phosphate and for use in the Menhaden fishing industry.

BELLOWS BAY A cove, 0.9 mi. (1.4 km) wide, in Currituck County, Fruitville Township at 36°29′27″N 75°57′56″W and located on the Barco map. The cove is in Currituck Sound at the south end of Mackay Island, 10.2 mi. (16.3 km) northwest of Corolla.

BELLS ISLAND An island, 0.5 mi. (0.8 km) long and 0.1 mi. (0.2 km) wide, in Dare County, Nags Head Township at 35°52′50″N 75°36′31″W and located on the Roanoke Island NE map. The marsh island is located in Roanoke Sound between Roanoke Island and Bodie Island just south of Headquarters Island, 5.3 mi. (8.9 km) south of Nags Head and 1.9 mi. (3 km) southwest of Whalebone Junction.

BEN DIXONS CREEK A cove, 0.05 mi. (0.08 km) wide, in Carteret County, Portsmouth Township at 35°04′15″N 76°04′07″W and located but not named on the Portsmouth map. The cove is just west northwest of the village of Portsmouth and 6.2 mi. (9.9 km) southwest of the village of Ocracoke.

BENS POINT A point of land in Dare County, Atlantic Township at 35°59′37″N 75°41′53″W and located but not named on the Manteo map. The point is the southern point of Colington Island, 1.2 mi. (1.9 km) south of the village of Colington and 4.6 mi. (7.4 km) northwest of Nags Head. **Other names** Bordens Point **Historical note** The name was originally Bordens Point, but after many generations the feature's name has been locally contracted to Bens Point.

BERMUDA ISLAND An island, less than 0.1 mi. (0.2 km) across, in Dare County, Atlantic Township at 36°02′55″N 75°42′15″W and located but not shown on the Kitty Hawk map. The island is in Kitty Hawk Bay 1 mi. (1.6 km) south of Kitty Hawk and 7 mi. (11.2 km) north northwest of Nags Head. **Other names** Bermuda Islands **Historical note** The name appears on early nineteenth century maps but the origin is unknown.

Bermuda Islands See Bermuda Island

BETSYS MARSH A marsh in Carteret County, Fruitville Township and located but not named on the Knotts Island map. The marsh was located at the site of Currituck Inlet about 3 mi. (4.8 km) east northeast of the village of Knotts Island. **Historical note** Historically, there was a tavern here.

BIG COLINGTON An historical island reference in Dare County, Atlantic Township at 36°00′20″N 75°43′05″W and located but not named on the Kitty Hawk map. The name is an historical reference to the west portion of Colington Island (q.v.). **Other names** Big Collington, Great Colenton, and Great Colington **Historical note** In the 1760s, a stream with its source near the center of Colington Island and which flowed north to Kitty Hawk Bay was extended south to Roanoke Sound thereby dividing Colington Island into two segments: the larger segment was referred to as Big Colington and the smaller segment was referred to as Little Colington (q.v.). The canalized stream was appropriately named Colington Cut (q.v.), but it has been known historically and locally as The Dividing Creek.

Big Colington Island See Big Colington

Big Collington See Big Colington

BIG DEEP MARSH ISLAND An island, 0.2 mi. (0.3 km) long, in Carteret County, Smyrna Township at 34°41′15″N 76°29′50″W and located on the Horsepen Point map. The marsh island is in Core Sound 0.5 mi. (0.8 km) northwest of Hogpen Bay and 3.5 mi. (5.6 km) east of the village of Harkers Island. **Other names** Long Deep Marsh Island

BIG FOOT SLOUGH CHANNEL A channel, 1.8 mi. (2.9 km) long, in Hyde County, Ocracoke Township at 35°08′42″N 75°59′45″W and located but not shown on the Howard Reef map. The channel is in Pamlico Sound 1.4 mi. (2.2 km) west of Howard Reef and 1.5 mi. (2.4 km) north of the village of Ocracoke. **Other names** Big Foot Slue

Big Foot Slue See Big Foot Slough Channel

BIG HILL A sand dune, 8 ft. (2.4 m) high, in Carteret County, Portsmouth Township at 35°03′53″N 76°03′50″W and located on the Portsmouth map. The dune is on south Portsmouth Island 0.3 mi. (0.5 km) south of the village of Portsmouth and 6.6 mi. (10.6 km) southwest of the village of Ocracoke.

Big Hill See Kill Devil Hill

Bight of Hatteras See Hatteras Bight

BIG ISLAND An island, 0.2 mi. (0.3 km) long and 0.2 mi. (0.3 km) wide, in Dare County, Kennekeet Township at 35°21′59″N 75°30′32″W and located on the Buxton map. This marsh island is in Pamlico Sound near the mouth of Mill Creek, 1.2 mi. (1.9 km) north of Avon.

BIG ISLAND An island, 0.6 mi. (1 km) long and 0.3 mi. (0.5 km) wide, in Dare County, Nags Head Township at 35°49′30″N 75°39′17″W and located but not named on the Wanchese map. The marsh island is at the southwest part of Roanoke Island, 1.5 mi. (2.4 km) southwest of Wanchese. **Historical note** The island was much more prominent in the seventeenth and eighteenth centuries when Roanoke Marshes (q.v.) existed.

BIG ISLAND An island, 0.2 mi. (0.3 km) long, in Dare County, Atlantic Township at 36°01′58″N 75°41′30″W and located but not named on the Kitty Hawk map. The island is in the north part of Colington Creek just west of Kill Devil Hills, 2.1 mi. (3.3 km) south of Kitty Hawk.

Big Kennakeet See Avon

Big Kill Devil Hill See Kill Devil Hill

Big Kinnakeet See Avon

Big Kinnakeet See Rodanthe

BIG MARSH An island, 0.4 mi. (0.6 km) long, in Carteret County, Sea Level Township at 34°49′20″N 76°21′45″W and located on the Styron Bay map. The marsh island is separated from Core Banks by Gutter Creek, 3.9 mi. (6.2 km) south of the mainland village of Atlantic.

BIG MARSH POINT A point of land in Carteret County, Sea Level Township at 34°49′29″N 76°21′53″W and located on the Styron Bay map. It is the northwest point of Big Marsh, 3.8 mi. (6.1 km) south of the mainland village of Atlantic.

BIG NARROWS A water passage in Currituck County, Poplar Branch Township at 36°17′05″N 75°51′10″W and located on the Mossey Islands map. The water passage is a narrow passage in Currituck Sound 2 mi. (3.2 km) southwest of Mossey Islands, 6.5 mi. (10.3 km) southwest of Corolla and 11.4 mi. (16.2 km) northwest of Duck. **Other names** Currituck Narrows

BIG PENGUIN ISLAND An island, 0.1 mi. (0.2 km) long and 0.2 mi. (0.3 km) wide, in Dare County, Nags Head Township at 35°54′38″N 75°36′53″W and located on the Roanoke Island map. The marsh island is in Roanoke Sound 3.2 mi. (5.1 km) south of Nags Head and 0.9 mi. (1.4 km) northwest of Whalebone Junction. **Historical note** See Penguin Islands for an explanatory note.

BIG SHOAL MARSH An island, 0.2 mi. (0.3 km) long, in Carteret County, Harkers Island Township at 34°40′57″N 76°36′44″W and located on the Harkers Island map. The island is in Back Sound 0.9 mi. (1.4 km) south of Middle Marshes, 3.1 mi. (5 km) west southwest of the village of Harkers Island, and 6.1 mi. (9.8 km) northwest of Barden Inlet.

BIG TIM ISLAND An island, 0.1 mi. (0.2 km) long and 0.5 mi. (0.8 km) wide, in Dare County, Nags Head Township at 35°47′42″N 75°33′42″W and located on the Oregon Inlet map. This marsh island is in Roanoke Sound, 0.4 mi. (0.6 km) north of Walter Slough, 0.2 mi. (0.3 km) northeast of Little Tim Island, and 5.9 mi. (9.6 km) southeast of Wanchese.

BIG YANKEE POND A cove, 0.2 mi. (0.3 km) long, in Currituck County, Poplar Branch Township at 36°14′55″N 75°47′26″W and located but not named on the Jarvisburg map. The cove is just north of Little Yankee Pond, 6.3 mi. (10.1 km) northwest of Duck and 9.1 mi. (14.6 km) south of Corolla. **Historical note** The origin of the name is unknown.

BILL SALTERS CREEK A cove, 0.1 mi. (0.2 km) long, in Carteret County, Portsmouth Township at 35°03′45″N 76°04′20″W and located on the Portsmouth map. The cove joins Willis Creek in southeast Casey Bay 0.7 mi. (1.1 km) southwest of the village of Portsmouth and 7.1 mi. (11.4 km) southwest of the village of Ocracoke.

BILLYS WOODS Woods in Dare County, Nags Head Township at

35°49′30″N 75°33′50″W and located but not named on the Oregon Inlet map. The wooded area is on Bodie Island north of Bodie Island Lighthouse and the pond at the Lighthouse, 2.8 mi. (4.5 km) northwest of Oregon Inlet and 4 mi. (6.4 km) east southeast of Wanchese. **Historical note** The wooded area was more extensive in the nineteenth century.

BIRD ISLAND An island in Carteret County, Beaufort Township at 34°42′25″N 76°40′25″W and located but not named on the Beaufort map. The island is the exposed part of Bird Shoal in Beaufort Inlet, 1 mi. (1.6 km) south southwest of the mainland town of Beaufort. **Historical note** The island has been in existence since the earliest maps of the area, but is often inundated at high water.

Bird Island See Bird Islands

BIRD ISLAND CHANNEL A former channel, about 2 mi. (3.2 km) long, in Carteret County, Beaufort township at 34°42′23″N 76°40′00″W and located but not shown on the Beaufort map. The channel separated Bird Island Shoal and Middle Ground, 1.2 mi. (1.9 km) south of the mainland town of Beaufort.

BIRD ISLANDS Islands, 1.4 mi. (2.3 km) long, in Dare County, Hatteras Township at 35°17′57″N 75°39′45″W and located on the Hatteras map. The islands are a chain of about 12 sand bars in Pamlico Sound 5.9 mi. (9.4 km) north of the village of Hatteras. **Other names** Bird Island

BIRD ISLAND SHOAL A shoal, about 2 mi. (3.2 km) long and less than 0.1 mi. (0.2 km) wide, in Carteret County, Beaufort Township at 34°42′00″N 76°38′35″W (east end), 34°42′38″N 76°40′43″W (west end), and 34°42′23″N 76°39′45″W (center) and located but not named on the Beaufort map. The shoal is situated between Bird Island Channel and Town Marsh Channel at the north end of Beaufort Inlet, 1 mi. (1.6 km) south of the mainland town of Beaufort. **Historical note** The feature was much wider in the nineteenth century.

Blackbeards Point See Springers Point

BLACK DUCK COVE A cove, 0.1 mi. (0.2 km) wide, in Currituck County, Poplar Branch Township and Dare County, Atlantic Township at 36°13′44″N 75°47′05″W and located on the Jarvisburg map. The cove is just north of the southeast end of Great Gap, 5 mi. (8 km) north northwest of Duck and 10.6 mi. (17 km) southwest of Corolla.

BLACKHALL BAY A cove, 0.6 mi. (1 km) wide, in Dare County, Nags Head Township at 35°54′35″N 75°42′00″W and located but not named on the Manteo map. The cove is in Croatan Sound just north of Pork Point 1.6 mi. (2.6 km) west of Manteo.

BLACK HAMMOCK A marsh, 1.7 mi. (2.7 km) long and 0.3 mi. (0.5 km) wide, in Dare County, Kennekeet Township at 35°20′21″N 75°31′00″W and located on the Buxton map. The marsh is on Hatteras Island between Avon and Askins Creek, 6 mi. (9.7 km) north of Cape Hatteras and 1.1 mi. (1.8 km) south of Avon. **Historical note** Hammock is a variation of the generic hummock and hammock is used throughout the southeastern United States. A hummock is a rounded hill and on the Outer Banks may be on land or in the water.

BLACKMAR GUT A harbor, 0.2 mi. (0.3 km) long and 0.05 mi. (0.08 km) wide, in Dare County, Kennekeet Township at 35°35′49″N 75°28′23″W and located on the Rodanthe map. The harbor trends east-west into

Chicamacomico Channel in Pamlico Sound 0.3 mi. (0.5 km) west of Rodanthe.

Blackmar Gut See Chicamacomico Channel

BLAIR CHANNEL A channel, 1 mi. (1.6 km) long, in Carteret County, Portsmouth Township and Hyde County, Ocracoke Township at 35°05′20″N 76°02′30″W and located but not shown on the Portsmouth map. The channel is in Ocracoke Inlet just east of Wallace Channel and 2.2 mi. (3.5 km) southwest of the village of Ocracoke. **Other names** Blairs Channel and Ship Channel

Blairs Channel See Blair Channel

BLINDS HAMMOCK Islands, 0.2 mi. (0.3 km) long, in Carteret County, Harkers Island Township at 34°38′54″N 76°31′53″W and located on the Harkers Island map. The marsh islands or hummocks are at the northwest corner of Blinds Hammock Bay and just west of Great Marsh Island, 3.5 mi. (5.6 km) south southeast of the village of Harkers Island and 1.2 mi. (1.8 km) north of Barden Inlet. **Historical note** The name is a reference to blinds used as camouflage while hunting. See Black Hammock for an explanatory note.

BLINDS HAMMOCK BAY A cove, 0.4 mi. (0.6 km) wide, in Carteret County, Harkers Island Township at 34°38′47″N 76°31′40″W and located on the Harkers Island map. The cove is in Back Sound just south of Sheep Island Slue 3.8 mi. (6.1 km) south southeast of the village of Harkers Island and 1.1 mi. (1.8 km) north of Barden Inlet.

BLOCKADE SHOAL A shoal in Dare County, Nags Head Township at 35°55′30″N 75°43′50″W and located but not named on the Manteo map. The shoal is in Croatan Sound at the northwest portion of Roanoke Island 3.5 mi. (5.6 km) northwest of Manteo. **Historical note** The feature acquired its name from the makeshift blockade of pilings and old sunken ships put here by confederate forces during The War Between the States to defend Roanoke Island.

BLOSSIE CREEK A water passage, 0.4 mi. (0.6 km) long, in Dare County, Nags Head Township at 35°48′50″N 75°34′07″W (north end), 35°48′47″N 75°33′50″W (south end), and 35°48′45″N 75°33′57″W (center) and located on the Oregon Inlet map. The water passage separates Off Island and Bodie Island and trends northwest-southeast 5 mi. (8 km) southeast of Wanchese. **Other names** Clubhouse Creek

BLOUNT BAY A cove, 1.1 mi. (1.8 km) long and 0.6 mi. (1 km) wide, in Dare County, Atlantic Township at 36°00′56″N 75°42′29″W and located on the Kitty Hawk map. The cove is at the north end of Colington Island just south of Kitty Hawk Bay, 2.2 mi. (3.5 km) west of the Wright Brothers Memorial and 3.3 mi. (5.3 km) south of Kitty Hawk.

Blue Hill See Bare Hill

BLUFF POINT A former point of land in Currituck County, Fruitville Township at 36°33′03″N 75°52′15″W and located but not shown on the Knotts Island map. The point was at the north side of Currituck Inlet just south of the North Carolina-Virginia boundary about 3.5 mi. (5.6 km) east northeast of the village of Knotts Island. **Other names** Cowpenpoint **Historical note** The feature and the name usage existed only during the early colonial period because Currituck Inlet had closed by 1731 and the point disappeared.

BLUFF SHOAL A shoal in Hyde County, Ocracoke Township at 35°18′00″N 76°05′15″W (north end), 35°09′30″N 76°06′30″W (south end), 35°13′31″N 76°05′23″W (center) and is located on chart number 11555. The shoal is in Pamlico Sound and extends from the mainland to Royal Shoal, 10.5 mi. (16.8 km) north northwest of Ocracoke Inlet and 9.1 mi. (14.4 km) northwest of the village of Ocracoke.

BOAT CREEK A cove, 0.1 mi. (0.2 km) wide, in Dare County, Kennekeet Township at 35°19′07″N 75°30′47″W and located on the Buxton map. The cove is in Pamlico Sound 5.1 mi. (8.3 km) north of Cape Hatteras and 2.1 mi. (3.4 km) south of Avon.

Bobby Island See Bobs Island

BOBS ISLAND An island, 0.2 mi. (0.3 km) long, in Dare County, Atlantic Township at 36°13′12″N 75°48′05″W and located but not named on the Jarvisburg map. The marsh island is in Currituck Sound, 5 mi. (8 km) northwest of Duck and 11.1 mi. (17.8 km) south of Corolla. **Other names** Bobby Island

BODIE ISLAND A former island, 10 mi. (16 km) long, in Dare County, Nags Head Township at 35°54′00″N 75°35′20″W (north end), 35°44′45″N 75°32′15″W (south end), and 35°53′30″N 75°35′00″W (center) and located on the Roanoke Island NE and Oregon Inlet maps. This former island is east of Roanoke Island and is now joined at the north end to Currituck Banks. It extends northwest from Oregon Inlet to the site of former Roanoke Inlet just south of Nags Head. **Other names** Bodies Island, Body Island, Bodys Island, Brodie Island, Cow Island, Essex Island, Etacrewac, Michards Island, and Misher Island. **Historical note** The

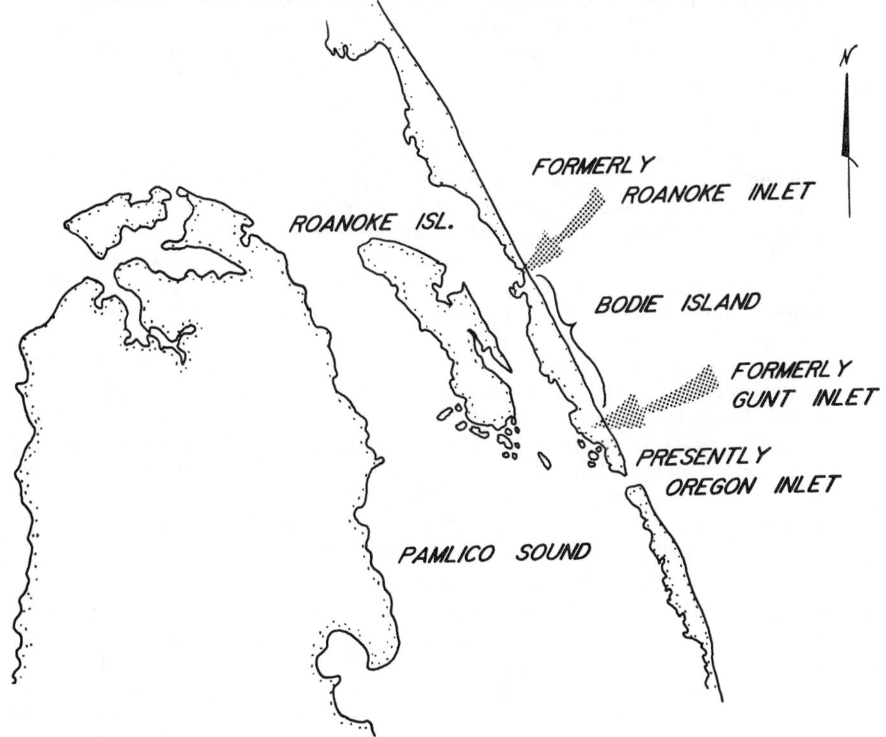

origin of the name is unclear but is usually said to be either that of a family name or that of a ship wrecked on the island, and the name appears on maps in the early eighteenth century. Another more likely possibility suggests that the name is descriptive. It was the practice in early Virginia to refer to certain units of land as a "body of land" and many of the early maps label this island Body Island. The original cartographic application may have merely been an attempt to record the description of a land grant or unit of land. The original southern limit of the island was Gunt Inlet (q.v.) but has varied over the years with the shifting inlets in the area. Today the southern boundary is Oregon Inlet (q.v.). The northern limit has also varied and has been extended as far north as Kitty Hawk, but is usually considered to have its north limit at the site of former Roanoke Inlet (q.v.)

Bodie Island See Pea Island

BODIE ISLAND BEACH An historical beach reference, 10 mi. (16 km) long, in Dare County, Nags Head Township and located but not named on the Roanoke Island NE and Oregon Inlet maps. The beach extends northwest from Oregon Inlet to the site of the former Roanoke Inlet just south of Nags Head. **Historical note** The term was popular in the late eighteenth and early nineteenth centuries, but is rarely used today.

Bodies Island See Bodie Island

Body Island See Bodie Island

Bodys Island See Bodie Island

BOG OPENING A marsh, 0.7 mi. (1.1. km) long, in Dare County, Kennekeet Township at 35°23′58″N 75°29′35″W and located but not named on the Little Kinnakeet map. The elongated marsh is on north Hatteras Island just south of Little Kinnakeet and 3.7 mi. (5.9 km) north of Avon.

Bogue Bank See Bogue Banks

BOGUE BANKS A barrier island, 25 mi. (40 km) long, at 34°42′15″N 76°56′19″W (east end) and 34°40′15″N 77°06′30″W (west end) and located on the Beaufort, Mansfield, Salter Path, and Swansboro maps. The barrier island trends east-west from Beaufort Inlet to Bogue Inlet and separates Bogue Sound from the Atlantic Ocean. **Other names** Bogue Bank, Borden Bank, Bordens Bank, Bordens Banks, Boug Bank, Cape Lookout Banks, and Stanford Islands **Historical note** The word Bogue has been reported by some authors to be a Choctaw Indian reference to a stream or a water passage. The term has evolved to refer to a swampy or marshy area. However, bogue may also be a derivation of a Spanish term that indicates movement to the leeward or side opposite the wind. The name Bogue is one of the oldest unchanged place names on the Outer Banks and the Spanish were known to frequently visit or raid places along the Outer Banks. Since the barrier islands here are oriented east-west in sharp contrast to those from Cape Henry in Virginia south to Cape Lookout, it is conceivable that this Spanish reference to "land to the leeward" could have found its way onto the maps and charts of the time because of its importance to navigation.

BOGUE INLET A water passage, 0.6 mi. (1 km) wide, in Carteret County, White Oak Township and Onslow County, Swansboro Township at 34°38′30″N 77°06′37″W and located on the Swansboro map. The inlet trends north-south from Bogue Sound to the Atlantic Ocean and separates Bogue Banks from Bear Island, 3.3 mi. (5.3 km) south of the mainland town of Swansboro. **Other names** Boug Inlet **Historical note** Bogue Inlet is one of three inlets that have been open continuously since before 1585. See Bogue Banks for an additional explanatory note.

BOGUE SOUND A lagoon, 26 mi. (41.6 km) long and 2.5 mi. (4 km) wide at the widest portion, in Onslow County, Swansboro Township and Carteret County, Morehead and White Oak townships at 34°42′45″N 76°42′15″W (east end), 34°40′15″N 77°07′15″W (west end), and 34°42′30″N 76°54′30″W (center) and located on the Beaufort, Mansfield, Salter Path, and Swansboro maps. The lagoon trends east-west from Back Sound at Beaufort to the White Oak River at Bogue Inlet and separates Bogue Banks from the mainland. **Historical note** See Bogue Banks for an explanatory note.

BONNYS STORE A former populated place in Currituck County, Fruitville Township at 36°29′07″N 75°55′20″W and located but not named on the Barco map. The locality was at the intersection of roads just east northeast of Knotts Landing and 1.7 mi. (2.7 km) south of the village of Knotts Island.

Borden Bank See Bogue Banks

Borden Inlet See Barden Inlet

Bordens Bank See Bogue Banks

BORDENS BANKS A former barrier island, approximately 20 mi. (32 km) long, in Carteret County, Morehead and White Oak townships at approximately 34°42′00″N 76°46′00″W (east end), 34°40′15″N 77°06′30″W (west end), and 34°40′36″N 76°56′30″W (center) and located but not named on the Mansfield, Salter Path and Swansboro maps. The barrier island was most of what is now Bogue Banks and extended from the site of Cheeseman Inlet to Bogue Inlet.

Bordens Banks See Bogue Banks

Bordens Inlet See Barden Inlet

Bordens Point See Bens Point

Botilla See Otilla

Botilla See Sound Landing

BOTTLE RUN POINT A point of land in Carteret County, Harkers Island Township at 34°40′53″N 76°35′07″W and located on the Harkers Island map. The Point is on a small marsh island in Back Sound 1.1 mi. (1.8 km) north northwest of Bald Hill Bay, 1.7 mi. (2.7 km) southwest of the village of Harkers Island, and 4.9 mi. (7.8 km) northwest of Barden Inlet.

Boug Bank See Bogue Banks

Boug Inlet See Bogue Inlet

BRANT ISLAND An island, 0.7 mi. (1.1 km) long, in Currituck County, Poplar Branch Township at 36°19′38″N 75°50′53″W and located on the Mossey Islands map. It is an elongated area of drier marsh at the extreme northwest extension of Mossey Islands, 3.5 mi. (5.6 km) south southwest of Corolla and 13.2 mi. (21.1 km) north northwest of Duck.

Brant Island See Elijah Lump

BRANT ISLAND POND A cove, 0.4 mi. (0.6 km) wide, in Currituck County, Poplar Branch Township at 36°19′42″N 75°50′37″W and located on the Mossey Islands map. The cove is located at the east side of Brant Island just west of Sanders Bay, 3.6 mi. (5.8 km) south southwest of Corolla and 12.9 mi. (20.6 km) north northwest of Duck.

BRANT ISLAND SHOAL A shoal, 7.3 mi. (11.7 km) long, in Carteret County, Portsmouth Township at 35°00′05″N 76°21′00″W and located on Chart number 11555. The shoal is in Pamlico Sound 17.5 mi. (28 km) west northwest of Ocracoke Inlet and 20.3 mi. (36.5 km) west northwest of the village of Ocracoke.

Brant Shoal Channel See Horse Island Channel

Braum Point Island See Baum Point Island

Breakwater Point See Power Sqaudron Spit

BRIGAND BAY A populated place in Dare County, Hatteras Township at 35°15′50″N 75°35′32″W and located but not named on the Buxton map. The community is on Hatteras Island, 3 mi. (4.8 km) west of Buxton and 6.5 mi. (10.5 km) northeast of the village of Hatteras.

BROAD CREEK A cove, 3.2 mi. (5.1 km) long and 0.5 mi. (0.8 km) wide, in Dare County, Nags Head Township at 35°50′57″N 75°37′04″W and located on the Manteo map. The cove trends northwest-southeast in Roanoke Sound 0.7 mi. (1.1 km) northeast of Wanchese, 5.8 mi. (9.4 km) southeast of Manteo.

BROAD CREEK POINT A peninsula, 1 mi. (1.6 km) long, in Dare County, Nags Head Township at 35°51′30″N 75°37′10″W and located on the Oregon Inlet map. The Peninsula is on southeast Roanoke Island at the northeast entrance of the mouth of Broad Creek 2 mi. (3.2 km) north northeast of Wanchese.

Brock Bay See Sanders Bay

Brodie Island See Bodie Island

BROOKS CREEK A cove, 0.1 mi (0.2 km) wide, in Carteret County, Harkers Island Township at 34°42′37″N 76°35′02″W and located on the Harkers Island map. The cove is in Back Sound at the northwest part of Harkers Island, 1.7 mi. (2.7 km) northwest of the village of Harkers Island and 4.1 mi. (6.6 km) east of the mainland town of Beaufort.

BROOKS CREEK A cove, 0.3 mi. (0.5 km) long and 0.1 mi. (0.2 km) wide, in Dare County, Hatteras Township at 35°16′06″N 75°35′50″W and located on the Buxton map. The cove is between Brooks Point and Kings Point 7.2 mi. (11.6 km) north northeast of the village of Hatteras, 4.2 mi. (6.7 km) west northwest of Cape Hatteras, and 3.2 mi. (5.1 km) west of Buxton.

BROOKS POINT A point of land in Dare County, Hatteras Township at 35°16′14″N 75°35′47″W and located on the Buxton map. The Point is a marsh point at the north entrance to Brooks Creek on the north shore of the south part of Hatteras Island 7.4 mi. (11.9 km) north northeast of the village of Hatteras, 4.2 mi. (6.7 km) west northwest of Cape Hatteras, and 3 mi. (5 km) west of Buxton.

BROWNS ISLAND An island, 1.6 mi. (2.6 km) long and 0.8 mi. (1.3 km) wide, in Carteret County, Harkers Island Township at 34°42′20″N 76°32′00″W and located on the Harkers Island map. The island is in Core Sound 1.1 mi. (1.8 km) south of the mainland, 1.7 mi. (2.7 km) northeast of the village of Harkers Island, and separated from Harkers Island by Westmouth Bay and Eastmouth Bay.

BUCK ISLAND An island, 0.1 mi. (0.2 km) wide, in Currituck County,

Fruitville Township at 36°29′20″N 75°58′20″W and located on the Barco map. It is located in Buck Island Bay at the south end of Mackay Island 3.2 mi. (5.1 km) southwest of the village of Knotts Island and 10.5 mi. (16.8 km) northwest of Corolla.

BUCK ISLAND BAY A cove, 0.7 mi. (1.1 km) wide, in Currituck County, Fruitville Township at 36°29′30″N 75°58′12″W and located on the Barco map. The cove is in the northwest part of Bellows Bay at the south end of Mackay Island, 2.9 mi. (4.6 km) southwest of the village of Knotts Island and 10.2 mi. (16.3 km) northwest of Corolla.

Buckle Island See Mon Island

Buckle Islands See Mon Island

BULKHEAD CHANNEL A channel, 0.6 mi. (1 km) long, in Carteret County, Beaufort Township at 34°42′50″N 76°40′40″W (north end), 34°42′18″N 76°40′42″W (south end), and 34°42′34″N 76°45′00″W (center) and located on the Beaufort map. The channel leads from Beaufort Inlet to Beaufort between Radio Island and Bird Island Shoal, 1 mi. (1.6 km) southwest of the mainland town of Beaufort.

BULKHEAD CHANNEL A former channel in Carteret County, Portsmouth Township at 35°06′40″N 76°06′55″W and located but not shown on the Portsmouth map. The channel was in Pamlico Sound and connected Flounder Slue to the open sound about 6.5 mi. (10.4 km) west of the village of Ocracoke.

Bum Point Island See Baum Point Island

BUNCH OF HAIR An island, 0.05 mi. (0.08 km) long, in Carteret County, Harkers Island Township at 34°39′29″N 76°33′14″W and located on the Harkers Island map. The island is just north of Shackleford Banks at the entrance to Johnsons Bay, 2.5 mi. (4 km) south of the village of Harkers Island and 2.5 mi. (4 km) northwest of Barden Inlet. **Historical note** The name is descriptive and refers to the appearance of the island.

BUNTON ISLAND Former islands in Dare County, Nags Head Township at approximately 35°49′00″N 75°40′15″W and located but not shown on the Wanchese map. The islands were formerly located in Croatan Sound and were remnants of Roanoke Marshes just southwest of Roanoke Island and about 2.5 mi. (4 km) southwest of Wanchese. **Historical note** The islands were in the former Roanoke Marshes (q.v.), and currently represent the shoals that are remnants of Roanoke Marshes.

BURDEN CHANNEL A channel, 1.1. mi. (1.7 km) long, in Carteret County, White Oak Township at 34°40′15″N 77°04′55″W and located on the Swansboro map. The channel trends northeast-southwest in Bogue Sound at the west end of Bogue Banks, 2.5 mi. (4 km) southeast of Swansboro, and connects Banks Channel and the Intracoastal Waterway. **Other names** Burthen Channel and Burthon Channel

BURNSIDE HEADQUARTERS An historical site in Dare County, Nags Head Township at 35°54′20″N 75°41′52″W and located on the Manteo map. The site is on western Roanoke Island 1.5 mi. (2.4 km) west of Manteo. **Historical note** This was the campsite from which the Union General, Ambrose Burnside, directed the defeat of Confederate forces and established control of the Outer Banks and the coastal area for the Union.

BURNT ISLAND An island, 0.5 mi. (0.8 km) long and 0.3 mi. (0.5 km) wide,

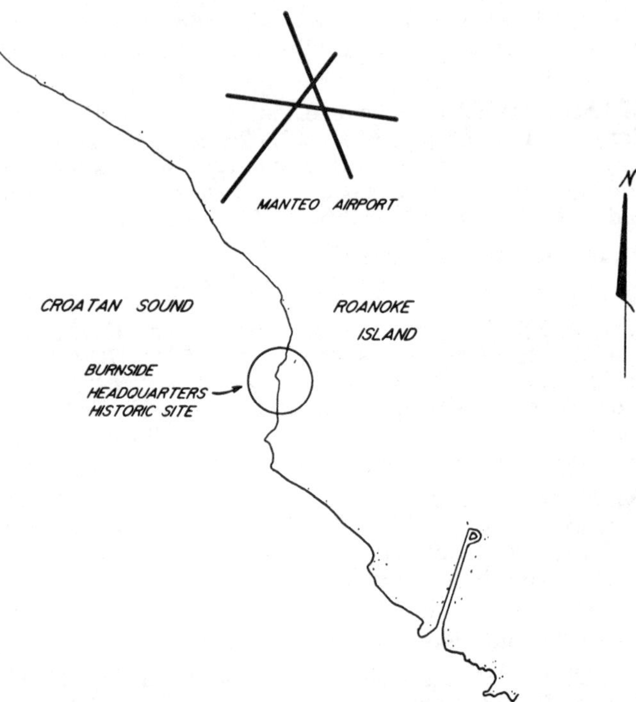

in Dare County, Atlantic Township at 36°02′15″N 75°42′06″W and located on the Kitty Hawk map. This marsh is in Kitty Hawk Bay just north of Sloop Island, 1.9 mi. (3 km) south of Kitty Hawk, 1.6 mi. (2.6 km) north of Colington, and 2.4 mi. (3.9 km) north of the Wright Brothers Memorial.

BURRIS BAY A cove, 0.6 mi. (1 km) across, in Currituck County, Poplar Branch Township at 36°16′57″N 75°49′58″W and located on the Mossey Islands map. The cove is situated between Big Narrows and Beasley Bay, 1.9 mi. (3 km) west of Currituck Banks, 6.5 mi. (10.4 km) south of Corolla and 9.3 mi. (14.9 km) northwest of Duck. **Other names** Burris Channel

Burris Channel See Burris Bay

Burthen Channel See Burden Channel

Burthon Channel See Burden Channel

BUSH ISLAND An island, less than 0.1 mi. (0.2 km) across, in Currituck County, Poplar Branch Township at 36°16′56″N 75°49′05″W and located on the Mossey Islands map. It is in Currituck Sound just west of Beasley Bay, 6.7 mi. (10.7 km) south of Corolla and 9.6 mi. (15.4 km) north northwest of Duck.

BUXTON A populated place, 10 ft. (3 m) high with a population of about 700 (summer 5000), in Dare County, Hatteras Township at 35°16′10″N 75°32′17″W and located on the Buxton map. The village is on the north shore of the south part of Hatteras Island, 1.5 mi. (2.6 km) northwest of Cape Hatteras, 6.1 mi. (9.9 km) south southwest of Avon, and 9.7 mi. (15.6 km) northeast of the village of Hatteras. **Other names** The Cape **Historical note** A post office was established here in 1873.

Buxton Channel See Buxton Harbor Channel

BUXTON HARBOR CHANNEL A channel, 4.6 mi. (7.4 km) long, in Dare County, Hatteras Township at 35°17′54″N 75°33′48″W (northwest end), 35°16′02″N 75°33′34″W (southeast end), and 35°16′58″N 75°33′41″W (center) and located on the Buxton map. The channel trends south in Pamlico Sound, 1.2 mi. (1.9 km) northwest of Buxton. **Other names** Buxton Channel, Cape Channel, and Muddy Slue **Historical note** The inner portion of the channel was originally called Cape Channel and is the remnant of one of the inlet channels of Chaneandepeco Inlet (q.v.).

Buxton Harbor Channel See Cape Channel

BUXTON LANDING A landing in Dare County, Hatteras Township at 35°16′15″N 75°32′25″W and located on the Buxton map. The landing is on Hatteras Island 0.2 mi. (0.3 km) north of Buxton.

Buxton Wood See Buxton Woods

BUXTON WOODS Woods, 1.2 mi. (1.9 km) long, 0.5 mi. (0.8 km) wide, and 17 ft. (5.1 m) high, at 35°15′37″N 75°32′15″W and located on the Buxton map. This wooded area is 0.7 mi. (1.1 km) south of Buxton and 1.3 mi. (2.1 km) north of Cape Hatteras. **Other names** Buxton Wood, Cape Hatteras Woods, and Hatteras Woods

BUZZARD BAY A bay, 1.1 mi. (1.7 km) wide, in Dare County, Atlantic Township at 35°59′32″N 75°41′14″W and located on the Manteo map. The bay is in Albemarle Sound just south of Colington Island, 4.2 mi. (6.7 km) northwest of Nags Head and 5.8 mi. (9.4 km) north of Manteo.

Buzzard Island See Sedge Island

BUZZARD LEAD A water passage, 0.8 mi. (1.3 km) long, in Currituck County, Poplar Branch Township at 36°18′15″N 75°49′35″W (east end), 36°18′20″N 75°50′08″W (west end), and 36°18′18″N 75°49′53″W (center) and located on the Mossey Islands map. It is a narrow water passage through Mossey Islands connecting the north extremity of Wells Creek and Wells Bay at Currituck Sound, 5.2 mi. (8.3 km) south of Corolla and 11.4 mi. (18.2 km) north northwest of Duck. **Historical note** The exact implication of the generic lead is not known but is probably a reference to a known passage through a marsh complex. The generic appears several times on the northern Outer Banks. Lead is also used as a nautical term referring to the course or length of a rope, and has been used to refer to an artificial water course.

BUZZARD POINT A point of land in Dare County, Atlantic Township at 35°59′47″N 75°40′40″W and located but not named on the Manteo map. The point is on Currituck Banks 1.3 mi. (2.1 km) south of the village of Colington and 4.2 mi. (6.7 km) northwest of Nags Head.

C

CABS CREEK A water passage, 0.6 mi. (1 km) long, in Carteret County, Harkers Island Township at 34°40′17″N 76°35′17″W and located on the Harkers Island map. The water passage trends southwest-northeast from Bald Hill Bay to Back Sound 2.3 mi. (3.7 km) south southwest of the village of Harkers Island and 4.4 mi. (7 km) northwest of Barden Inlet.

Caffee Inlet See Caffeys Inlet

Caffey Inlet See Caffeys Inlet

CAFFEYS INLET A former water passage, 0.1 mi. (0.2 km) long, in Dare

County, Atlantic Township at 36°13′30″N 75°46′27″W and located but not shown on the Jarvisburg map. The water passage formerly cut through Currituck Banks, 4.3 mi. (6.9 km) north northwest of Duck **Other names** Caffee Inlet, Caffey Inlet, Caffreys Inlet, Cartheys Inlet, Coffeys Inlet, Providence Inlet, Smith Inlet, South Inlet, Trinety Harbor and Trinitie Harbor. **Historical note** The inlet was open from about 1770 to 1810, and was named for George Caffey who owned a considerable amount of land through which the inlet cut its passage.

Caffreys Inlet See Caffeys Inlet

CAGGS CREEK A water passage, 0.4 mi. (0.6 km) long, in Carteret County, Smyrna Township at 34°41′15″N 76°29′17″W and located on the Horsepen Point map. The water passage is in Core Sound and separates an unnamed marsh island from Core Banks 4 mi. (6.4 km) east of the village of Harkers Island.

CALIFORNIA A populated place, 5 ft. (1.5 m) high with a population of about 300, in Dare County, Nags Head Township at 35°54′15″N 75°40′45″W and located on the Manteo map. The community is on north central Roanoke Island and is part of the town of Manteo, 0.6 mi. (1 km) west southwest of the center of Manteo. **Historical note** The origin of the name is not known or at least not remembered, but the name is still in local use today. California is probably a site where freed slaves were temporarily settled during the War Between the States and referred to as "Town of Blacks." The name may also reflect the desire of many freed slaves to move westward to California where economic opportunities were available.

CAMP CASS WILLIAMS A camp in Hyde County, Ocracoke Township at 35°08′07″N 75°54′37″W and located on the Howard Reef map. The camp is just south of Quokes Point, 8.6 mi. (13.8 km) southwest of Hatteras Inlet and 5.1 mi. (8.1 km) northeast of the village of Ocracoke. **Historical note** See Ira Morris Camp for an explanatory note.

CAMP GARY BRAGGS A camp, 5 ft. (1.5 m) high, in Hyde County, Ocracoke Township at 35°08′50″N 75°52′23″W and located on the Green Island map. The camp is on Ocracoke Island seaward of Knoll Creek, 7.6 mi. (12.1 km) northeast of the village of Ocracoke. **Historical note** See Ira Morris Camp for an explanatory note.

CAMP WASHINGTON A former military camp in Carteret County, Portsmouth Township and located but not shown on the Portsmouth map. The camp was one of the main Confederate encampments on the Outer Banks and was located on Portsmouth Island at Portsmouth. **Historical note** The camp was abandoned with the fall of Fort Hatteras on August 29, 1861.

CAMP WINFIELD A former encampment in Dare County, Hatteras Township at 35°12′58″N 75°41′10″W and located but not shown on the Hatteras map. The camp was located near Fort Totten in the eastern part of the village of Hatteras. **Historical note** The camp was a disembarking site for Union troops moving northward to Roanoke Island during The War Between the States.

CANVASBACK POINT A point of land in Currituck County, Poplar Branch Township at 36°16′13″N 75°49′24″W and located on the Mossey Islands map. It is the northwest point of Indian Gap Island just south of Jarvis Channel, 2.6 mi. (4.2 km) south of Three Dunes, 7.5 mi. (12 km) south of Corolla and 9.3 mi. (14.9 km) northwest of Duck. **Other names** Canvas Back Point **Historical note** This point was probably named for the presence of large quantities of the Canvasback Duck. The Mossey Islands area is a frequent stop by many migrating birds along the Atlantic Flyway as many of the place names indicate.

Canvas Back Point See Canvasback Point

CANVASBACK POND A lake, 0.4 mi. (0.6 km) long and 0.1 mi. (0.2 km) wide, in Currituck County, Poplar Branch Township at 36°18′53″N 75°50′05″W and located on the Mossey Islands map. The lake is located on the north portion of Mossey Islands, 4.3 mi. (6.9 km) south southwest of Corolla and 12.2 mi. (19.5 km) north northwest of Duck. **Historical note** See Canvasback Point for an historical note.

Cape Amidas See Cape Kenrick

Cape Canrik See Cape Kenrick

Cape Cenrick See Cape Kenrick

CAPE CHANNEL A channel, 3.8 mi. (6.1 km) long, in Dare County, Hatteras Township at 35°18′40″N 75°37′45″W (northwest end), 35°17′54″N 75°33′48″W (southeast end), and 35°18′17″N 75°35′47″W (center) and located but not named on the Buxton and Hatteras maps. The channel extends northwest in Pamlico Sound from Buxton Harbor Channel and is 2.5 mi. (4 km) north northwest of Buxton. **Other names** Buxton Harbor Channel

Cape Channel See Buxton Harbor Channel

Cape Channel See Chaneandepeco Inlet

CAPE CREEK A cove, 0.4 mi. (0.6 km) wide, in Dare County, Hatteras Township at 35°16′14″N 75°31′30″W and located on the Buxton map. The cove is in Pamlico Sound 1 mi. (1.6 km) west of Buxton and 1.8 mi. (2.9 km) north of Cape Hatteras. **Historical note** The feature is the remnant of Chaneandepeco Inlet (q.v.) and during storms is subject to overwash and sound surge.

Cape di Virginia Australe See Cape Lookout (cape)

Cape Feare See Cape Lookout (cape)

Cape Harbour See Lookout Bight

Cape Hattera See Cape Hatteras

CAPE HATTERAS A cape in Dare County, Hatteras Township at 35°13′10″N 75°31′53″W and located on the Cape Hatteras map. The cape is on Hatteras Island 4.4 mi. (7 km) south of Buxton and 4.3 mi. (6.9 km) east of Frisco. **Other names** Cape Hattera, Cape Hope, Cape of Engano, Cape on Currituck Banks, Cape Saint John, Croatoan, Hatorask, and Hatoraske **Historical note** The origin of the name is for the Hatteras Indians but the meaning of Hatteras is generally vague and unclear. The name may refer to an area of sparse vegetation.

Cape Hatteras See Cape Kenrick

CAPE HATTERAS BANKS A former barrier island in Hyde County, Ocracoke Township and Dare County, Hatteras Township at 35°24′23″N 75°29′30″W (northeast end), 35°09′00″N 75°51′30″W (southwest end), and 35°16′30″N 75°40′30″W (center) and located but not shown on the Cape Hatteras, Hatteras, and Green Island maps. This former barrier island extended from Cape Hatteras southwest to Old Hatteras Inlet (q.v.) including the present south portion of Hatteras Island from Cape Hatteras to Hatteras Inlet and the northeast portion of Ocracoke Island for approximately 5 mi. (8 km).

Cape Hatteras Banks See Hatteras Island

Cape Hatteras Indian Town See Indian Town

Cape Hatteras Island See Hatteras Island

Cape Hatteras Shoals See Diamond Shoals

Cape Hatteras Spit See Hatteras Shoals

Cape Hatteras Woods See Buxton Woods

CAPE HILLS An area of sand dunes in Carteret County, Harkers Island Township at approximately 34°36′15″N 76°32′15″W and located but not named on the Cape Lookout map. The dunes are at Cape Lookout in the vicinity of the former village of Cape Lookout about 6.5 mi. (10.4 km) south of the village of Harkers Island.

Cape Hills See Diamond City

Cape Hills See Cape Lookout (former populated place)

Cape Hope See Cape Hatteras

Cape Hope See Cape Lookout (cape)

Cape Inlet See Barden Inlet

Cape Inlet See Chaneandepeco Inlet

Cape Kaneraick See Cape Kenrick

Cape Kendrick See Cape Kenrick

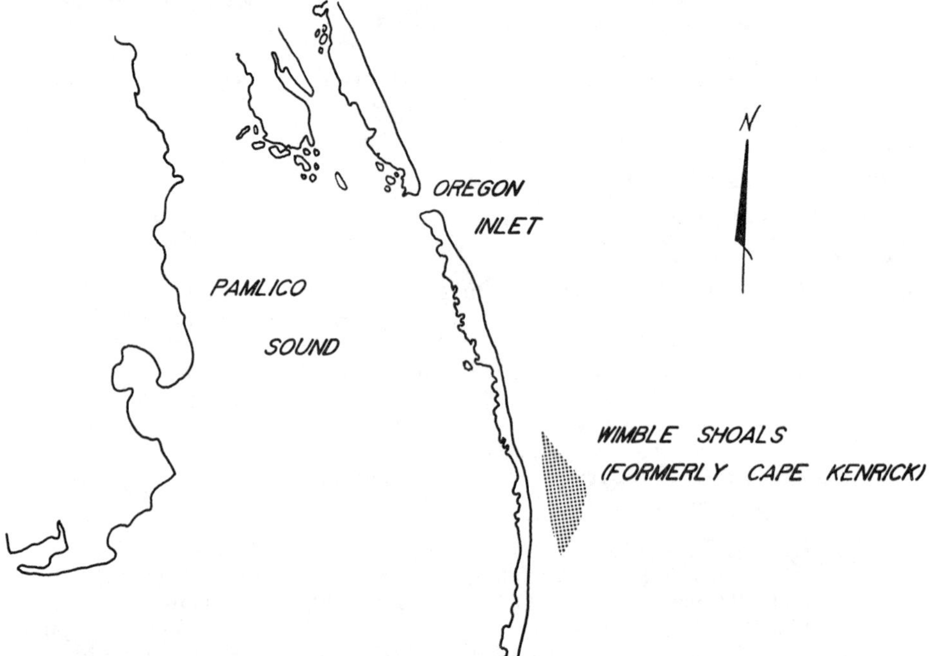

CAPE KENRICK A former cape in Dare County, Kennekeet Township at 35°32′45″N 75°25′45″W and located but not shown on the Rodanthe map. This feature was formerly the east projection of the present area of north Hatteras Island and south Pea Island 3 mi. (4.8 km) southwest of Rodanthe and 20 mi. (32 km) north northeast of Cape Hatteras. **Other names** Cape Amidas, Cape Canrik, Cape Cenrick, Cape Hatteras, Cape Kaneraick, Cape Kendrick, and Wimble Shoals. **Historical note** This prominent cape existed until the middle part of the seventeenth century when it disappeared, and today Wimble Shoals (q.v.) are the remnants of Cape Kenrick. This feature is sometimes confused with Cape Hatteras which developed after Cape Kenrick disappeared. See Kenricks Mounts for a further explanation.

Cape Kenrick See Salvo

CAPE LOOKOUT A former populated place, 10 ft. (3 m) high, in Carteret County, Harkers Island Township at 34°36′02″N 76°32′15″W and located on the Cape Lookout map. The former community was located on Cape Lookout at the south tip of Core Banks, 6 mi. (9.7 km) south of the village of Harkers Island. **Other names** Cape Hills and Cape Lookout Woods **Historical note** Today the former community of Cape Lookout is abandoned, but as late as 1950 it had a population of approximately 50, and the post office that was established here in 1910 has also been discontinued.

CAPE LOOKOUT A cape, 1.9 mi. (3 km) long, 1.1 mi. (1.8 km) wide and approximately 25 ft. (7.5 m) high, in Carteret County, Harkers Island Township at 34°36′11″N 76°32′14″W and located on the Cape Lookout map. The cape is at the south tip of Core Banks just east of Onslow Bay, 6.3 mi. (10.1 km) south of the village of Harkers Island. **Other names** Cape di Virginia Australe, Cape Feare, Cape Hope, Cape Look Out, Cape of Fear, Cape of Feare, Cape of Southern Virginia, Cape of Trafalgar, Promontorium Tremendium, and The Colonies' Gibralter. **Historical note** The French, who were instrumental in building Fort Hancock (q.v.) on this cape in the seventeenth century, referred to the area as The Colonies' Gibralter because of its strategic location in the seventeenth and eighteenth centuries.

Cape Look Out See Cape Lookout (cape)

Cape Lookout Bank See Cape Lookout Shoals

Cape Lookout Banks See Bogue Banks

Cape Lookout Banks See Cape Lookout Shoals

Cape Lookout Banks See Core Banks

Cape Lookout Bay See Lookout Bight

Cape Lookout Bight See Lookout Bight

Cape Lookout Harbor See Lookout Bight

CAPE LOOKOUT GROUNDS An historical reference to an area of open sea that is east and south of Cape Lookout at approximately 34°34′30″N 76°25′30″W. **Historical note** The area was extensively used for whaling until the late nineteenth century when the whales disappeared. This method of shore-based whaling on the Outer Banks was quite different from that of New England. The local older men would watch for whales from high sand dunes, and when a whale was sighted, the "whalers" would put to sea in their long boats to capture the whale. The men would harpoon the whale by hand (later by gun) and tow the whale to shore where it would be beached at high tide. The two-week job of processing or trying the whale was always considered a community project and the profits were shared accordingly.

CAPE LOOKOUT SHOALS Shoals, 9 mi. (14.5 km) long and 2 mi. (3.2 km) wide, in Carteret County, Harkers Island Township at 34°30′00″N 76°28′30′W and partially located but not named on the Cape Lookout map. These shoals are in the Atlantic Ocean just southeast of Cape Lookout. **Other names** Cape Lookout Bank, Cape Lookout Banks and Frying Pan Shoals

Cape Lookout Woods See Cape Lookout (former populated place)

Cape of Engano See Cape Hatteras

Cape of Fear See Cape Lookout (cape)

Cape of Feare See Cape Lookout (cape)

Cape of Southern Virginia See Cape Lookout (cape)

Cape of Trafalgar See Cape Lookout (cape)

Cape on Currituck Banks See Cape Hatteras

CAPE POINT A point of land in Carteret County, Harkers Island Township at 34°34′57″N 76°32′01″W and located on the Cape Lookout map. The point is the southernmost tip of Core Banks at the south tip of Cape Lookout 1.6 mi. (2.6 km) south of the former community of Cape Lookout and 7.6 mi. (12.2 km) south of the village of Harkers Island. **Historical note** The name was originally more descriptive for purposes of referring to the furthest projection of land of a prominent cape. The reference has evolved to a place name.

CAPE POINT A point of land in Dare County, Hatteras Township at 35°14′40″N 75°31′38″W and located on the Cape Hatteras map. The point is the extreme south tip of Cape Hatteras 2.7 mi. (4.3 km) south of Buxton. **Other names** Cove Point, Point of Cape Hatteras, Point of the Cape and The Point **Historical note** See Cape Point, Carteret County for an explanatory note.

Cape Saint John See Cape Hatteras

Cape Woods See Frisco Woods

CAPSIES CREEK A cove, 0.7 mi. (1.1 km) wide, in Currituck County, Fruitville Township at 36°32′57″N 75°55′00″W and located on the Knotts Island map. The cove is in Back Bay at the northeast end of Knotts Island 2.7 mi. (4.3 km) north of the village of Knotts Island.

Caratock Inlet See Currituck Inlet

Caratuk Inlet See Currituck Inlet

Caratuk Inlet See New Currituck Inlet

Caritock Inlet See Currituck Inlet

Carlile Island See Colington Island

Carlyle Island See Colington Island

Carolana See Carolina

CAROLINA A former region that represented the land granted to the eight

Lords Proprietors in 1663 by Charles II King of England and the proprietors named the grant in honor of Charles II. The charter included all the land from Virginia to Florida and from the Atlantic to the Pacific oceans. **Other names** Carolana

Carolina Banks See Outer Banks

Carolina Outer Banks See Outer Banks

Carolina River See Albemarle Sound

Carotuck Inlet See Currituck Inlet

Carotuck River See Currituck Inlet

CAROVA A populated place, 2.3 mi. (3.7 km) in extent with a population of about 20, in Currituck County, Fruitville Township at 36°31′45″N 75°52′15″W and located but not named on the Knotts Island map. This scattered community is just south of the North Carolina-Virginia boundary, 3.2 mi. (5.1 km) east northeast of the village of Knotts Island and 13 mi. (20.8 km) north northwest of Corolla. **Other names** Carova Beach, Corova, Corova Beach, and South Shore **Historical note** There are about 20 or 30 year-round residents who have been here for about ten years. The only access is by boat or four-wheel drive vehicles. The origin of the name is not known for sure, but it is suspected to be a contraction of Carolina and the abbreviation for Virginia which is Va, thus indicating its proximity to the North Carolina-Virginia boundary.

Carova Beach See Carova

CARROT ISLAND An island, 2 mi. (3.2 km) long, in Carteret County, Beaufort Township at 34°42′20″N 76°37′07″W (east end), 34°42′30″N 76°38′50″W (west end), and 34°42′20″N 76°38′00″W (center) and located on the Beaufort and Harkers Island maps. The island is in Back Sound, 2 mi. (3.2 km) from the mainland town of Beaufort and 4.4 mi. (7 km) west of the village of Harkers Island. **Other names** Cart Island

CARROT ISLAND CHANNEL A former channel, about 2.5 mi. (4 km) long, in Carteret County, Beaufort Township at 34°42′27″N 76°39′07″W and located but not shown on the Beaufort map. The channel separated Carrot Island and Horse Island from Bird Island Shoal just southeast of the mainland town of Beaufort and 5.3 mi. (8.5 km) west of the village of Harkers Island. **Other names** Carrot Slough

Carrot Slough See Carrot Island Channel

CARTERET An intended populated place in Dare County, Nags Head Township and located but not shown on the Manteo map. A charter was granted in 1723 and the location was on the northeast portion of Roanoke Island, but the charter lasted only until about 1733, and the town never developed. **Other names** Roanoke Town **Historical note** This was the name of one of two attempts to establish a port town on Roanoke Island. The town failed because Roanoke Inlet was "shoaling up" as a result of changes in currents caused by the natural closing of inlets through the north portion of Currituck Banks, and by the 1730s there was no direct or reliable inlet through the barrier island in the Roanoke Island area. Oregon Inlet did not open until 1846. The proposed town was to be named for Sir John Carteret, one of the eight Lords Proprietors of Carolina.

CARTERET COUNTY A civil division, 536 square mi. (857.6 square km)

with a population of 31,603, including Portsmouth, Cedar Island, Atlantic, Sea Level, Stacy, Davis, Smyrna, Straits, Beaufort, Harlowe, Morehead, White Oak, Newport, Merrimon, Harkers Island, and Marshallberg townships at 34°48′00″N 76°33′00″W. The civil division was formed in 1772 from Craven County and is the southernmost county on the Outer Banks. It is bounded by Jones, Craven, Pamlico, and Hyde counties. **Historical note** The county was named for Sir John Carteret, one of the original eight Lords Proprietors of Carolina.

Cartheys Inlet See Caffeys Inlet

Cart Island See Carrot Island

CASEY BAY A cove, 0.3 mi. (0.5 km) wide, in Carteret County, Portsmouth Township at 35°03′53″N 76°04′34″W and located on the Portsmouth map. The cove is in Pamlico Sound and separates Evergreen Island from Sheep Island, 0.8 mi. (1.3 km) west of the village of Portsmouth and 6.4 mi. (10.2 km) southwest of the village of Ocracoke.

CASEY ISLAND An island, 0.3 mi. (0.5 km) long, in Carteret County, Portsmouth Township at 35°04′38″N 76°04′40″W and located on the Portsmouth map. The island is in Pamlico Sound 0.6 mi. (1 km) north of the village of Portsmouth and 5.4 mi. (8.6 km) southwest of the village of Ocracoke. **Other names** Caseys Island

Caseys Island See Casey Island

CASEYS POINT A point of land in Carteret County, Portsmouth Township at 35°04′40″N 76°04′10″W and located but not named on the Portsmouth map. This point is the west point of Casey Island and is 0.5 mi. (0.8 km) north of the village of Portsmouth and 5.7 mi. (9.1 km) southwest of the village of Ocracoke.

CASON POINT A point of land in Currituck County, Fruitville Township at 36°31′30″N 75°54′37″W and located on the Knotts Island map. This point is on Knotts Island 1.3 mi. (2.1 km) northeast of the village of Knotts Island. **Historical note** Early maps of Knotts Island indicate the surname Cason or Casun in this area.

Castle See Shell Castle

Castle Rock See Shell Castle

CATFISH POINT A point of land in Carteret County, Harkers Island Township at 34°36′50″N 76°32′30″W and located but not named on the Cape Lookout map. The point of land is at the south end of Core Banks on the north shore of Cape Lookout 1.5 mi. (2.4 km) north of Cape Point and 4.8 mi. (7.7 km) south southeast of the village of Harkers Island.

Catfish Point See Power Squadron Spit

CAT ISLAND An island in Carteret County, White Oak Township at 34°41′10″N 76°58′16″W and located on the Salter Path map. The island is in Bogue Sound 4.3 mi. (6.9 km) west of Salter Path, and 13.9 mi. (22.3 km) west of Atlantic Beach. **Other names** Gull Island

CAT ISLAND An island, 0.1 mi. (0.2 km) wide, in Dare County, Kennekeet Township at 35°38′17″N 75°28′57″W and located on the Pea Island map. The island is in Pamlico Sound just northwest of Round Hammock Point and 3.1 mi. (5 km) northwest of Rodanthe. **Other names** Logerhead Shoal and Loggerhead Shoal **Historical note** The island represents the remnants of the primary shoal at Loggerhead Inlet (q.v.) but today the feature is small.

CAT ISLAND A former island in Carteret County, White Oak Township at 34°40′58″N 76°57′38″W and located but not shown on the Salter Path map. The island was in Bogue Sound 4.3 mi. (6.9 km) west of Salter Path. **Historical note** Historically, there were two features named Cat Island (q.v.) in close proximity in this part of Bogue Sound. This particular Cat Island has disappeared leaving the other Cat Island 0.7 mi. (1.1 km) to the northwest, the only Cat Island in the area.

Cedar Bay See Cedar Bush Bay

CEDAR BUSH BAY A cove, 0.6 mi. (1 km) wide, in Dare County, Nags Head Township at 35°49′45″N 75°39′45″W and located on the Pea Island map. The cove is in Croatan sound just southwest of Roanoke Island and 1.9 mi. (3.1 km) southwest of Wanchese. **Other names** Cedar Bay

CEDAR HAMMOCK An island, 0.3 mi. (0.5 km) long, in Carteret County, Harkers Island Township at 34°39′37″N 76°32′20″W and located on the Harkers Island map. This marsh island is in Back Sound at the northwest end of Sheep Island Slue 2.6 mi. (4.2 km) south southeast of the village of Harkers Island and 2 mi. (3.2 km) north of Barden Inlet. **Historical note** See Black Hammock for an explanatory note.

CEDAR HAMMOCK A peninsula, 1.3 mi. (2.1 km) wide, in Carteret County, Morehead Township at 34°42′35″N 76°44′45″W and located on the Beaufort map. The peninsula is a marsh area in Bogue Sound now connected to Bogue Banks by man-made land at Atlantic Beach 1.7 mi. (2.7 km) southwest of the mainland town of Morhead City. **Historical note** See Black Hammock for an explanatory note.

CEDAR HAMMOCK A marsh, 0.2 mi. (0.3 km) long, in Carteret County, Stacy Township at 34°49′08″N 76°21′50″W and located on the Styron Bay map. This marsh area is located just west of Core Banks in Core Sound 4.1 mi. (6.6 km) south of the mainland village of Atlantic. **Historical note** See Black Hammock for an explanatory note.

CEDAR HAMMOCK A marsh, 0.5 mi. (0.8 km) long and 0.2 mi. (0.3 km) wide, in Dare County, Kennekeet Township at 35°39′54″N 75°29′17″W and located on the Pea Island map. The marsh is just north of Wreck Creek 5 mi. (8 km) north northwest of Rodanthe. **Historical note** See Black Hammock for an explanatory note.

CEDAR HAMMOCK CREEK A former water passage in Carteret County, Morehead Township at 34°42′15″N 76°44′00″W (east end), 34°42′37″N 76°45′07″ (west end), and 34°42′20″N 76°44′30″W (center) and located but not shown on the Beaufort and Mansfield maps. The water passage connected Hoop Pole Creek and Money Island Bay just north of Atlantic Beach and was 1.2 mi. (1.9 km) south southwest of the mainland town of Morehead City. **Historical note** The feature's remnants may be seen as coves in the man-made areas of Cedar Hammock (q.v.).

Cedar Hammock Island See No Ache Island

CEDAR INLET A former water passage, 0.5 mi. (0.8 km) long, in Carteret County, Stacy Township at 34°49′17″N 76°22′04″W and located on the Styron Bay map. The former water passage was formerly located in Core Sound, separated Outer Grass Lump from Big Marsh, and connected Old Channel to Core Sound, 4 mi. (6.4 km) south of the mainland village of Atlantic. **Other names** Hunting Quarter Inlet, Normans Inlet, Porters

Inlet, and Sand Inlet. **Historical note** The inlet was open from approximately 1725 to 1865.

CEDAR ISLAND An island, 0.1 mi. (0.2 km) long, in Dare County, Nags Head Township at 35°49′05″N 75°34′32″W and located on the Oregon Inlet map. The island is in Roanoke Sound 0.2 mi. (0.3 km) west of Cedar Point, 1.6 mi. (2.6 km) northeast of Duck Island, and 4 mi. (6.4 km) east southeast of Wanchese.

CEDAR ISLAND An island, 0.4 mi. (0.6 km) long and 0.3 mi. (0.5 km) wide, in Dare County, Nags Head Township at 35°54′15″N 75°36′29″W and located on the Roanoke Island NE map. The island is in Roanoke Sound 3.7 mi. (5.9 km) south of Nags Head, 0.6 mi. (1 km) west of Whalebone Junction, and supports the causeway to Bodie Island. **Other names** Horse Islands **Historical note** The original name was Horse Islands and originally there were several islands that have become one.

CEDAR POINT A peninsula in Dare County, Nags Head Township at 35°49′07″N 75°34′23″W and located on the Oregon Inlet map. The peninsula is on southwest Bodie Island just northwest of Georges Creek, 0.4 mi. (0.6 km) west of the Bodie Island Lighthouse, and 4.2 mi. (6.7 km) west southwest of Wanchese.

CEDAR POINT BEACH A populated place in Carteret County, White Oak Township at 34°40′15″N 77°03′00″W and located on the Swansboro map. The community is on the sound side of west Bogue Banks and is 5 mi. (8 km) southeast of the mainland town of Swansboro.

Chacandepeco Inlet See Chaneandepeco Inlet

CHAIN SHOT ISLAND An island, 0.2 mi. (0.3 km) long, at 34°59′23″N 76°14′09″W and located on the Wainwright Island map. The island is in Core Sound 4.6 mi. (7.4 km) west of Swash Inlet, 11.2 mi. (17.9 km) southwest of the village of Portsmouth, and 17.2 mi. (27.5 km) southwest of the village of Ocracoke. **Other names** Chainshot Island **Historical note** The feature was named in the early eighteenth century and was named for a kind of cannon shot consisting of two balls or half balls united by a short chain, and formerly used in naval warfare to cut a ship's rigging or sails. The island's shape historically resembled a "chainshot" but has changed its shape over the years.

Chainshot Island See Chain Shot Island

Chancandepeco Inlet See Chaneandepeco Inlet

CHANEANDEPECO INLET A former water passage in Dare County, Kennekeet Township at 35°16′15″N 75°31′15″ and located but not shown on the Buxton map. The water passage connected Pamlico Sound to the Atlantic Ocean through Hatteras Island 1.1 mi. (1.8 km) east of Buxton, and 2.3 mi. (3.7 km) north of Cape Hatteras. **Other names** Cape Channel, Cape Inlet, Chacandepeco Inlet, Chancandepeco Inlet, and The Haulover. **Historical note** The inlet opened prior to 1585 and closed about 1650. The origin of the name is possibly a Spanish corruption of an Algonquian word referring to a shallow area.

Charotuck Inlett Bar See Eastern Shoals

CHEESEMAN INLET A former water passage in Carteret County, Morehead Township at 34°42′00″N 76°46′00″W and located but not shown on the Mansfield map. The water passage connected Bogue Sound to the Atlantic Ocean through Bogue Banks 1.6 mi. (2.6 km) west of Atlantic

Beach, 3.8 mi. (6.1 km) west southwest of the mainland town of Morehead City, and 5 mi. (8 km) west of Beaufort Inlet. **Historical note** The inlet was generally open between 1750 and 1810.

Chicahauk See Kitty Hawk

Chicamacomico See Rodanthe

Chicamacomico See Waves

CHICAMACOMICO BANKS A former barrier island, 19 mi. (30.4 km) long in Dare County, Kennekeet Township at 35°40′30″N 75°29′15″W (north end), 35°24′23″N 75°29′30″W (south end), and 35°32′00″N 75°29′23″W (center) and located but not named on the Pea Island, Rodanthe and Little Kinnakeet maps. The former island included the portion of present Hatteras Island that extends north from the former community of Little Kinnakeet near the former Chaneandepeco Inlet to former New Inlet at the south end of Pea Island. **Other names** Chickinnacomac

Chicamacomico Banks See Hatteras Island

Chicamacomico Banks See Pea Island

CHICAMACOMICO CHANNEL A channel in Dare County, Kennekeet Township at 35°35′42″N 75°28′45″W and located but not shown on the Rodanthe map. The channel is in Pamlico Sound and is the approach to Blackmar Gut, the harbor at Rodanthe on Pea Island. **Other names** Blackmar Gut, Chicamocomico Channel, and The Harbor **Historical note** This is the only name still in current use that uses the original Indian name of this area.

Chicamacomico Inlet See Chickinacommock Inlet

Chicamocomico Channel See Chicamacomico Channel

Chichinock-cominock See Rodanthe

Chicimacomico See Rodanthe

Chicimacomico See Salvo

Chickahauk See Kitty Hawk

Chickahawk See Kitty Hawk

Chickamicomico See Rodanthe

Chickamicomico See Waves

CHICKEHAUK An historical area. This is the Anglicized version of the Indian name for the area from the vicinity of Duck south to Whalebone Junction which is the major tourist area of the Outer Banks today. Kitty Hawk is probably a further corruption of a variation of Chickehauk.

Chickehauk See Kitty Hawk

Chickehauk Island See Currituck Banks

Chickinacommack Inlet See New Inlet

CHICKINACOMMOCK INLET A former water passage in Dare County, Kennekeet Township at 35°37′00″N 75°28′00″W and located on the Rodanthe map. The water passage connected Pamlico Sound to the Atlantic Ocean through Hatteras Island 1.5 mi. (2.4 km) north of Rodanthe and 11 mi. (17.6 km) south of Oregon Inlet. **Other names** Chick Inlet, Chicamacomico Inlet, Chickinockcominock Inlet, Chickinock-comonock Inlet, Chickinoke Inlet, and Chicomok Inlet **Historical**

note The inlet opened in the 1650s and closed just before 1775.

Chickinacommock Inlet See New Inlet

Chick Inlet See Chickinacommock Inlet

Chick Inlet See New Inlet

Chickinnacomac See Chicamacomico Banks

Chickinockcominock Inlet See Chickinacommock Inlet

Chickinockcominok Inlet See New Inlet

Chickinock-comonock Inlet See Chickinacommock Inlet

Chickinocominock Inlet See New Inlet

Chickinoke Inlet See Chickinacommock Inlet

Chickonocomack Bank See Hatteras Island

Chicky See Rodanthe

Chicomok Inlet See Chickinacommock Inlet

Chiconomack Bank See Hatteras Island

Choratuck Inlet See Currituck Inlet

Choretuck Inlet See Currituck Inlet

Chorotuck Inlet Bar See Currituck Inlet Bar

Chowane River See Albemarle Sound

Chowanoke See Croatoan Island

Chowan River See Albemarle Sound

Citie of Raleigh See Fort Raleigh

Cittie of Raleigh See Fort Raleigh

Cittie of Raleigh in Virginia See Fort Raleigh

CLAM SHOAL A shoal, 3 mi. (4.8 km) long, in Dare County, Hatteras Township at 35°17′55″N 75°38′57″W and located but not shown on the Hatteras map. The shoal is in Pamlico Sound 4 mi. (6.4 km) northeast of the village of Hatteras and 5.5 mi. (8.9 km) northwest of Buxton. **Historical note** The exposed area of this shoal is referred to as Bird Island (q.v.).

CLARK REEF A shoal, 0.5 mi. (0.8 km) long, in Hyde County, Ocracoke Township at 35°09′45″N 75°53′42″W and located but not shown on the Howard Reef map. The shoal is in Pamlico Sound 0.9 mi. (1.4 km) north of The Knoll and 3.7 mi. (5.9 km) northeast of the village of Ocracoke.

Clarks See Salvo

CLARKS BAY A cove in Dare County, Kennekeet Township at 35°31′53″N 75°28′47″W and located on the Rodanthe map. The cove is in Pamlico Sound just north of No Ache and 0.8 mi. (1.3 km) south southwest of Salvo.

Clarksville See Salvo

Clubhouse Creek See Austin Creek

Clubhouse Creek See Blossie Creek

COASTAL PLAIN A physiographic or landform region in which the Outer Banks are situated at the extreme east end in North Carolina. The coastal plain is a flat sandy soil area stretching about 150 mi. (230 km) inland in North Carolina to the piedmont region near Raleigh. The plain is made up of two zones: the submerged shelf, and the exposed plain, but generally only the exposed portion is referred to as the Coastal Plain.

COAST GUARD CREEK A cove, 0.05 mi. (0.08 km) wide, in Carteret County, Portsmouth Township at 35°04′09″N 76°03′20″W and located on the Portsmouth map. The cove is in Pamlico Sound at the northeast part of Portsmouth Island 0.4 mi. (0.6 km) east of the village of Portsmouth and 6 mi. (9.7 km) southwest of the village of Ocracoke.

Cockle Creek See Cockrel Creek

Cockle Creek See Silver Lake

COCKLE MARSH ISLAND An island, 0.3 mi. (0.5 km) long, in Carteret County, Harkers Island Township at 34°40′37″N 76°30′25″W and located on the Harkers Island map. The island is in Core Sound 3.3 mi. (4.3 km) east southeast of the village of Harkers Island and 3.3 mi. (4.3 km) north northeast of Barden Inlet. **Historical note** Cockle has many meanings but on the Outer Banks the reference is generally to the bi-valved mollusk with ribbed shells common to the region.

COCKREL CREEK A water passage, 0.4 mi. (0.6 km) wide, in Hyde County, Ocracoke Township at 35°10′21″N 75°49′10″W and located on the Green Island map. The water passage is in Pamlico Sound 0.8 mi. (1.3 km) southwest of Green Island, 3.9 mi. (6.2 km) southwest of Hatteras Inlet, and 10.9 mi. (17.4 km) northeast of the village of Ocracoke. **Other names** Cockle Creek and The Creek **Historical note** The term cockrel is a corruption of the word cockle. See Cockle Marsh Island for a further explanatory note.

COCKREL CREEK ISLAND An island, 0.1 mi. (0.2 km) long, in Hyde County, Ocracoke Township at 35°10′17″N 75°49′10″W and located on the Green Island map. The marsh island is just northeast of Cockrel Creek, 3.8 mi. (6.1 km) southwest of Hatteras Inlet and 11 mi. (17.6 km) northeast of the village of Ocracoke. **Historical note** See Cockle Marsh Island and Cockrel Creek for further explanatory notes.

Cockrel Pond Creek See Silver Lake

CODDS CREEK A water passage, 0.4 mi. (0.6 km) long, in Carteret County, Smyrna Township at 34°41′36″N 76°29′02″W and located on the Horsepen Point map. The water passage is in Core Sound at the entrance to Try Yard Creek 4.2 mi. (6.7 km) east of the town of Harkers Island. **Historical note** Codd is a sixteenth century English term that refers to the bag-like inner part of a bay or marsh and is used extensively in the early Virginia records. The evidence for this meaning is supported by nearby Try Yard Creek (q.v.) which is also a sixteenth century English application.

Coffeys Inlet See Caffeys Inlet

COLINGTON A populated place, 20 ft. (6.1 m) high and with a population of about 150, in Dare County, Atlantic Township at 36°00′53″N 75°42′05″W and located on the Kitty Hawk map. The community is on Colington Island 3.8 mi. (6.1 km) south of Kitty Hawk, 1.9 mi. (3.1 km) west southwest of the Wright Brothers Memorial, and 5.7 mi. (9.1 km) northwest of Nags Head. **Other names** Collington **Historical note** The community is named for the island on which it is located, and a post office was established in 1889 but is now discontinued.

Colington Bay See Colington Creek

COLINGTON CREEK A water passage, 3.5 mi. (5.6 km) long, at 36°02′30″N 75°41′45″W (north end), 35°59′45″N 75°41′10″W (south end), and 36°01′45″N 75°41′23″W (center) and located on the Kitty Hawk and Manteo maps. The water passage connects Kitty Hawk Bay and Buzzard Bay and separates Colington Island from the barrier island, just east of Colington, 3 mi. (4.8 km) south of Kitty Hawk, and 1.1 mi. (2.6 km) west of the Wright Brothers Memorial. **Other names** Colington Bay and Collington Creek

COLINGTON CUT A water passage, 0.8 mi. (1.3 km) long, in Dare County, Atlantic Township at 36°00′33″N 75°42′03″W (north end), 35°59′57″N 75°41′46″W (south end), 36°00′00″N 75°41′55″W (center) and located on the Kitty Hawk and Manteo maps. The water passage is a canalized stream that divides Colington Island into two sections and connects Blount Bay on the north and Buzzard Bay on the south, 1.7 mi. (2.7 km) south southwest of the Wright Brothers Memorial and 3.1 mi. (5 km) north northwest of Nags Head. **Other names** Colington Cut Ditch, Colington Ditch, Dividing Creek, and The Dividing Creek. **Historical note** The feature was canalized by extending the stream south in the eighteenth century, and is oftentimes locally referred to as The Dividing Creek.

Colington Cut Ditch See Colington Cut

Colington Ditch See Colington Cut

COLINGTON HARBOUR A harbor, 0.2 mi. (0.3 km) long and 0.2 mi. (0.3 km) wide, in Dare County, Atlantic Township at 36°01′06″N 75°43′30″W and located but not named on the Kitty Hawk map. The harbor is at the northwest part of Colington Island, 2.3 mi. (3.7 km) south southwest of Kitty Hawk and 7.3 mi. (11.7 km) northwest of Nags Head. **Historical note** The name is a recent one, therefore, the spelling is not from the English of the sixteenth or seventeenth centuries, but is a colorful name of recent application.

COLINGTON ISLAND An island, 2.1 mi. (3.4 km) long and 2.5 mi. (4 km) wide, in Dare County, Atlantic Township at 36°00′00″N 75°42′00″W and located on the Kitty Hawk and Manteo Maps. The island is located in Roanoke Sound near the mouth of Albemarle Sound just west of the barrier island, 4.5 mi. (7.2 km) south of Kitty Hawk and 2 mi. (3.2 km) west of the Wright Brothers Memorial. **Other names** Carlile Island, Carlyle Island, Colleton Island, Collington Island, and Collingtons Island **Historical note** The feature was named for Sir John Colleton to whom the island was granted in 1663. The name was changed to Carlile Island for a short time for Christopher Carlile, stepson of Sir Francis Washington who accompanied Sir Francis Drake to the Outer Banks in 1586, but Carlile Island was dropped in favor of Colington Island.

COLINGTON ISLAND SHOAL A shoal in Dare County, Atlantic Township at 35°58′30″N 75°43′30″W and located but not shown on the Manteo map. The shoal is at the junction of Croatan and Albemarle Sounds 3.6 mi. (5.8 km) east southeast of Colington Island and 4.1 mi. (6.6 km) northwest of Manteo.

COLINGTON SHOAL A shoal, about 2 mi. (3.2 km) long and an average of 6 ft. (1.9 meters or 1 fathom) deep at mean water level, in Dare County, Nags Head and Croatan townships at 36°56′45″N 75°45′47″W and located but not shown on the Manteo map. The shoal is in Albemarle Sound, 5.3

mi. (8.5 km) northwest of Manteo.

Colleton Island See Colington Island

Collington See Colington

Collington Creek See Colington Creek

Collington Island See Colington Island

Collingtons Island See Colington Island

COLONY LAKE A lake, 0.1 mi. (0.2 km) across, in Dare County, Atlantic Township at 36°01′14″N 75°42′57″W and located but not named on the Kitty Hawk map. The lake is on the northwest part of Colington Island, 1.4 mi. (2.2 km) west northwest of the village of Colington and 3 mi. (4.8 km) south of Kitty Hawk.

CONCH SHOAL MARSH An island, 0.05 mi. (0.08 km) long, in Carteret County, Harkers Island Township at 34°39′14″N 76°32′57″W and located on the Harkers Island map. The island is a marsh area just north of Shackleford Banks and just east of Johnsons Bay, 3 mi. (4.8 km) south of the village of Harkers Island and 2.1 mi. (3.4 km) northwest of Barden Inlet. **Historical note** Conch refers to any large spiral-shelled marine gastroped mollusks (clams and oysters) which are commonly found on the Outer Banks.

Conetto Inlett See Currituck Inlet

COQUINA BEACH A beach in Dare County, Nags Head Township at 34°49′55″N 75°33′20″W and located but not named on the Oregon Inlet map. The beach is on Bodie Island 3.8 mi. (6.1 km) north northwest of Oregon Inlet, 4.9 mi. (7.8 km) east of Wanchese, and 9.5 mi. (15.3 km) south southeast of Nags Head. **Historical note** The beach was established as a swimming area and named by the National Park Service. The name originates from a shellfish of the conch family found on the Outer Banks.

Corahtuck Banks See Currituck Banks

Coranine Sound See Core Sound

Coratock Banks See Currituck Banks

Coratuck Inlet See Currituck Inlet

Coratut Banks See Currituck Banks

Core Bank See Core Banks

CORE BANKS Barrier beaches in Carteret County, Portsmouth, Atlantic, Sea Level, Stacy, Davis, Smyrna, and Harkers Island townships at 34°58′07″N 76°09′15″W (north end), 34°34′57″N 76°32′01″W (south end), and 34°47′00″N 76°23′30″W (center) and located on the Wainwright Island, Atlantic, Styron Bay, Davis, Horsepen Point, Harkers Island, and Cape Lookout maps. These islands extend northeast from Cape Lookout and Barden Inlet to Swash Inlet just south of Portsmouth Island. **Other names** Cape Lookout Banks, Core Bank, Coree Banks, Croatoan Island, Endesoakes, Ocracock Island, Portsmouth Bank, Portsmouth Banks, Salvage Island, Shoals Bank, and Wococon Island. **Historical note** The feature is named for the Coree Indians who were known to have inhabited this area. The Coree Indians had become extinct by the early seventeenth century as a result of their warlike nature with the colonists and neighboring Indian tribes.

CORE BEACH An historical area vaguely applied to various undefined portions of Core Banks south of Portsmouth Island and north of Cape Lookout. The term is still used today by older residents but is rapidly falling into disuse.

Core Beach See Portsmouth Island

Coree Banks See Core Banks

Corenines Sound See Core Sound

CORE SOUND A lagoon, 27 mi. (33.1 km) long and 3 mi. (4.8 km) wide, in Carteret County, Cedar Island, Portsmouth, Atlantic, Sea Level, Stacy, Davis, Smyrna, and Harkers Island townships at 34°59′00″N 76°12′30″W (north end), 34°40′45″N 76°31′15″W (south end), and 35°49′00″N 76°22′00″W (center) and located on the Wainwright Island, Atlantic, Styron Bay, Davis, Horsepen Point, and Harkers Island maps. The lagoon extends south from Pamlico Sound to Back Sound at Cape Lookout and separates the mainland from Core Banks. **Other names** Coranine Sound, Corenines Sound, and The Sound **Historical note** See Core Banks for an explanatory note.

Core Sound See Beaufort Inlet

Core Sound See The Straits

Core Sound Inlet See Beaufort Inlet

Coretank See Currituck Sound

COROLLA A populated place, with a population of about 35, in Currituck County, Fruitville Township at 36°22′45″N 75°50′00″W and located on the Corolla map. The village is on Currituck Banks 4.8 mi. (7.7 km) east of the mainland village of Waterlilly and 17 mi. (27.3 km) north of Duck. **Other names** Currituck Beach and Whales Head. **Historical note** The post office department named its post office Corolla when it was established here in 1895 and gradually the former village names of Currituck Beach and Whales Head fell into disuse. The origin of the name is unknown or at least lost, but the name refers to the inner leaves or petals of a flower, and local residents accept this as the reason for naming but give no other explanation. The name Currituck Beach was generally used to refer to the beach at Corolla while the name Whales Head was used to refer to the village at Currituck Beach. The term Whales Head is reported by some to be a reference to the shape of the local barchane or crescent shaped dunes in the area, but this is not verified by local investigation.

Corotuck River See Currituck Inlet

Corova See Carova

Corova Beach See Carova

Corratuck Banks See Currituck Banks

CORYS A former populated place in Currituck County, Fruitville Township at 36°32′19″N 75°57′50″W and located on the Knotts Island map. The community was formerly on the northwest edge of Great Marsh 2.9 mi. (4.1 km) northwest of the village of Knotts Island. **Historical note** Today Corys is abandoned without even a trace of buildings, but as late as 1950 there were a few families living there. The name is reported to be that of a family but is more than likely a variation of Coropeake, an early variation of an Indian name used in this area.

Cove Point See Cape Point (Dare County, Hatteras Township)

Cowe Island See Cow Island (former barrier island)

COW ISLAND An island, 0.1 mi. (0.2 km) long, in Carteret County, Harkers Island Township at 34°39′45″N 76°34′02″W and located on the Harkers Island map. The marsh island is in Back Sound just north of Shackleford Banks, 2.2 mi. (3.5 km) south of the village of Harkers Island, and 3.2 mi. (5.1 km) northwest of Barden Inlet.

COW ISLAND A former barrier island in Dare County, Nags Head Township just east of Roanoke Island and in the present vicinity of Whalebone Junction. **Other names** Cowe Island and Lucks Island **Historical note** Cow Island was the northernmost of three small barrier islands formed by the historical inlets Gunt, and Roanoke in the present vicinity of Bodie Island and Oregon Inlet.

Cow Island See Bodie Island

Cowpen Creek See Fort Macon Creek

Cow Pen Creek See Fort Macon Creek

COWPEN ISLAND An island, 0.3 mi. (0.5 km) wide, in Carteret County, Smyrna Township at 34°42′37″N 76°28′23″W and located on the Horsepen Point map. The marsh island is in Core Sound just west of Core Banks and 4.8 mi. (7.7 km) east of the village of Harkers Island.

COWPEN POINT A point of land in Carteret County, Portsmouth Township at 34°58′07″N 76°11′01″W and located on the Wainwright Island map. It is a sandy point on the soundside area of an unnamed shoal between the Pilontary Islands and Cricket Island 9.2 mi. (14.7 km) southwest of the village of Portsmouth and 15.2 mi. (24.3 km) southwest of the village of Ocracoke. **Other names** Cowpenpoint

Cowpenpoint See Bluff Point

Cowpenpoint See Cowpen Point

CRAB CLAW SPIT A peninsula, 1.1 mi. (1.8 km) long, in Dare County, Nags Head Township at 35°56′17″N 75°41′55″W and located but not named on the Manteo map. The sand spit is in Roanoke Sound at the north end of Roanoke Island, 2.4 mi. (3.8 km) northwest of Manteo. **Other names** Sand Spit **Historical note** The feature's name is descriptive of its shape. As with the formation of any spit, material is being deposited by longshore drift which is a process that moves eroded material along the shore, as the result of angular wave action.

CRANE ISLAND A former island, approximately 11 mi. (17.6 km) long, in Carteret County at about 34°50′00″N 76°22′00″W. The island was in Core Sound about 2 mi. (3.2 km) west of Core Banks, about 20 mi. (32 km) north northeast of Cape Lookout and about 30 mi. (48 km) southwest of the village of Ocracoke.

Crane Island See Harkers Island

Craney Island See Harkers Island

Crany Island See Harkers Island

CREEDS HILL A hill, 9 ft. (2.7 m) high, in Dare County, Hatteras Township at 35°14′29″N 75°34′57″W and located on the Cape Hatteras map. The hill is located just north of Hatteras Bight, 3.1 mi. (5 km) west northwest of Cape Hatteras and 2.3 mi. (3.4 km) east of Frisco.

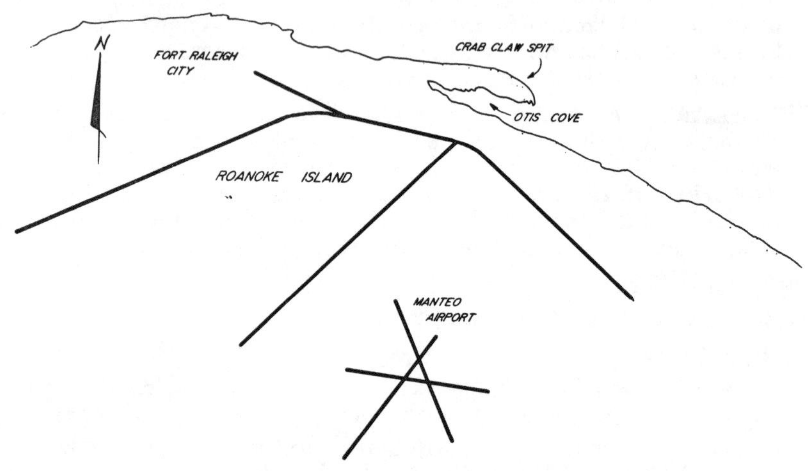

CRICKET ISLAND An island, 0.5 mi. (0.8 km) wide, in Carteret County, Portsmouth Township at 34°57′34″N 76°22′14″W and located on the Wainwright Island map. The marsh island is between the Pilontary Islands and Sand Island 9.9 mi. (15.9 km) southwest of the village of Portsmouth and 15.9 mi. (22.5 km) southwest of the village of Ocracoke.

CRICKET ISLAND POINT A point of land in Carteret County, Portsmouth Township at 34°57′34″N 76°11′38″W and located on the Wainwright Island map. This marsh point is on Cricket Island 10.2 mi. (16.3 km) southwest of the village of Portsmouth and 15.2 mi. (25.9 km) southwest of the village of Ocracoke.

Croat See Etacrewac

CROATAMUNG A former barrier island that is now part of Currituck Banks. It extended north from the vicinity of Kitty Hawk to the barrier island just east of Knotts Island in the general area of the present North Carolina and Virginia boundary. **Other names** Arundells Ile, Etacrewac, and Lucks Island

Croatamung See Currituck Banks

Croatamung See Lucks Island

Croatan See Croatoan Island

Croatan See Indian Town

Croatan Island See Portsmouth Island

CROATAN SHORES A populated place in Dare County, Atlantic Township at 36°01′45″N 75°40′00″W and located on the Kitty Hawk map. The community is located 3.3 mi. (5.3 km) southeast of Kitty Hawk and 4.1 mi. (6.6 km) southeast of Kitty Hawk Beach.

Croatan Shores See Kill Devil Hills (populated place)

CROATAN SOUND A strait, 11.3 mi. (18.2 km) long, in Dare County, Nags Head and Croatan townships at 35°56′15″N 75°44′45″W (northwest end), 35°46′30″N 75°41′15″W (southeast end), and 35°53′00″N 75°43′00″W (center) and located on the Manteo and Wanchese maps. The water passage trends northwest-southeast from Albemarle Sound to Pamlico Sound and separates the mainland and Roanoke Island. **Other names** Back Bay, Croatoan Sound, Croetan Sound, Occam (Algonquian term meaning "the opposite shore"), and The Narrows

Croatoan See Cape Hatteras

Croatoan See Hatteras Island

CROATOAN ISLAND A former barrier island in Dare and Hyde counties that consisted of the south portion of Hatteras Island and a small portion of north Ocracoke Island. It extended north and northeast from Old Hatteras Inlet (q.v.) to just north of Cape Hatteras near the former Chaneandepeco Inlet (q.v.), and Hatteras Inlet now bisects what used to be Croatoan Island. **Other names** Abbots Island, Chowanoke, Croatan, Raonack, and Roanack **Historical note** The feature is named for an Indian village formerly located in the vicinity of Cape Hatteras and the name could mean residence of the chief. This application is less extensive than that used by White on his return voyage searching for the Lost Colonists. White seems to have placed the northern limit about 18 mi. (28.8 km) further north than later cartographic application.

Croatoan Island See Core Banks

Croatoan Island See Portsmouth Island

Croatoan Sound See Croatan Sound

Croetan Sound See Croatan Sound

Cross Shoal See Austin Reef

CROSS SHOAL CHANNEL A channel, 0.6 mi. (1 km) long, in Carteret County, Atlantic Township at 34°51′47″N 76°18′53″W and located on the Styron Bay map. The channel is in Core Sound 2 mi. (3.2 km) southeast of the mainland village of Atlantic.

Crotan See Portsmouth Island

Crow Inlet See New Currituck Inlet

CROW ISLAND A former island, about 1 mi. (1.6 km) across, in Currituck County, Fruitville Township and located but not shown on the Barco and Corolla maps. The island was located in Currituck Sound about 6 mi. (9.6 km) southeast of Knotts Island at New Currituck Inlet approximately 5 mi. (8 km) north northeast of Monkey Island. In 1833 the island began to become inundated and by 1861 had become merely tidal marshes.

Curatock Inlet See Currituck Inlet

Curhuk Banks See Currituck Banks

Curratuck Inlet See Currituck Inlet

Currchuck Inlet See New Currituck Inlet

Currehuck Inlet See Currituck Inlet

Curretuck Inlet See Currituck Inlet

Curritue Inlet See Currituck Inlet

Currituck See Currituck Banks

Currituck Bank See Currituck Banks

CURRITUCK BANKS A barrier spit in Currituck County, Fruitville and Poplar Branch townships, and Dare County, Atlantic Township at 36°42′45″N 75°52′15″W (north end), 35°54′00″N 75°52′00″W (south end), and 36°16′23″N 75°30′08″W (center) and located on the Knotts Island, Barco, Corolla, Mossey Islands, Jarvisburg, Martin Point, Point Harbor, Kitty Hawk, Manteo, and Roanoke Island NE maps. The barrier spit extends north from Bodie Island near Whalebone Junction to North Bay in Virginia. **Other names** Arundells Ile, Chickehauk Island, Corahtuck Banks, Coratock Banks, Coratut Banks, Corratuck Banks, Croatamung, Curhuk Banks, Currituck, Currituck Bank, Currituck Liberty Plains, False Cape, Goade Island, Iland of Saint John, Ile Goade, Liberty Plains, Lucks Island, Nags Head Banks, North Bank, North Banks, North Banks of Currituck, Point Bacon, and Sand Bank **Historical note** The name is thought to be derived from the Algonquin word Carotank or Coratank referring to wild geese. The suffix means "wealth" and most likely refers to the profusion of wild geese in the area. Some authors also believe that the word may imitate the sound of the water fowl of the region.

Currituck Banks See Lucks Island

CURRITUCK BEACH A beach in Currituck County, Fruitville Township at 36°22′30″N 75°49′25″W and located on the Corolla and Mossey Islands maps. The beach is at Corolla on Currituck Banks 5 mi. (8 km) east of the mainland village of Waterlilly, and 16.8 mi. (27 km) north of Duck. **Historical note** The name is oftentimes applied to the beach at Corolla, and the community of Corolla was sommetimes known as Currituck Beach until a post office was established and the community gradually adopted Corolla as the name of the village as well as the post office.

Currituck Beach See Corolla

CURRITUCK COUNTY A civil division, at 36°21′00″N 75°53′00″W. It is the northeast most county in North Carolina and is bounded by Dare and Camden Counties as well as the City of Virginia Beach, Virginia and includes Fruitville, Poplar Branch, Moyock and Crawford townships.

CURRITUCK INLET A former water passage in Currituck County, Fruitville Township at 36°33′00″N 75°52′15″W and located but not shown on the Knotts Island map. The former water passage connected Currituck Sound and the Atlantic Ocean through Currituck Banks just south of the North Carolina - Virginia boundary. **Other names** Caratock Inlet, Caratuk Inlet, Caritock Inlet, Carotuck Inlet, Carotuck River, Choratuck Inlet, Choretuck Inlet, Conetto Inlett, Coratuck Inlet, Corotuck River, Curatock Inlet, Curratuck Inlet, Currehuck Inlet, Curretuck Inlet, Curritue Inlett, Currituck Inlett, Old Currituck Inlet, Old Inlet, Port Currituck, and Trinitie Harbor. **Historical note** The inlet was open prior to 1585 but closed in 1731. It was selected as the starting point for the boundary between North Carolina and Virginia, but by the time the boundary commission actually began surveying the boundary, the North Carolina residents claimed the inlet had "shoaled up" to the north and had migrated southward, therefore, the boundary was surveyed 200 yards north of the inlet.

Currituck Inlet See New Currituck Inlet

CURRITUCK INLET BAR Former shoals in Currituck County, Fruitville Township at 36°30′00″N 75°52′10″W and located but not named on the Knotts Island map. The shoals and breakers area was formerly located at the entrance to Currituck Inlet before it closed. **Other names** Chorotuck Inlet Bar

Currituck Inlett See Currituck Inlet

Currituck Liberty Plains See Currituck Banks

Currituck Narrows See Big Narrows

CURRITUCK SOUND A lagoon, 30 mi. (48 km) long and 4 mi. (6.4 km) wide, in Dare County, Atlantic Township and Currituck County, Fruitville and Popular Branch Townships at 36°20′54″N 75°51′25″W and located on the Barco, Corolla, Mossey Islands, Jarvisburg, Martin Point, and Point Harbor maps. The lagoon connects Back Bay in Virginia to Albemarle Sound and separates the mainland from Currituck Banks. **Other names** Coretank, Northwest River, Occam, Port Currituck, River San Bartolome, and Titpano **Historical note** The sound was known locally by the Indians as Titepano an Algonquin word generally meaning swirling waters. The sound has become fresh water since Currituck and New Currituck Inlets (q.v.) closed.

Cutoff Island See Off Island

CUT THROUGH A water passage, 0.5 mi. (0.8 km) long, in Dare County, Nags Head Township at 35°48′57″N 75°38′02″W and located on the Wanchese map. The water passage separates unnamed marsh islands just south of Roanoke Island 2 mi. (3.2 km) south of Wanchese. **Historical note** The term is descriptive and is often applied to features that provide passages for water craft among the marsh islands. Some more permanent such passages have retained the descriptive term as a proper name.

CUT THROUGH A water passage, 0.2 mi. (0.3 km) long, in Dare County, Nags Head Township at 35°49′14″N 75°36′57″W and located on the Oregon Inlet map. The water passage is in Roanoke Sound and trends northeast-southwest through unnamed marsh islands 2.4 mi. (3.8 km) south southeast of Wanchese. **Historical note** See Cut Through above for an explanatory note.

CUTTIN SAGE LAKE A cove, less than 0.1 mi. (0.2 km) wide, in Hyde County, Ocracoke Township at 35°07′12″N 76°58′31″W and located on the Ocracoke map. It is a small cove with a very narrow opening to Pamlico Sound 0.3 mi. (0.5 km) east of Northern Pond and 0.5 mi. (0.8 km) northeast of the village of Ocracoke. **Historical note** The "g" in Cutting has been dropped which is a common practice in spoken language throughout the U.S., but is not usually written as such. While sage is a common plant of the mint family, the word is probably a mispronunciation of sedge, a common plant found in marshes on the Outer Banks and cuttin sedge is a common term used in the area.

D

Daniels Marshes See Roanoke Marshes

DANIEL SWASH A water passage, 0.7 mi. (1.1 km) long, in Carteret County, Portsmouth Township at 35°02′04″N 75°06′15″W and located on the Portsmouth map. The water passage is in Pamlico Sound and trends east southeast-west northwest from Portsmouth Island to Pamlico Sound 3.5 mi. (5.6 km) southwest of the village of Portsmouth and 9.5 mi. (15.1 km) southwest of the village of Ocracoke. **Historical note** Swash is the advancement of water up the beach after the breaking of a wave (wave surge). On the Outer Banks swash oftentimes refers to an area of overwash.

DARE BANKS An area. A relatively recent term applied to Bodie Island and southern Currituck Banks generally from Whalebone Junction to Southern Shores. It is applied commercially and used as a reference in the tourist industry.

Dare Coast See Outer Banks

DARE COUNTY A civil division, 391 square mi. (526.6 km) with a population of 6,995 at 35°54′00″N 75°54′00″W. The county was formed in 1870 from Currituck, Tyrell, and Hyde counties, and is bounded by Currituck, Camden, Tyrell and Hyde counties and contains Atlantic, Nags Head, Kennekeet, Hatteras, Croatan, and East Lake townships. **Historical note** The county was named for Virginia Dare, the first English child to be born in America.

Dare Dunes See Dunes of Dare

Davers Island See Harkers Island

DAVIDS POINT A point of land in Dare County, Kennekeet Township at 35°33′43″N 75°28′29″W and located on the Rodanthe map. The point is a marsh point on north Hatteras Island 0.1 mi. (0.2 km) east of Great Island and 0.4 mi. (0.6 km) southwest of Waves.

DAVIS CHANNEL A channel, 2.5 mi. (4 km) long, in Dare County, Kennekeet Township at 35°46′00″N 75°32′15″W (northeast end), 35°44′10″N 75°34′00″W (southwest end), and 35°45′14″N 75°33′17″W (center) and located on the Oregon Inlet map. The channel is in Pamlico Sound just west of Pea Island and 7.6 mi. (12.2 km) southeast of Wanchese. **Other names** Davis Slough

Davis Slough See Davis Channel

DEAL ISLAND A marsh in Dare County, Fruitville Township at 36°32′45″N 75°53′30″W and located on the Knotts Island map. The marsh is 1 mi. (1.6 km) west of Currituck Banks and 3.1 mi. (5 km) northeast of the village of Knotts Island

DEALS A former populated place in Currituck County, Fruitville Township at 36°30′28″N 75°52′00″W and located on the Corolla map. The former community was on Currituck Banks 4 mi. (6.4 km) south of the North Carolina-Virginia boundary and 7 mi. (11.2 km) north northwest of Corolla. **Other names** Wash Woods **Historical note** The community was originally known as Wash Woods because there are stumps on the beach from a former wooded area. In 1907 the Post Office Department established a Post office here and called it Deals. Gradually, the post office name was adopted as the community name. The name is a surname in the area, but as with many of these late nineteenth and early twentieth century post office names no record exists as to the origin. The post office was discontinued in 1917 and today there is little evidence of the former community.

Deep Creek See Drum Creek

DEEP DITCH A water passage, 0.8 mi. (1.3 km) long, in Dare County, Atlantic Township at 36°00′18″N 75°41′02″W (north end), 35°59′45″N 75°40′18″W (south end), and 36°00″04″N 75°40′50″W (center) and located but not named on the Kitty Hawk and Manteo maps. The water passage separates Walker Island from Currituck Banks and is 4.3 mi. (6.9 km) northwest of Nags Head.

DEEP DITCH POINT A point of land in Dare County, Atlantic Township at 35°59′45″N 75°41′00″W and located but not named on the Manteo map. The point is the southern point of Walker Island and is located 4 mi. (6.4 km) northwest of Nags Head.

DEEP NECK A water passage, 0.4 mi. (0.6 km) long, in Currituck County, Poplar Branch Township at 36°15′59″N 75°48′14″W (north end), 36°15′40″N 75°48′00″W (south end), and 36°15′53″N 75°48′02″W (center) and located on the Mossey Islands map. This pronounced water passage is just south of Tar Cove Marsh at the sound side of Currituck Banks, 8 mi. (12.8 km) northwest of Duck and 8 mi. (12.8 km) south of Corolla. **Other names** Deep Neck Creek **Historical note** Neck, as a generic, is usually used for a protuberance of land as in nearby coastal Virginia and Maryland, but in this case refers to a water passage.

Deep Neck Creek See Deep Neck

DEEP WEAR POINT A point of land in Dare County, Nags Head Township at 35°53′38″N 75°41′17″W and located but not named on the Manteo map. The Point is 1.5 mi. (2.4 km) northwest of Ashbee Harbor and 1.5 mi. (2.4 km) southwest of Manteo. **Historical note** The name appears on early maps and could be a corruption of weir (a fishing apparatus). The reference, however, is more likely a term in use in the seventeenth and eighteenth centuries when wear referred to bring a ship about or into the wind.

Deer Creek See Deer Pond

DEER POND A cove, 0.3 mi. (0.5 km) wide, in Carteret County, Smyrna Township at 34°44′37″N 76°26′17″W and located on the Horsepen Point map. The cove is in Core Sound just east of Johnson Creek and 3.8 mi. (6.1 km) south of the mainland town of Davis. **Other names** Deer Creek

DEMPS ISLAND A former island in Dare County, Nags Head Township at approximately 35°54′55″N 75°36′25″W and located but not shown on the Roanoke Island NE map. The small island was in Roanoke Sound just east of the Penguin Islands about 1 mi. (1.6 km) northwest of Whalebone Junction and about 3.5 mi. (5.3 km) south southeast of Nags Head. **Historical note** There is no trace of the island today.

DENNISS ISLAND A former barrier island at 36°33′00″N 75°52′15″W (north end), 36°23′30″N 75°49′45″W (south end), and 36°28′15″N 75°51′00″W (center) and located but not named on the Knotts Island and Corolla maps. The former barrier island is now part of Currituck Banks but was bounded on the north by Currituck Inlet and on the south by Musketo Inlet, both of which are now closed.

DEVIL SHOALS An area of shoals, 1 mi. (1.6 km) long, in Dare County, Hatteras Township at 35°18′05″N 75°35′10″W (northwest end), 35°17′35″N 75°34′20″W (southeast end), and 35°17′50″N 75°34′45″W (center) and located but not shown on the Buxton map. The shoals are in Pamlico Sound, 2.5 mi. (4 km) northwest of Buxton.

DIAMOND CITY A former populated place in Carteret County, Harkers Island Township at 34°38′40″N 76°32′15″W and located but not shown on the Harkers Island map. This former village was on east Shackleford Banks 3 mi. (4.8 km) north northwest of Cape Lookout, 1.1 mi. (1.8 km) west of Barden Inlet, and 4 mi. (6.4 km) south southeast of the village of Harkers Island. **Other names** Cape Hills, Eastern End, Lookout Woods and The Eastern End **Historical note** The name was derived from the diamond-shaped pattern of the nearby lighthouse at Cape Lookout, and was suggested by Joe Etheridge former superintendant of the life saving station at Diamond City. The community was a scattered or dispersed community extending from Barden Inlet west over much of the island. The major economy was based on the whaling and fishing industry. The village became deserted after several devastating storms in the 1890's especially the hurricane of 1899, after which most of the residents moved to the village of Harkers Island. See Cape Lookout Grounds for a description of whaling Outer Banks style.

DIAMOND CITY HILLS Sand dunes, 15 ft (4.5 m) high, in Carteret County, Harkers Island Township at 34°38′43″N 76°32′15″W and located on the Harkers Island map. These dunes are located on Shackleford Banks 1.1 mi. (1.8 km) west northwest of Barden Inlet and 3.8 mi. (6.1 km) south southeast of the village of Harkers Island.

Diamond Shoal See Diamond Shoals

Diamond Shoal See Inner Shoals

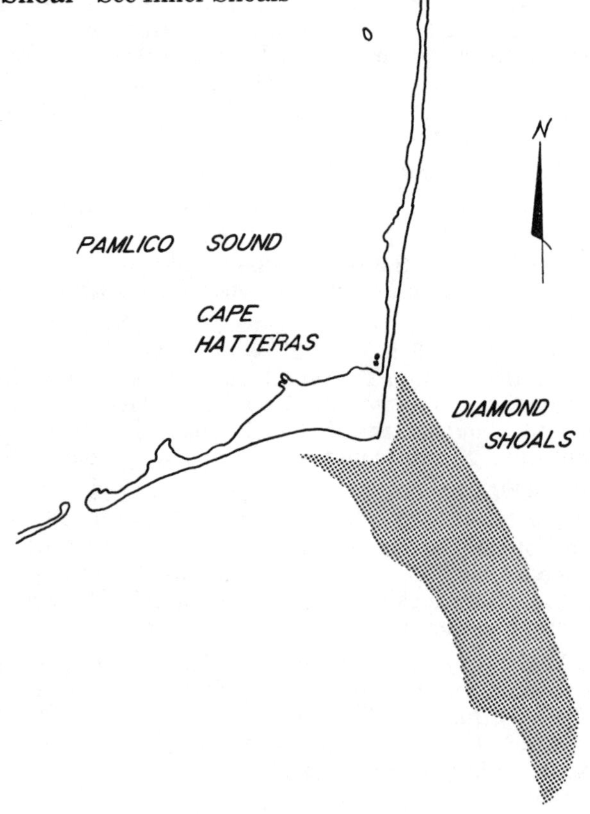

DIAMOND SHOALS Shoals, 25 mi. (40 km) long, in Dare County, Hatteras Township at 35°11′00″N 75°29′30″W and located on the Cape Hatteras map. The shoals extend southeast from Cape Hatteras into the Atlantic Ocean 4.8 mi. (7.5 km) southeast of Buxton. **Other names** Cape Hatteras Shoals, Diamond Shoal, Graveyard of Ships, Graveyard of the Atlantic, Hatteras Shoals, Point of the Diamonds, Sholes of Hatteras, The Diamond, The Diamonds, The Graveyard, The Shoals, and Torpedo Junction (originiated from the high degree of activity of German submarines in the area during World War II). **Historical note** Diamond Shoals is actually made up of a series of three shoals - Hatteras Shoals (q.v.), Inner Diamond Shoal (q.v.), and Outer Diamond Shoal (q.v.). Hatteras Shoals is separated from Inner Diamond Shoal by Hatteras Slough, and Diamond Slough separates Inner and Outer Diamond Shoals. The name originates from the somewhat diamond shape created by the shoals. These shoals are the area at which the warm waters of the Gulf Stream and cold waters of the Labrador Current Extension meet causing constantly changing hydrography. These shoals were recognized as dangerous to shipping from very early in the settlement of North America and the area was termed "the Graveyard of the Atlantic" by Alexander Hamilton in 1773. Alexander Hamilton was also responsible for the first attempt at establishing a lighthouse at Cape Hatteras to warn ships approaching the dreaded Diamond Shoals.

DIAMOND SLOUGH A channel in Dare County, Hatteras Township at 35°10′30″N 75°27′10″W and located but not named on Chart 11555. The channel is a natural channel between Inner Diamond Shoal and Outer Diamond Shoal. **Other names** Hatteras Slough and Outer Slue Channel

DICKS CAMP A camp in Hyde County, Ocracoke Township at 35°08′34″N 75°53′45″W and located on the Howard Reef map. The camp is located on the southwest bank of Try Yard Creek 0.3 mi. (0.5 km) northeast of Parkers Hill, 7.7 mi. (12.3 km) west of Hatteras Inlet, and 6 mi. (9.7 km) northeast of Ocracoke. **Historical note** See Ira Morris Camp for an explanatory note.

Dividing Creek See Colington Cut

DOCTORS CREEK A cove, 0.2 mi. (0.3 km) long, in Carteret County, Portsmouth Township at 35°04′15″N 76°03′42″W and located on the Portsmouth map. The cove is in Pamlico Sound 0.2 mi. (0.3 km) northeast of the village of Portsmouth and 6.2 mi. (9.9 km) southwest of the village of Ocracoke.

Dog Island See Dog Islands

DOG ISLANDS Islands in Carteret County, Morehead Township at 34°41′40″N 76°54′22″W and located on the Salter Path map. The series of three of four islands are in Bogue Sound 1.2 mi. (1.9 km) northwest of Salter Path and 10.5 mi. (16.8 km) west of Atlantic Beach. **Other names** Dog Island **Historical note** These islands were originally one island but have since divided into three or four islands.

DOG POINT CREEK A water passage, 0.5 mi. (0.8 km) long, in Dare County, Atlantic Township at 36°01′05″N 75°42′00″W and located but not named on the Kitty Hawk map. The tidal passage is the southwest section of a water passage that trends northeast from Blount Bay to Sloop Creek just northwest of the village of Colington and 3.3 mi. (5.3 km) south of Kitty Hawk.

Dolbys Point See Baum Point (Dare County, Nags Head Township)

Dollys Point See Baum Point (Dare County, Nags Head Township)

DORLAND LUMP An island, less than 0.1 mi. (0.2 km) across, in Dare County, Kennekeet Township at 35°40′44″N 75°30′23″W and located but not named on the Pea Island map. The small marsh island is in Pamlico Sound 0.5 mi. (0.8 km) south of Jack Shoal, 1.6 mi. (2.6 km) north northwest of the site of New Inlet and 6.1 mi. (9.8 km) northwest of Rodanthe. **Historical note** The feature is considerably smaller than in the nineteenth century.

DOTTY POND A lake, 0.2 mi. (0.3 km) long and less than 0.1 mi. (0.2 km) wide, in Currituck County, Poplar Branch Township at 36°18′42″N 75°49′09″W and located on the Mossey Islands map. It is located on the marshy sound side of Curritucks Banks just west of the northern most dune of Three Dunes, 4.5 mi. (7.2 km) south of Corolla and 11.3 mi. (18.1 km) north northwest of Duck. **Other names** Potty Pond

DOUGHS CREEK A stream, 1.3 mi. (2.1 km) long, in Dare County, Nags Head Township at 35°54′34″N 75°40′06″W and located on the Manteo map. The stream heads at 35°55′31″N 75°40′37″W, 0.6 mi. (1 km) west of Mother Vineyard on Roanoke Island and flows south to Shallowbag Bay at Manteo.

DOUGLAS ISLAND Marsh and hummocks, 0.5 mi. (0.8 km) long and 0.3 mi. (0.5 km) wide, in Dare County, Kennekeet Township at 35°42′09″N 75°30′07″W and located on the Pea Island map. The feature is made up of two areas of high ground surrounded by a marsh area just south of Terrapin Creek, 5.8 mi. (9.3 km) south of Oregon Inlet and 6.8 mi. (10.9 km) north northwest of Rodanthe.

DOUGLAS POINT A point of land in Carteret County, Davis Township at 34°45′57″N 76°25′53″W and located on the Davis map. The point is on an unnamed marsh island between Stone Point and Shingle Point 2.9 mi. (4.6 km) south southeast of the mainland town of Davis.

Doxeys Pond See Doxeys Salthouse

DOXEYS SALTHOUSE A marsh, 1 mi. (1.6 km) long, in Currituck County, Poplar Branch Township at 36°14′49″N 75°47′07″W and located on the Jarvisburg map. It is a marsh area with open water and located on the sound side of Currituck Banks just east of Little Yankee Pond, 6.3 mi. (10.1 km) northwest of Duck and 9.3 mi. (14.9 km) south of Corolla. **Other names** Doxeys Pond and Spit House

DRAIN ISLANDS Islands, 0.1 mi. (0.2 km) long and 0.05 mi. (0.08 km) wide, in Dare County, Kennekeet Township at 35°24′54″N 75°29′35″W and located on the Little Kinnakeet map. These marsh islands are located at the mouth of The Drain 0.7 mi. (1.1 km) north of Little Kinnakeet and 4.7 mi. (7.5 km) north of Avon.

DRUM CREEK A former water passage in Carteret County, Morehead Township at 34°42′23″N 76°41′53″W and located but not shown on the Beaufort map. The water passage connected Morehead City Channel and Bogue Sound and was located just north of Goat Island 1.8 mi. (3.9 km) south of the mainland town of Morehead City. **Other names** Deep Creek **Historical note** See Drum Inlet for a possible explanation of the use and application of the word drum.

DRUM INLET A water passage, 0.3 mi. (0.5 km) wide, in Carteret County,

Atlantic Township at 34°51′15″N 76°18′52″W and located but not shown on the Styron Bay map. The water passage connects Core Sound and the Atlantic Ocean at Cross Shoal Channel 2.8 mi. (4.5 km) southeast of former Drum Inlet and 1.9 mi. (3 km) south southeast of the mainland village of Atlantic. **Other names** New Drum Inlet, New Inlet, and Old Drum Inlet **Historical note** The inlet was opened in its present location in 1971 by the U.S. Army Corps of Engineers when the old location 2.8 mi. (4.5 km) northwest of the present location closed. The true origin of the name may never be known, but is thought to refer to the Drum fish (so called because of the drumming noise that it makes) common to the Atlantic coast. This accepted use may be misleading because the term drum has been applied to many inlets since the early eighteenth century, and there are archaic references to the word drum that may have relevance to its application and use on the Outer Banks. In the early eighteenth century a drum also referred to a sieve and may have been applied to inlets whose processes resembled the action of a sieve. Another possibility is that during the nineteenth century the term drum referred to a cylinder or canvas used as a storm signal.

Drum Inlet See Old Drum Inlet (Carteret County, Portsmouth and Atlantic townships)

Drum Inlet See Old Drum Inlet (Carteret County, Smyrna Township)

DRUM SHOALS A shoal, 0.5 mi. (0.8 km) long, in Carteret County, Morehead Township at 34°42′37″N 76°46′22″W and located on the Mansfield map. The shoal is in Bogue Sound 0.5 mi. (0.8 km) north of Bogue Banks, 2.1 mi. (3.3 km) west of Atlantic Beach, and 3.5 mi. (5.6 km) southwest of Morehead City. **Historical note** See Drum Inlet for an explanatory note.

DRY SAND SHOAL A former shoal area in Carteret County, Portsmouth Township at 35°03′50″N 76°01′45″W and located but not shown on the Portsmouth map. The shoal was an extension of Portsmouth Island into Ocracoke Inlet about 1.75 mi. (2.8 km) east of the village of Portsmouth and 4 mi. (6.4 km) southwest of the village of Ocracoke. **Historical note** Much of the feature is now inundated, but remnants including Vera Cruz Shoal (q.v.) remain.

Dry Sand Shoal See Vera Cruz Shoal

Dry Shoal Point See Vera Cruz Shoal

DUCK A populated place, with a population of about 100, in Dare County, Atlantic Township at 36°09′50″N 75°45′05″W and located on the Jarvisburg map. This village is on south Currituck Banks 16 mi. (25.6 km) north northwest of Nags Head and 15.1 mi. (24.2 km) south southeast of Corolla. **Historical note** The village was named for the large numbers and varieties of ducks found in the area. A post office was established here in 1890 but is now discontinued.

DUCK HOLE A lake, 0.1 mi. (0.2 km) across, in Currituck County, Poplar Branch Township at 36°18′36″N 75°49′47″W and located on the Mossey Islands map. It is located in Mossey Islands 4.7 mi. (7.5 km) south of Corolla and 11.4 mi. (18.2 km) north northwest of Duck. **Historical note** The name is indicative of feeding areas for ducks in this "hunting area" along The Atlantic Flyway.

DUCK ISLAND An island, 0.8 mi. (1.3 km) long and 0.5 mi. (0.8 km) wide, in Dare County, Nags Head Township at 35°48′04″N 75°35′43″W and located on the Oregon Inlet map. This marsh island is located in Roanoke Sound 2 mi. (3.2 km) west of Herring Shoal and 4.4 mi. (7 km) southeast of Wanchese.

DUCK ISLAND FLATS Tidal flats, in Dare County, Nags Head Township at 35°48′23″N 75°35′00″W and located but not named on the Oregon Inlet map. These shoal areas are sometimes exposed and sometimes covered with water and the number of exposed fouls or muddy flats varies. This tidal flats area is 0.7 mi. (1.1 km) east of Duck Island, 3.2 mi. (5.1 km) northwest of Oregon Inlet and 4 mi. (6.4 km) southeast of Wanchese.

DUCK LANDING A landing in Dare County, Atlantic Township at 36°09′43″N 75°45′04″W and located but not named on the Jarvisburg map. The landing is on the sound side at Duck, 16.7 mi. (26.7 km) northwest of Nags Head.

DUCKPOND A cove, 0.2 mi. (0.3 km) wide, in Currituck County, Fruitville Township at 36°30′56″N 75°58′30″W and located on the Knotts Island map. The cove is in North Landing River 0.7 mi. (1.1 km) north northwest of Mackay Island and 2.7 mi. (4.3 km) west of the village of Knotts Island. **Historical note** The name is descriptive and refers to one of the many ponds and coves that provide food and a rest stop for migrating birds along the Atlantic Flyway migration routes.

Duck Pond See Duck Ponds

DUCK POND CREEK A stream, 1.5 mi. (2.4 km) long, in Dare County, Atlantic Township at 36°03′03″N 75°42′27″W and located on the Kitty Hawk map. The stream heads at 36°04′27″N 75°43′17″W, 0.9 mi. (1.4 km) west of Kitty Hawk and flows south to Kitty Hawk Bay 8.2 mi. (13.1 km) northwest of Nags Head. **Historical note** See Duckpond for an explanatory note.

DUCK PONDS A lake, 0.4 mi. (0.6 km) long and 0.02 mi. (0.03 km) wide, in Dare County, Hatteras Township at 35°12′49″N 75°41′24″W and located on the Hatteras map. The lake is just northeast of Isaac Pond 0.5 mi. (0.8 km) south of the village of Hatteras. **Other names** Duck Pond **Historical note** See Duckpond for an explanatory note.

DUCK WOODS Woods in Dare County, Atlantic Township at 36°08′45″N 75°44′20″W and located but not named on the Jarvisburg, Martin Point, and Kitty Hawk maps. The feature is a wooded area on Currituck Banks extending south from Duck to the south boundary of Southern Shores, 16 mi. (25.6 km) north northwest of Nags Head and 17 mi. (27.2 km) south southeast of Corolla.

DUCK WOODS POND A lake, 0.7 mi. (1.2 km) long and less than 0.05 mi. (0.08 km) wide, in Dare County, Atlantic Township at 36°06′20″N 76°44′15″W and located but not named on the Kitty Hawk map. This elongated lake is on Currituck Banks in the village of Southern Shores, 3.3 mi. (5.5 km) northwest of Kitty Hawk.

Duffys Point See Baum Point (Dare County, Nags Head Township)

Duges Island See Guthries Hammock

DUGS An historical reference. The term first appears on Moll's map of 1729 and recurs on several later maps. It is applied in various places but most often to the southernmost of three islands in the Oregon Inlet area. **Historical note** Some authors and cartographers have assumed this to be a place name and have added the generic "island" or "inlet" accordingly. The name is merely descriptive and appropriately appears in the early references without a generic. The term was applied to places with distinctive and pronounced sand dunes. The word "dug" is a sixteenth century somewhat derogatory term that referred to female breasts, especially the teat or nipple. The terms dugs and paps were liberally used by English seamen in the sixteenth and seventeenth centuries as a descriptive term for formations that resembled the female breast.

DULLS POINT A point of land in Dare County, Kennekeet Township at 35°41′44″N 75°29′54″W and located on the Pea Island map. This marsh point is on Pea Island and on the center shore of Terrapin Creek Bay 6.3 mi. (10.2 km) south of Oregon Inlet and 7.3 mi. (11.7 km) north northwest of Rodanthe.

DUMP ISLAND An island, 0.5 mi. (0.8 km) long, in Dare County, Atlantic Township at 34°53′34″N 76°17′09″W and located on the Atlantic map. The elongated island is in Core Sound 1.1 mi. (1.8 km) north of Old Drum Inlet (Portsmouth and Atlantic townships) and 3.1 mi. (5 km) east of the mainland village of Atlantic.

DUNCAN POINT A point of land in Dare County, Hatteras Township at 35°13′16″N 75°40′14″W and located on the Hatteras map. The point is at the south entrance to Sandy Bay 1.2 mi. (1.9 km) east of the village of Hatteras.

DUNES OF DARE Sand dunes in Dare County, Nags Head Township. Dunes of Dare is a general and collective term used to refer to all of the sand dunes in and around the Nags Head area. The name is somewhat historical and not used extensively today. **Other names** Dare Dunes and Nags Head Dunes

Dunstan Marsh See Dunston Island

DUNSTON ISLAND An island, less than 0.1 mi. (0.2 km) across, in Dare County, Atlantic Township at 36°02′37″N 75°41′27″W and located but not named on the Kitty Hawk map. The marsh island is in the southeast part of Kitty Hawk Bay, 1.6 mi. (2.6 km) south southeast of Kitty Hawk. **Other names** Dunstan Marsh

Dunton Hill See Luark Hill

DURANT POINT A point of land in Dare County, Hatteras Township at 35°14′00″N 75°40′54″W and located on the Hatteras map. The point is at the north entrance to Sandy Bay 1.1 mi. (1.8 km) east of the village of Hatteras. **Other names** Durants Point

Durants Point See Durant Point

DYKES CREEK A canalized stream, 0.2 mi. (0.3 km) long, in Dare County, Nags Head Township at 35°53′40″N 75°38′23″W and located but not named on the Manteo map. The stream is at the east shore of Roanoke Island just south of the entrance to the Roanoke Sound Bridge and 2.2 mi. (3.5 km) southeast of Manteo. **Other names** McKnights Creek

E

EAGLE NEST BAY A cove, 0.4 mi. (0.6 km) wide, in Dare County Kennekeet Township at 35°43′55″N 75°30′47″W and located on the Pea Island map. The cove is in Pamlico Sound off Pea Island and trends northeast-southwest between Eagle Nest Point and Goat Island Point 3.7

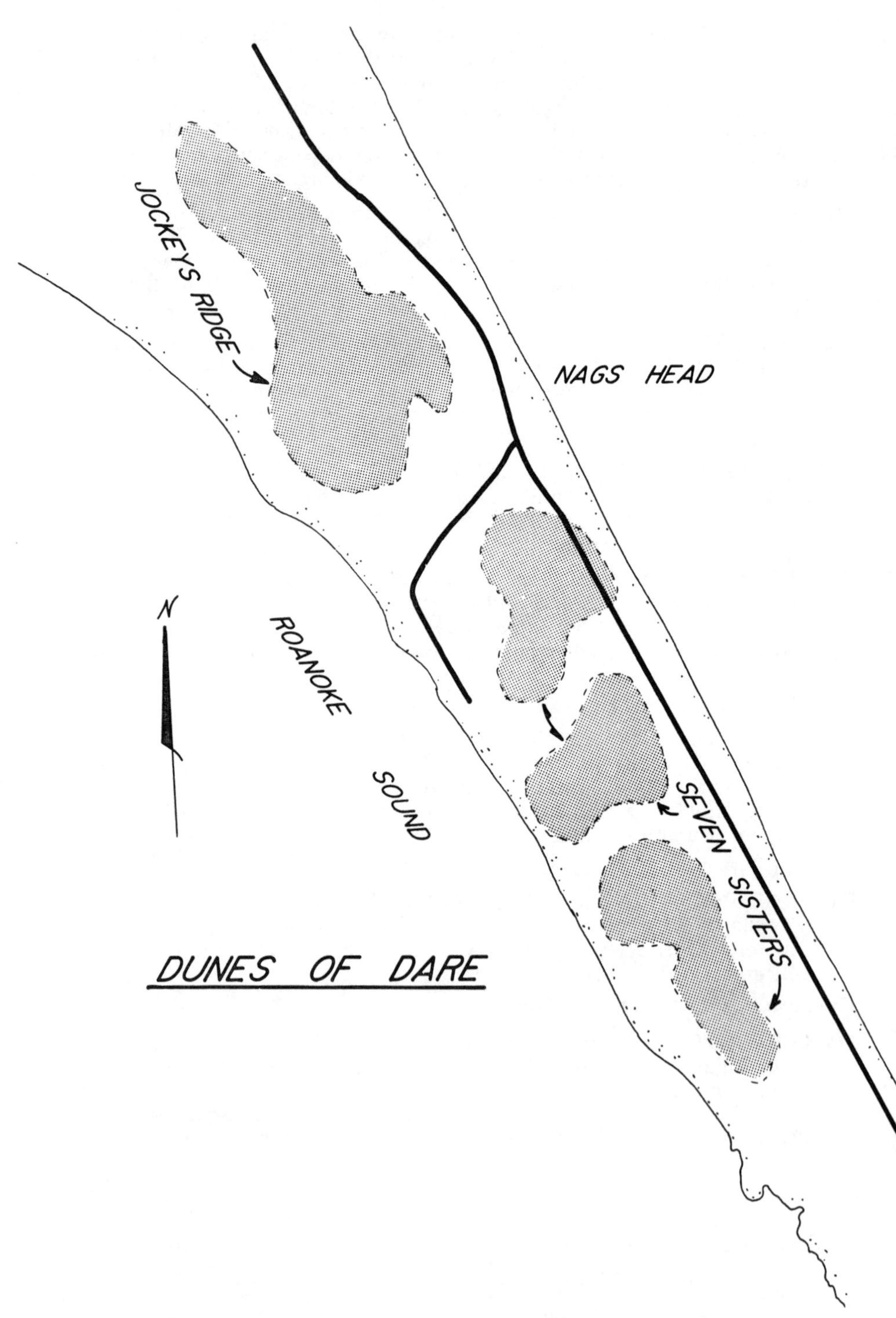
JOCKEYS RIDGE
NAGS HEAD
N
ROANOKE
SOUND
SEVEN SISTERS
DUNES OF DARE

mi. (5.9 km) south of Oregon Inlet and 9.9 mi. (15.8 km) north northwest of Rodanthe. **Other names** Eagles Nest Bay

EAGLE NEST POINT A point of land in Dare County, Kennekeet Township at 35°44′10″N 75°31′04″W and located on the Pea Island map. It is the north entrance point of Eagle Nest Bay 3.5 mi. (5.6 km) south of Oregon Inlet and 10.2 mi. (16.3 km) north northwest of Rodanthe.

Eagles Nest Bay See Eagle Nest Bay

Eagleston See Eagleton

EAGLETON A former populated place in Dare County, Atlantic Township at 36°01′15″N 75°42′45″W and located on the Kitty Hawk map. The community was on Colington Island 0.9 mi. (1.5 km) northwest of Colington and 2.5 mi. (4 km) west of the Wright Brothers Memorial. **Other names** Eagleton Point and Eagleston **Historical note** This feature name generally refers to the scattered settlement on the northwest part of Colington Island and not to a specific community. Locally the names Eagleton and Eagleton Point seem to be used interchangeably. The name originates from local reference to the large number of Osprey that nest in the area or at least used to nest in the area. The Osprey is a large bird of prey often referred to as Sea Eagle, Fishing Eagle, or Fish Hawk.

EAGLETON POINT A point of land in Dare County, Atlantic Township at 36°01′20″N 75°43′44″W and located on the Kitty Hawk map. The point is at the south entrance of Kitty Hawk Bay and the northwest point of Colington Island 2 mi. (3.2 km) west of the village of Colington and 3.4 mi. (5.4 km) southwest of Kitty Hawk. **Other names** North Point **Historical note** See Eagleton for an explanatory note.

Eagleton Point See Eagleton

EASTERN CHANNEL A former channel, 10-15 ft. (3-5 m) wide, in Dare County, Nags Head Township and located but not shown on the Wanchese map. The channel was the easternmost passage through Roanoke Marshes (q.v.) and was located about 2 mi. (3.2 km) west of Wanchese. **Historical note** The name is descriptive and was first used as mere description but continued use led to it being established as an accepted proper name. There are conflicting reports as to the width, but at least 10 ft. (3 m) is certain. Many residents of Roanoke Island have tales of their great-grandparents walking to the mainland by carrying a fence post to assist in crossing the channel, but there is no proof that this was possible. In fact, it is doubtful that it was even attempted. Today there is not a trace of Eastern Channel since most of Roanoke Marshes was inundated as a result of the closing of Roanoke Inlet. See Roanoke Marshes for an additional explanation.

Eastern End See Diamond City

Eastern Rocks See Oyster Rocks

EASTERN SHOALS Former shoals in Currituck County, Fruitville Township and located but not shown on the Knotts Island map. These shoals were in the Atlantic Ocean near the entrance to Currituck Inlet but today only remnants of the shoals remain. **Other names** Charotuck Inlett Bar

EAST MOUTH BAY A cove in Carteret County, Harkers Island Township at 34°41′53″N 76°32′04″W and located on the Harkers Island map. The cove is in Core Sound and separates Harkers Island from Browns Island

1.5 mi. (2.4 km) east northeast of the village of Harkers Island. **Other names** Eastmouth Bay

Eastmouth Bay See East Mouth Bay

EEL CREEK A tidal stream, 0.4 mi. (0.6 km) long, in Currituck County, Poplar Branch Township at 36°14′05″N 75°47′30″W and located but not named on the Jarvisburg map. The tidal stream is just east of Great Gap, 5.4 mi. (8.6 km) north northwest of Duck and 10.1 mi. (16.2 km) southeast of Corolla. **Historical note** Local usage does not indicate whether the feature was named for its shape or for eels caught here. Eel catching was an economic activity at one time in this area, however, all of the catch was shipped northward and "Bankers" never really liked to eat eel.

EGG SHOAL A shoal, 0.1 mi. (0.2 km) long, in Dare County, Hatteras Township at 35°15″25″N 75°42′50″W and located but not shown on the Hatteras map. The shoal is in Pamlico Sound 2.3 mi. (3.7 km) north northwest of the village of Hatteras. **Other names** Egg Shoals and Shell Island

Egg Shoals See Egg Shoal

ELIJAH CREEK A former water passage in Dare County, Morehead Township at 34°42′30″N 76°41′45″W and located but not shown on the Beaufort map. The water passage connected Morehead City Channel and Back Sound and was located just southeast of Elijah Lump, 2 mi. (3.2 km) southeast of the mainland town of Morehead City.

ELIJAH LUMP A hummock, 19 ft. (5.9 m) high, in Carteret County, Morehead Township at 34°42′35″N 76°41′58″W and located but not named on the Beaufort map. The hummock is in Bogue Sound at Morehead City Channel, 1.5 mi. (2.4 km) southeast of the mainland town of Morehead City. **Other names** Brant Island **Historical note** The feature was formerly surrounded by water, but has become completely surrounded by a tidal flat during the past fifteen years.

EMERALD ISLE A populated place in Carteret County, White Oak Township at 34°40′40″N 76°56′55″W and located on the Salter Path map. The community is on Bogue Banks 4.5 mi. (7.2 km) south southwest of Salter Path. **Historical note** Emerald Isle was incorporated in 1957.

Endesoakes See Core Banks

ENDESOECES An historical area. The name is an Indian word that appeared on some of the early maps as a reference to the area of Portsmouth Island.

ENGAGEMENT HILL A sand dune, 68 ft. (20.7 m) high, in Dare County, Nags Head Township at 35°57′45″N 75°38′17″W and located on the Manteo map. The dune is just south of Jockeys Ridge 0.7 mi. (1.1 km) northwest of Nags Head. **Historical note** The name is said to have originated from young couples who visited the sand dune and, as the story goes, found it easy to become engaged because of the spectacular view of both the ocean and the sound.

Essex Island See Bodie Island

Essex Island See Etacrewac

ETACREWAC A former barrier island in Dare County, Nags Head and Atlantic townships. The former barrier island extended from the south tip of Bodies Island at the present site of Oregon Inlet north to the south portion of Currituck Banks in the vicinity of Kitty Hawk. **Other names** Croat and Essex Island **Historical note** This Indian name has been applied generally to various areas in the north parts of the Outer Banks by early European mapmakers, and is an Algonquian word meaning area of evergreen type trees. The application of Etacrewac as a place tends to support some theories that an inlet existed in the general vicinity of Kitty Hawk Bay during historic times, however, the proof is inconclusive and early maps of the area are at best confusing and unclear as to whether such an inlet ever existed.

Etacrewac See Bodie Island

Etacrewac See Croatamung

Etacrewac See Nags Head

ETHRIDGES POINT A former point of land in Dare County, Nags Head Township at 35°56′50″N 75°43′07″W and located but not shown on the Manteo map. The former point is now located just north of Roanoke Island about 1 mi. (1.6 km) northeast of Northwest Point and 3.6 mi. (5.8 km) northwest of Manteo. **Other names** North Point of Roanoke Island **Historical note** The existence of this former named feature is indicative of the erosion on the north end of Roanoke Island. The feature was completely submerged by the mid-nineteenth century. This erosion also suggests that since no trace of the Lost Colony site has ever been found, the site may be just north of the present shoreline. Any trace of the site is likely to have been obliterated by the tides and currents.

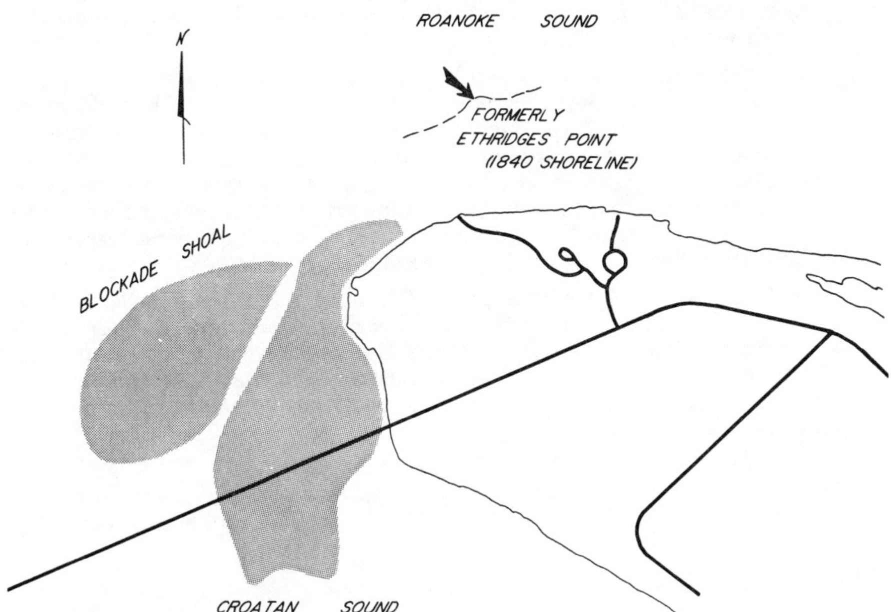

EVERGREEN ISLAND An island, 0.6 mi. (1 km) wide, in Carteret County, Portsmouth Township at 35°03′30″N 76°04′25″W and located on the Portsmouth map. The island is in Pamlico Sound southwest of Portsmouth Island between Evergreen Slough and The Haulover 6.9 mi. (11 km) southwest of the village of Ocracoke.

EVERGREEN SLOUGH A water passage, 0.5 mi. (0.8 km) long, in Carteret County, Portsmouth Township at 35°03′36″N 76°04′30″W and located on the Portsmouth map. The water passage trends north in Pamlico Sound from Portsmouth Island to Casey Bay 0.9 mi. (1.4 km) southwest of the village of Portsmouth and 6.7 mi. (10.7 km) southwest of the village of Ocracoke.

Eyers Rock See Ayers Rock

F

False Cape See Currituck Banks

FIRST CREEKS A system of about five tidal streams in Dare County, Nags Head Township at 35°53′30″N 75°41′00″W and located but not named on the Manteo map. The tidal streams are at northwest Roanoke Island in Croatan Sound, 1 mi. (1.6 km) north of Ashbee Harbor and 1.5 mi. (2.4 km) south of Manteo. **Historical note** The name has been in use since the eighteenth century.

FIRST GRASS A point of land in Hyde County, Ocracoke Township at 35°05′30″N 75°59′23″W and located on the Ocracoke map. The point is on Ocracoke Island 1.7 mi. (2.7 km) southwest of the village of Ocracoke. **Historical note** The sparse vegetation on Ocracoke Island is evident in this descriptive name. It was an early method of determining areas of grass or "scrag" trees. In this case the feature is the first grass area encountered after leaving the village of Ocracoke, and travelling northeast toward the village of Hatteras.

FIRST HAMMOCK HILLS Sand dunes, 0.4 mi. (0.6 km) long, located in Hyde County, Ocracoke Township at 35°07′32″N 75°56′02″W and located on the Howard Reef and Ocracoke maps. The series of three hills on Ocracoke Island are just south of Sand Hole Creek, 10.1 mi. (16.2 km) southwest of Hatteras Inlet and 3.2 mi. (4.2 km) northeast of the village of Ocracoke. **Historical note** The same principle may be applied to this feature as related in the explanatory note listed with First Grass. See Black Hammock for an additional explanatory note.

FISHING CREEK A water passage, 0.5 mi. (0.8 km) long, at 34°42′06″N 76°41′37″W and located on the Beaufort map. The water passage trends east-west at the east end of Bogue Banks between Goat Island and Tombstone Point 1.9 mi. (3 km) southeast of the mainland town of Morehead City and 2.5 mi. (4 km) east of Atlantic Beach.

FISHING SHOAL A former shoal in Hyde County, Ocracoke Township and Dare County, Hatteras Township at 35°11′23″N 75°45′00″W and located but not shown on the Green Island and Hatteras maps. The shoal was at the entrance to Hatteras Inlet, 3.8 mi. (6.1 km) southwest of the village of Hatteras

Five Fathoms Bank See Wimble Shoals

FLAG ISLAND An island, 0.1 mi. (0.2 km) across, in Dare County, Atlantic Township at 36°13′16″N 75°46′59″W and located but not named on the Jarvisburg map. This small marsh island is in Currituck Sound, 4.4 mi. (7 km) northwest of Duck and 11.2 mi. (17.9 km) south of Corolla.

Florida Current See Gulf Stream

FLOUNDER ROCK A former rock in Carteret County, Portsmouth Township at approximately 35°06′00″N 76°05′45″W and located but not shown on the Portsmouth map. The rock was in Pamlico Sound just southwest of North Rock about 4.5 mi. (7.2 km) west of the village of Ocracoke. **Other names** Flounder Slue Rock

FLOUNDER SLUE A former channel, about 1 mi. (1.6 km) long, in Carteret County, Portsmouth Township at 35°05′55″N 76°04′55″W and located but not shown on the Portsmouth map. The channel was in Pamlico Sound, 2 mi. (3.2 km) north northwest of the village of Portsmouth and 4.7 mi. (7.5 km) west of the village of Ocracoke. **Historical note** The feature formerly connected Wallace Channel (q.v.) to Ship Channel (q.v.) and the open sound. Today, Flounder Slue is the northwest part of Wallace Channel.

Flounder Slue Rock See Flounder Rock

FORT BARTOW A former fort, 2 acres in extent, in Dare County, Nags Head Township at 35°54′15″N 71°45′00″W and located but not shown on the Manteo map. The fort was located 1.5 mi. (2.4 km) southwest of Manteo in the general vicinity of the General Burnside National Historic Site. **Historical note** This was one of many confederate forts built on the Outer Banks during The War Between the States. Fort Bartow was bombarded by Union forces on February 7, 1862.

FORT BLANCHARD A former fort, 2 acres in extent, in Dare County, Nags Head Township at 35°52′28″N 75°43′00″W and located but not shown on the Manteo map. The former fort was just northwest of Sunnyside, 0.3 mi. (0.5 km) southeast of William B. Umstead Bridge and Weir Point, and 200 yards south of Fort Huger. **Historical note** Fort Blanchard was the smallest Confederate fort on Roanoke Island and it surrendered on February 8, 1862.

FORT CLARK A former fort, 5 ft. (1.5 m) high and 2 acres in extent, in Dare County, Hatteras Township at 35°11′56″N 75°43′50″W and located on the Hatteras map. The former fort was 0.5 mi. (0.8 km) northeast of Inlet Peninsula at the southwest tip of Hatteras Island 2.6 mi. (4.2 km) southwest of the village of Hatteras. **Other names** Battery Clark **Historical note** The fort was constructed in 1861 on the east side of Hatteras Inlet to protect the inlet from Union vessels, but the fort fell on August 29, 1861 after a two-day seige. Some ruins of the fort are still visible, but constant inundation is removing all traces of the fort.

Fort Dobb See Fort Macon

Fort Ellis See Fort Hatteras

Forten Island See Fortin Island

Forter Island See Fortin Island

FORT GRANVILLE A former fort in Carteret County, Portsmouth Township and located but not shown on the Portsmouth map. The fort was located somewhere on Portsmouth Island and probably at the village of Portsmouth. **Historical note** The fort was to be built to protect the coast from enemy raids, and the decision to build the fort was a result of King George's War (1744-1748). The fort was begun in 1755-1756, but was most likely never completed.

Fort Hampton See Fort Macon

FORT HANCOCK A former fort in Carteret County, Harkers Island Township and located but not named on the Cape Lookout map. The fort was on the south end of Core Banks at Cape Lookout, but no trace of the fort exists today. **Other names** Old Ruins **Historical note** Two French captains named De Cottineau and De Cambray in the eighteenth century noted that Cape Lookout Harbor or Lookout Bight (q.v.) was the only safe harbor between Cape Henry in Virginia and Cape Fear in the extreme south portion of North Carolina and they referred to Cape Lookout Harbor or Lookout Bight as The Colonies' Gibralter. For this reason they approached North Carolina officials to allow the French to build a fort at Cape Lookout, but found the idea already being considered by North Carolina and the Continental Congress. Since no money had been appropriated for construction of the fort, De Cottineau convinced the North Carolina officials to let him build the fort which he and the French completed. The fort, however, was named for Enock Hancock who owned the land on which the fort was built.

FORT HATTERAS A former fort, 2 acres in extent, and located but not shown on the Hatteras map. The fort was located on the south tip of Hatteras Island 2 mi. (3.2 km) southwest of the Hatteras Ferry Landing near former Fort Clark 3 mi. (4.8 km) southwest of the village of Hatteras. **Other names** Fort Ellis **Historical note** The fort was constructed in 1861 on the east side of Hatteras Inlet, and fell to Union forces on August 29, 1861 after a two-day seige. There is no trace of the fort because of constant inundation.

FORT HUGER A former fort, 2 acres in extent, in Dare County, Nags Head Township at 35°53′33″N 75°43′00″W and located but not shown on the Manteo map. The fort was located on Roanoke Island just northwest of Sunnyside, 0.3 mi. (0.5 km) south of William B. Umstead Bridge and Weir Point, and 200 yards from Fort Blanchard. **Historical note** Fort Huger was the principle Confederate fort on Roanoke Island, and it was surrendered on February 8, 1862.

FORTIN BAY A cove, 0.3 mi. (0.5 km) wide, in Carteret County, Davis Township at 34°46′45″N 76°24′30″W and located on the Davis map. The cove is in Core Sound and separates Fortin Island and the north portion of Great Island, 3.3. mi. (5.3 km) east southeast of the mainland town of Davis.

FORTIN ISLAND An island, 0.3 mi. (0.5 km) long and 0.2 mi. (0.3 km) wide, in Carteret County, Davis Township at 34°46′47″N 76°24′42″W and located on the Davis map. This marsh island is located in Core Sound 0.4 mi. (0.6 km) west of Great Island and 3 mi. (4.8 km) east southeast of the mainland town of Davis. **Other names** Forten Island and Forter Island

FORT MACON A fort in Carteret County, Morehead Township at 34°41′45″N 76°40′45″W and located on the Beaufort map. The fort is at the east end of Bogue Banks 2.9 mi. (4.4 km) southeast of the mainland town of Morehead City and 3.5 mi. (5.6 km) east of Atlantic Beach. **Other names** Fort Dobb and Fort Hampton **Historical note** The fort was built 1826-1834 to protect Beaufort Inlet, and was still used as a coaling station as late as World War I. Today it is maintained as a state park.

FORT MACON CREEK A cove, 0.1 mi. (0.2 km) across, in Carteret County, Morehead Township at 34°41′52″N 76°40′57″W and located on the Beaufort map. The cove is in Core Sound at the east end of Bogue Banks at

Fort Macon 2.5 mi. (4 km) southeast of the mainland town of Morehead City and 3.1 mi. (4.9 km) east of Atlantic Beach. **Other names** Cowpen Creek and Cow Pen Creek **Historical note** The original name was Cowpen Creek but with the decline of stock grazing and the influence of nearby Fort Macon, the name was changed.

FORT MORGAN A former fort in Carteret County, Portsmouth Township and located but not named on the Portsmouth map. It was located on Beacon Island in Ocracoke Inlet approximately 3.8 mi. (6 km) west of the village of Ocracoke. **Other names** Fort Ocracoke **Historical note** The fort was built on or near the previous site of Beacon Island Fort (q.v.). No evidence of the fort remains, but it was constructed on Beacon Island in 1861 as part of a system of forts to protect the Outer Banks from Union forces. It was abandoned when Fort Hatteras fell on August 29, 1861.

Fort Ocracoke See Beacon Island Fort

Fort Ocracoke See Fort Morgan

FORT OREGON A former fort in Dare County, Kennkeet Township and located but not shown on the Oregon Inlet map. It was located on Pea Island approximately 14 mi. (22.4 km) south southeast of Nags Head. **Historical note** The fort was built on the south shore of Oregon Inlet in 1861 to protect the Inlet from Union forces. The former site has been completely obliterated because of the south migration of Oregon Inlet.

FORT RALEIGH A former fort, 20 acres in extent, in Dare County, Nags Head Township at 35°56′17″N 75°42′32″W and located on the Manteo map. The fort was located on northeast Roanoke Island 3 mi. (4.8 km) north northwest of Manteo. **Other names** Citie of Raleigh, Cittie of Raleigh, Cittie of Raleigh in Virginia, and New Fort in Virginia. **Historical note** The fort is actually an earthen fort reconstructed in 1950 by the National Park Service in a manner thought to be similar to that of the original fort constructed by the Roanoke Island colonists or the Lost Colony. The actual site of the fort is thought to be near the reconstructed fort but has never been located.

FORT RALEIGH CITY A populated place, 15 ft. (4.6 m) high, in Dare County, Nags Head Township at 35°56′14″N 75°42′38″W and located on the Manteo map. The community is located on the north end of Roanoke Island at Fort Raleigh National Historic Site 2.5 mi. (4 km) northwest of Manteo. **Historical note** This feature is the name of an old subdivision that still retains a small clustered community, and although the name appears on older maps it is not in local usage today.

FORT RALEIGH NATIONAL HISTORIC SITE A park in Dare County, Nags Head Township at 35°56′23″N 75°42′35″W and located on the Manteo map. The park is on north Roanoke Island, 2.9 mi. (4.7 km) northwest of Manteo. **Historical note** The park is used to display information about the Lost Colony and contains a reconstruction of the type of fort constructed by the first colony, (not the Lost Colony) however, the actual site is probably off the north shore since considerable erosion has occurred. See Etheridges Point.

FORT RUSSELL A former fort in Dare County, Nags Head Township and located but not shown on the Manteo map. This was a small Confederate fort somewhere near the center of Roanoke Island constructed on a natural causeway through marshes and swamps connecting the north and south portions of Roanoke Island.

FORT TOTTEN A former fort in Dare County, Hatteras Township at 35°12′48″N 75°40′45″W and located but not named on the Hatteras map. The fort was located on Hatteras Island, 1 mi. (1.6 km) southeast of the village of Hatteras **Historical note** The fort was a temporary one erected during the occupation by Union forces during The War Between the States.

FORT WOOL A former encampment in Dare County, Hatteras Township and located but not shown on the Hatteras map. It was a temporary encampment of Union troops just east of the village of Hatteras.

Foster Channel See Fosters Channel

FOSTERS CHANNEL A water passage in Currituck County, Poplar Branch Township at 36°17′37″N 75°50′13″W (southeast end), 36°18′04″N 75°50′37″W (northwest end), and 36°17′51″N 75°50′25″W (center) and located on the Mossey Islands map. It is located in Currituck Sound joining Lone Oak Channel at the south end of Mossey Islands 5.7 mi. (9.1 km) south southwest of Corolla and 11.1 mi. (17.8 km) north northwest of Duck. **Other names** Foster Channel

Fresh Pond See Fresh Ponds

FRESH POND HILL A hill in Currituck County, Fruitville Township at 36°30′05″N 75°51′50″W and located on the Corolla map. The hill is on Currituck Banks near Wash Woods 4 mi. (6.4 km) south of the North Carolina and Virginia boundary and 7.5 mi. (12 km) north northwest of Corolla.

FRESH PONDS Lakes, 125 acres in extent, in Dare County, Atlantic and Nags Head townships at 35°59′23″N 75°39′23″W and located on the Manteo map. The lakes are located 2 mi. (3.2 km) south of the Wright Brothers Memorial, 3 mi. (4.8 km) northwest of Nags Head, and 5.8 mi. (9.3 km) south of Kitty Hawk. **Other names** Fresh Pond, Great Fresh Pond, The Great Fish Ponds and The Great Fresh Ponds **Historical note** The ponds are possibly remnants of a former inlet, and this is further supported by the fact that the ponds were historically connected to Roanoke Sound by The Run (q.v.).

FRISCO A populated place, 5 ft. (1.5 m) high with a population of about 300, in Dare County, Hatteras Township at 35°14′19″N 75°37′10″W and located on the Cape Hatteras map. The village is on the west shore of Hatteras Island 4.4 mi. (7 km) west of Cape Hatteras, 5.1 mi. (8.2 km) southwest of Buxton, and 2.8 mi. (4.5 km) northeast of the village of Hatteras. **Other names** Trent and Trent Woods **Historical note** The original name was Trent but the post office name was changed in 1898 by the Post Office Department to avoid confusion with another village named Trent on the mainland, and eventualy the community name disappeared and the post office name came to be used. The name Frisco is said to have been suggested by the first postmaster, a man named Wallace, who was a sailor that had spent a considerable amount of time in San Francisco. Wallace had been shipwrecked on Hatteras Island where he later married and settled. It is believed that Wallace suggested the name Frisco for the post office because of his fondness for San Francisco. Actually, he may have suggested San Francisco which the Post Office probably rejected in favor of the shorter form Frisco.

FRISCO DUNE A sand dune, 36 ft. (11.1 m) high, in Dare County, Hatteras Township at 35°13′55″N 75°37′40″W and located but not named on the

Hatteras map. The dune is on Hatteras Island just south of Frisco, 3.8 mi. (6.1 km) east northeast of the village of Hatteras.

FRISCO WOODS Woods in Dare County, Hatteras Township at 35°14′15″N 75°37′30″W and located but not named on the Cape Hatteras and Hatteras maps. A wooded area in the vicinity of Frisco 4 mi. (6.4 km) east northeast of the village of Hatteras and 4.5 mi. (7.2 km) west of Cape Hatteras. **Other names** Cape Woods, Little Grove, and Trent Woods

Frying Pan Island See Sloop Island

Frying Pan Shoals See Cape Lookout Shoals

Fulker Island See Fulker Islands

FULKER ISLANDS Former islands in Dare County, Nags Head Township at 34°52′40″N 75°42′15″W and located but not shown on the Manteo map. The islands were formerly in Croatan Sound approximately 2.5 mi. (4 km) Southwest of Manteo. **Other names** Fulker Island and Fulkners Island **Historical note** The feature has disappeared but was formerly the exposed portion of Fulker Shoal. It is quite possible that the islands were remnants of the former Roanoke Marshes (q.v.).

FULKER SHOAL A former shoal in Dare County, Nags Head Township at 35°53′00″N 75°42′00″W and located but not shown on the Manteo map. The shoal was formerly in Croatan Sound approximately 2.5 mi. (4 km) southwest of Manteo. The feature no longer exists but was probably part of the now submerged Roanoke Marshes (q.v.). **Other names** Fulkers Shoal and Fulkners Shoal

Fulkers Shoal See Fulker Shoal
Fulkners Island See Fulker Island
Fulkners Shoal See Fulker Shoal
Full Moon Shoal See Outer Diamond Shoal

G

GALES ISLAND A former island in Hyde County, Ocracoke Township at 35°05′45″N 76°00′30″W and located but not shown on the Portsmouth map. The island was in Pamlico Sound, 1.8 mi. (2.9 km) southwest of the village of Ocracoke and 2 mi. (3.2 km) north northeast of Ocracoke Inlet. **Other names** Gates Island **Historical note** The feature is actually the highest part of Qualk Shoal (q.v.) which is occasionally bare at low water.

GALES SHOAL A former shoal in Carteret County, Portsmouth Township at 35°05′45″N 76°02′45″W and located but not shown on the Portsmouth map. The shoal was located in Ocracoke Inlet just south of Beacon Island, 3.2 mi. (5.1 km) west southwest of the village of Ocracoke.

Gant Inlet See Gunt Inlet

GAP POINT A point of land in Hyde County, Ocracoke Township at 35°07′17″N 75°58′54″W and located on the Ocracoke map. The point is on Ocracoke Island 0.4 mi. (0.6 km) north of Ocracoke.

GARR ISLAND A former island in Dare County, Kennekeet Township at 35°45′10″N 75°31′27″W and located but not named on the Oregon Inlet map. The island was just west of Pea Island, 2 mi. (3.2 km) south of Oregon Inlet and 12.4 mi. (19.8 km) north of Rodanthe.

Gaskins Creek See Shallowbag Bay

Gates Island See Gales Island

GEORGE GILGOS CREEK A cove, 0.05 mi. (0.08 km) long, in Carteret County, Portsmouth Township at 35°04′02″N 76°04′07″W and located on the Portsmouth map. The cove joins Warren Gilgos Creek just east of Baymarsh Thorofare 0.3 mi. (0.5 km) west southwest of the village of Portsmouth and 6.7 mi. (10.7 km) southwest of the village of Ocracoke.

GEORGE HILLS Sand dunes, 14 ft. (4.2 m) high, in Carteret County, Portsmouth Township at 35°57′44″N 76°10′54″W and located on the Wainwright Island map. The dunes are located on Core Banks just northeast of Cricket Island 9.5 mi. (15.2 km) southwest of the village of Portsmouth and 15.5 mi. (24.8 km) southwest of the village of Ocracoke.

GEORGES CREEK A cove, 0.2 mi. (0.3 km) long, in Dare County, Nags Head Township at 35°49′02″N 75°34′17″W and located on the Oregon Inlet map. The cove is 0.4 mi. (0.6 km) east of the Bodie Island Lighthouse and 4.3 mi. (6.9 km) east southeast of Wanchese.

GIBBS POINT A point of land in Dare County, Kennekeet Township at 35°21′43″N 75°30′44″W and located on the Buxton map. The point is a marsh point on Hatteras Island just south of Big Island and 0.9 mi. (1.5 km) north northwest of Avon. **Historical note** The feature was most likely named for Henry Gibbs who had a land grant in this area of Hatteras Island in 1716.

Gibs Creek See Shallowbag Bay

Gibson Creek See Shallowbag Bay

Gingite Creek See Jeanguite Creek

Ginguite Bay See Jeanguite Creek

Ginguite Creek See Jeanguite Creek

Goade Island See Currituck Banks

GOAT ISLAND An island, 0.3 mi. (0.5 km) long, at 34°42′17″N 76°42′00″W and located on the Beaufort map. The island is located at the east end of Bogue Banks and the west end of Fishing Creek 1.5 mi. (2.4 km) southeast of the mainland town of Morehead City and 2.2 mi. (3.5 km) east of Atlantic Beach.

GOAT ISLAND An island, 0.2 mi. (0.3 km) long and 0.1 mi. (0.2 km) wide, in Currituck County, Poplar Branch Township at 36°15′10″N 75°48′38″W and located on the Mossey Islands map. It is a small irregular island separating Little Goat Island Bay and Goat Island Bay, 7.1 mi. (11.4 km) northwest of Duck and 8.5 mi. (13.6 km) south of Corolla.

GOAT ISLAND A marsh, 0.3 mi. (0.5 km) long and 0.5 mi. (0.8 km) wide, in Dare County, Kennekeet Township at 35°43′45″N 75°30′42″W and located on the Pea Island map. The marsh is located 0.6 mi. (1 km) north of Goose Island, 4 mi. (6.4 km) south of Oregon Inlet, and 9.6 mi. (15.3 km) north northwest of Rodanthe.

GOAT ISLAND BAY A cove, 0.7 mi. (1.1 km) wide and 0.4 mi. (0.6 km) long, in Currituck County, Poplar Branch Township at 36°15′00″N 75°48′30″W and located on the Mossey Islands map. The bay is in Currituck Sound 3.8 mi. (6.1 km) south of Three Dunes, 6.8 mi. (10.1 km) northwest of Duck and 8.9 mi. (14.2 km) south of Corolla.

GOAT ISLAND BAY A cove, 0.3 mi. (0.5 km) across, in Dare County, Kennekeet Township at 35°43′35″N 75°30′45″W and located on the Pea Island map. The cove is between two marsh areas named Goat Island and Goose Island, 4.2 mi. (6.7 km) south of Oregon Inlet and 9.4 mi. (15 km) north northwest of Rodanthe.

GOAT ISLAND POINT A point of land in Dare County, Kennekeet Township at 35°43′45″N 75°30′52″W and located on the Hatteras map. The point is on the west tip of Goat Island 3.9 mi. (6.3 km) south of Oregon Inlet at the entrance of Eagle Nest Bay 9.6 mi. (15.3 km) north northwest of Rodanthe.

GOOSE CREEK A cove, 0.1 mi. (0.2 km) wide, in Dare County, Hatteras Township at 35°12′23″N 75°42′43″W and located on the Hatteras map. The cove is in Pamlico Sound 1.5 mi. (2.4 km) southwest of the village of Hatteras.

GOOSE CREEK SHOALS A shoal, 0.7 mi. (1.1 km) long, in Carteret County, White Oak Township at 34°41′00″N 77°01′15″W and located on the Swansboro map. The shoal is a normally dry shoal in Bogue Sound 6 mi. (9.7 km) east southeast of the mainland town of Swansboro.

GOOSE ISLAND An island, 0.8 mi. (1.3 km) long and 0.3 mi. (0.5 km) wide, in Carteret County, Davis Township at 34°45′19″N 76°26′10″W and located on the Davis map. This marsh island is located in Core Sound 1 mi. (1.6 km) east of Core Banks and 3.2 mi. (5.1 km) southeast of the mainland town of Davis.

GOOSE ISLAND A marsh, 0.5 mi. (0.8 km) across, in Dare County, Kennekeet Township at 34°43′23″N 75°30′42″W and located on the Pea Island map. The marsh is located 0.6 mi. (1 km) south of Goat Island Bay, 4.5 mi. (7.2 km) south of Oregon Inlet, and 9.1 mi. (14.5 km) north northwest of Rodanthe.

GOOSE ISLAND An island, 0.1 mi. (0.2 km) wide, in Dare County, Atlantic Township at 36°13′32″N 75°46′34″W and located on the Jarvisburg map. This marsh island is just west of Currituck Banks near the site of former Caffeys Inlet. The feature is 4.6 mi. (7.4 km) north northwest of Duck and 11 mi. (17.6 km) southeast of Corolla. **Other names** Water Bush Island

GOOSE ISLAND POINT A point of land in Dare County, Kennekeet Township at 35°43′07″N 75°30′45″W and located on the Pea Island map. The feature is a marsh point on Goose Island and the north point of The Trench 4.6 mi. (7.4 km) south of Oregon Inlet and 8.1 mi. (13.1 km) north northwest of Rodanthe.

GOOSE SHOAL A shoal in Dare County, Atlantic Township at 36°02′28″N 75°44′00″W and located but not shown on the Kitty Hawk map. The shoal is just south of Stove Island in the north part of the entrance to Kitty Hawk Bay, 2.5 mi. (4 km) southwest of Kitty Hawk and 4.8 mi. (7.7 km) south of Southern Shores.

Gordons Ile See Ocracoke Island

Gordons Ile See Wococon

Gore Sound See Beaufort Inlet

GOULDS LUMP An island, 0.2 mi. (0.3 km) across, in Dare County, Kennekeet Township at 35°39′43″N 75°29′25″W and located on the Pea Island map. The island is located in Pamlico Sound just south of Wreck

Creek and 4.8 mi. (7.7 km) north northwest of Rodanthe. **Historical note** Lump is a local descriptive term used throughout the Outer Banks, especially from Ocracoke southward, and it refers to a small island, hummock, or a high portion of ground and sometimes even a shoal.

GRANTS COVE A cove, 0.2 mi. (0.3 km) wide, in Dare County, Atlantic Township at 36°02′50″N 75°43′02″W and located but not named on the Kitty Hawk map. The cove is in Kitty Hawk Bay at its north shore, 1.6 mi. (2.6 km) southwest of Kitty Hawk and 4.1 mi. (6.6 km) south of Southern Shores.

Graveyard of Ships See Diamond Shoals

Graveyard of the Atlantic See Diamond Shoals

GRAYS ROCK A rock in Currituck County, Poplar Branch Township at 36°19′15″N 75°52′44″W and located on Chart number 12205. This rock is in Currituck Sound 1.1 mi. (1.8 km) east of the mainland town of Aydlett and 4.3 mi. (6.8 km) southwest of Corolla.

GREAT BEACH POND A cove, 0.2 mi. (0.3 km) across, in Currituck County, Fruitville Township at 36°21′22″N 75°49′51″W and located on the Mossey Islands map. The cove is located in Currituck Sound just south of Whale Head Bay, formed by recent deposition in Currituck Sound, and located 1.3 mi. (2.4 km) south of Corolla and 14.5 mi. (23.2 km) north northwest of Duck.

Great Colenton See Big Colington

Great Colington See Big Colington

Great Fresh Pond See Fresh Ponds

GREAT GAP A water passage, 1 mi. (1.6 km) long, in Currituck County, Poplar Branch Township and Dare County, Atlantic Township at 36°13′35″N 75°48′02″W (northwest end), 36°13′40″N 75°47′05″W (southeast end), and 36°13′47″N 75°47′30″W (center) and located but not named on the Jarvisburg map. The water passage extends from near Currituck Banks to Pine Island Bay and Shoe Hole Bay in Currituck Sound, 5.2 mi. (8.3 km) northwest of Duck and 10.4 mi. (16.6 km) south of Corolla. **Other names** The Lead **Historical note** Since this feature trends generally northwest from near the site of Caffeys Inlet, this water passage is probably the remnant of Caffeys Inlet's north channel. See New Currituck Inlet for an explanatory note about inlet channels.

GREAT GAP ISLAND An island, 0.2 mi. (0.3 km) long, in Dare County, Atlantic Township and Currituck County, Poplar Branch Township at 36°13′40″N 75°47′35″W and located but not named on the Jarvisburg map. The island is at Great Gap in Currituck Sound, 5 mi. (8 km) northwest of Duck and 10.6 mi. (17 km) south of Corolla.

Great Hammock Swash See Merkle Hammock

GREAT ISLAND An island, 1.5 mi. (2.4 km) long and 0.3 mi. (0.5 km) wide, in Carteret County, Davis Township at 34°46′23″N 76°24′25″W and located on the Davis map. This elongated marsh island is located in Core Sound 0.4 mi. (0.6 km) west of Core Banks just south of Horse Island and 3.5 mi. (5.6 km) east southeast of the mainland town of Davis

GREAT ISLAND An island, 0.4 mi. (0.6 km) long and 0.05 mi. (0.08 km) wide, in Dare County, Hatteras Township at 35°16′49″N 76°31′20″W and located on the Buxton map. The elongated marsh island is in Pamlico

Sound 0.2 mi. (0.3 km) northeast of Bald Point, 1.5 mi. (2.4 km) northeast of Buxton, and 2.4 mi. (3.8 km) north of Cape Hatteras.

GREAT ISLAND An island, 0.4 mi. (0.6 km) long and 0.1 mi. (0.2 km) wide, in Dare County, Kennekeet Township at 35°33′37″N 75°28′36″W and located on the Rodanthe map. This marsh island is located in Pamlico Sound 0.5 mi. (0.8 km) southwest of Waves and 0.1 mi. (0.2 km) west of Davis Point.

GREAT ISLAND BAY A cove, 0.7 mi. (1.1 km) long and 0.3 mi. (0.5 km) wide, in Carteret County, Davis Township at 34°45′32″N 76°25′14″W and located on the Davis map. The cove is in Core Sound 1.3 mi. (2.1 km) southwest of Great Island and 3.5 mi. (5.6 km) southeast of the mainland town of Davis.

GREAT ISLAND CREEK A water passage, 0.8 mi. (1.3 km) long, in Carteret County, Davis Township at 34°46′54″N 76°24′14″W and located on the Davis map. The water passage is in Core Sound and separates Horse Island and Great Island, 3.5 mi. (5.6 km) east of the mainland town of Davis.

GREAT ISLAND POINT A point of land in Carteret County, Davis Township at 34°47′01″N 76°24′32″W and located on the Davis map. The point is the north point of Great Island at the entrance to Great Island Creek 3 mi. (4.8 km) east of the mainland town of Davis.

GREAT MARSH A marsh, 4.5 mi. (7.2 km) long and 3.7 mi. (5.9 km) wide, in Currituck County, Fruitville Township at 36°31′45″N 75°57′00″W and located on the Knotts Island map. It separates Knotts Island from the mainland and Mackay Island from the southern part of Knotts Island 2 mi. (3.2 km) northwest of the village of Knotts Island.

GREAT MARSH ISLAND An island, 0.4 mi. (0.6 km) long, in Dare County, Harkers Island Township at 34°38′57″N 76°31′24″W and located on the Harkers Island map. The irregularly shaped island is in Back Sound 3.8 mi. (6.1 km) south southeast of the village of Harkers Island and 1.2 mi. (1.9 km) north of Barden Inlet.

Great Shell Rock See North Rock

GREAT SHOAL A shoal in Carteret County, Smyrna Township at 34°44′06″N 76°27′15″W and located on the Horsepen Point map. The shoal is in Core Sound just north of Horsepen Point 7.3 mi. (11.7 km) northeast of the village of Harkers Island.

Great Swash See Terrapin Shoal

Great Swash See The Great Swash

GREEN ISLAND A former island, 0.5 mi. (0.8 km) long and 0.05 mi. (0.08 km) wide, in Dare County, Kennekeet Township at 35°45′57″N 75°32′07″W and located on the Oregon Inlet map. The marsh island was in Pamlico Sound 0.8 mi. (1.3 km) west of Pea Island, 0.4 mi. (0.6 km) south of the Herbert Bonner Bridge which spans Oregon Inlet, and 8.1 mi. (12.8 km) southeast of Wanchese. **Other names** Inner Green Island and Little Green Island **Historical note** The island ceased to exist in 1975.

GREEN ISLAND A marsh, 0.5 mi. (0.8 km) long, in Hyde County, Ocracoke Township at 35°10′37″N 75°48′24″W and located on the Green Island map. The marsh area is on Ocracoke Island 3.1 mi. (5 km) southwest of Hatteras Inlet and 11.7 mi. (18.7 km) northeast of the village of Ocracoke.

Other names Outer Green Island **Historical note** The feature was historically an island but today is a marsh attached to Ocracoke Island. The feature was locally named because of its contrasting vegetation with the surrounding area.

Green Island See Grun Island

GREEN ISLAND CHANNEL A channel, 2.2 mi. (3.5 km) long, in Dare County, Kennekeet Township at 35°46′00″N 75°31′50″W (north end), 35°44′15″N 75°31′40″W (south end), and 35°45′14″N 75°31′47″W (center) and located on the Oregon Inlet map. The channel is in Pamlico Sound just west of Pea Island, 1.8 mi. (2.9 km) south of Oregon Inlet and 8.4 mi. (17.4 km) south southeast of Wanchese.

GREEN ISLANDS Former islands in Dare County, Nags Head Township at approximately 35°53′40″N 75°37′10″W and located on the Roanoke Island NE map. The islands are located at the Causeway, 1.4 mi. (2 km) west southwest of Whalebone Junction and 4.3 mi. (6.9 km) east southeast of Manteo. **Historical note** The present islands of Grun, Pond, House and other small marsh islands were historically referred to as Green Islands.

GREENS POINT A point of land in Dare County, Kennekeet Township at 35°35′47″N 75°28′25″W and located on the Rodanthe map. It is a marsh point at the north entrance to Blackmar Gut 0.4 mi. (0.6 km) northwest of Rodanthe.

Greenvills Rode See Old Hatteras Inlet

GREYS ISLAND An island, 0.1 mi. (0.2 km) across, in Currituck County, Poplar Branch Township at 36°15′02″N 75°49′14″W and located on the Mossey Islands and Jarvisburg maps. It is a small marsh island in Currituck Sound just west of Goat Island Bay, 6.9 mi. (14.2 km) northwest of Duck and 8.9 mi. (11.2 km) south of Corolla.

Griffin See Nags Head

GRUN ISLAND An island, 0.2 mi. (0.3 km) long and 0.3 mi. (0.5 km) wide, in Dare County, Nags Head Township at 35°53′37″N 75°37′20″W and located on the Roanoke Island NE map. This marsh island is located in Roanoke Sound 4.4 mi. (7 km) south of Nags Head, 0.4 mi. (0.6 km) south of The Causeway, and 1.7 mi. (2.7 km) west southwest of Whalebone Junction. **Other names** Green Island **Historical note** Grun is probably a transcribing error because this island was originally part of a group known as Green Islands (q.v.). Another more colorful explanation also relies on clerical error. The name could have originally been Grunt which refers to the Grunter Fish so named because of the sound it makes when removed from the water.

Guinguys Creek See Jeanguite Creek

GULF STREAM An ocean current that originates in the Gulf of Mexico and flows through the Straits of Florida to join the Antilles Current where it then flows north along the Atlantic Coast of the United States to the vicinity of the Outer Banks. At Cape Hatteras the current veers northeast after colliding and mixing with the cold Labrador Current Extension and then flows northeast to the area of the Grand Banks off the coast of Newfoundland where it turns east toward Europe and becomes known as the North Atlantic Drift. **Other names** Florida Current, Gulph Stream, Ocean River, and The Great River **Historical note** The mixing of the

Gulf Stream and the Labrador Current Extension causes considerable turmoil and unpredictable hydrography in the Diamond Shoals area.

GULL ISLAND An island, 0.6 mi. (1 km) long and 0.3 mi. (0.5 km) wide, in Dare County, Kennekeet Township at 35°28′20″N 75°31′27″W and located on the Little Kinnakeet map. The marsh island is in Pamlico Sound 2.2 mi. (3.5 km) west of Hatteras Island, 9.8 mi. (15.8 km) southwest of Rodanthe, and 8.9 mi. (14.1 km) northwest of Avon. **Other names** Gull Shoal and Gull Shore

GULL ISLAND A former island in Carteret County, Harkers Island Township at approximately 34°40′40″N 76°33′45″W and located but not shown on the Harkers Island map. The island was centrally located in Back Sound between Shackleford Banks and Harkers Island 1.2 mi. (1.9 km) south of the village of Harkers Island. **Historical note** The island was a prominent feature until the mid-nineteenth century. Today there is no trace of the feature.

Gull Island See Cat Island (34°41′10″N 76°58′16″W)

GULL ISLAND BAY A cove, 0.4 mi. (0.6 km) long, in Dare County, Kennekeet Township at 35°28′30″N 75°29′02″W and located on the Little Kinnakeet map. The cove is in Pamlico Sound 2.4 mi. (3.9 km) north northeast of Gull Island and 7.8 mi. (12.6 km) south of Rodanthe.

Gull Shoal See Gull Island

Gull Shore See Gull Island

Gulph Stream See Gulf Stream

Gun Inlet See Gunt Inlet

GUNNING HAMMOCK ISLAND An island, 0.5 mi. (0.8 km) long, in Carteret County, Harkers Island Township at 34°40′20″N 76°30′02″W and located on the Horsepen Point and Harkers Island maps. The island is in Core Sound just south of Little Deep Marsh and 3.8 mi. (5.1 km) east southeast of the village of Harkers Island. **Historical note** The name is a reference to hunting.

GUNT INLET A former water passage in Dare County, Nags Head Township at 35°49′30″N 75°33′00″W and located but not shown on the Oregon Inlet map. It formerly connected Pamlico Sound to the Atlantic Ocean through Bodie Island approximately 2 mi. (3.2 km) north of Oregon Inlet and approximately 11.8 mi. (18.9 km) south southeast of Nags Head. **Other names** Gant Inlet, Gun Inlet, Hatoras Inlet, Hatorask Inlet, New Inlet, Old Inlet, Old Inlett, Port Ferdinando, Port Fernando, Vieu Passage, and View Passage **Historical note** The inlet formed the southern limit of the original extension of Bodie Island (q.v.) but closed in the 1770s. Some authors and historians believe this to be the inlet through which the original or "lost" colonists passed. Note the two variant names Vieu Passage and View Passage listed above. View is actually an error in transcribing the French name Vieu which means old. See Grun Island for a colorful explanation of the name origin. The actual origin is likely a shortened form of gunter which is a method using rings and hoops for sliding a top mast up and down on a lower mast. Oftentimes seamen applied nautical terminology as place names.

Gunt Inlet See New Inlet

Guthrie Hammock See Guthries Hammock

GUTHRIES HAMMOCK A hummock, 0.8 mi. (1.3 km) long and 0.2 mi. (0.3 km) wide, in Carteret County, Smyrna Township at 34°44′42″N 76°25′54″W and located on the Horsepen Point map. The hummock is located at Core Banks 1.5 mi. (2.4 km) northeast of Great Shoal and 3.4 mi. (5.4 km) south of the mainland town of Davis. **Other names** Duges Island and Guthrie Hammock **Historical note** Historically, there was a semi-permanent settlement here, but today it is totally uninhabited. The hammock is one of the few stands of vegetation on Core Banks. The variant name Duges Island is a variation and reference to Duggs or Dugs (q.v.) which was a sixteenth century English reference to teats or the female breast and further identifies this feature as a landmark on this barrier beach. See Black Hammock for an explanatory note.

GUTTER CREEK A water passage, 1 mi. (1.6 km) long, in Carteret County, Stacy Township at 34°49′17″N 76°21′20″W and located on the Styron Bay map. The water passage separates Core Banks from Big Marsh and connects Old Channel to Core Sound 3.9 mi. (6.2 km) south of the mainland village of Atlantic.

H

HALFWAY POINT A point of land in Currituck County, Fruitville Township at 36°29′03″N 75°58′32″W and located on the Barco map. The Point is the south point of Mackay Island 10.6 mi. (17 km) northwest of Corolla and 3 mi (4.8 km) west of the village of Knotts Island. **Other names** Morses Point **Historical note** The point was originally named Morses Point but the name was changed to Halfway Point because it was approximately halfway along the old steamship route between Norfolk and Nags Head, and the name Morse was then applied to another point of land northward.

HAMILTONS SHOAL A former shoal in Carteret County, Morehead Township at approximately 34°40′30″N 76°41′30″W and located but not shown on the Beaufort map. The shoal was at the western approach to Beaufort Inlet about 3 mi. (4.8 km) south southwest of the mainland town of Beaufort. **Historical note** The feature no longer exists.

HAMMOCK OAKS Former woods in Hyde County, Ocracoke Township at 35°07′37″N 75°55′42″W and located on the Howard Reef map. This wooded area was just south of Island Creek 9.7 mi. (15.5 km) southwest of Hatteras Inlet and 3.6 mi. (5.8 km) northeast of the village of Ocracoke. **Other names** Second Hammock Hills **Historical note** The feature has now disappeared, but originally referred to a stand of trees. See Black Hammock for an explanatory note.

Hammocks Ditch See Midgetts Ditch

HAMMOCK WOODS Woods, 1 mi. (1.6 km) long, in Dare County, Ocracoke Township at 35°07′53″N 75°55′00″W and located on the Howard Reef map. This wooded area is on Ocracoke Island 4.7 mi. (7.5 km) northeast of the village of Ocracoke. **Historical note** See Black Hammock for an explanatory note.

HARBOR ISLAND An island, 0.1 mi. (0.2 km) wide, in Carteret County, Cedar Island Township at 34°59′14″N 76°13′19″W and located on the Wainwright Island map. The irregularly shaped island is in Core Sound between Chain Shot Island and Wainwright Island 4 mi. (6.4 km) west of

Swash Inlet, 10.6 mi. (17 km) southwest of the village of Portsmouth, and 16.6 mi. (26.7 km) southwest of the village of Ocracoke. **Other names** Barbage Island and Harbour Island **Historical note** Historically, the island was much larger or about 2 mi. (3.2 km) across, and the name originates from the ideal "harbor" created by the island's original irregular shape. The name was originally spelled Harbour because of its very early application by the English, but has since adopted the American spelling.

Harbour Island See Harbor Island

HARD WORKING LUMPS A shoal in Carteret County, Harkers Island Township at 34°39′38″N 76°33′43″W and located on the Harkers Island map. The shoal is in Back Sound just off Shackleford Banks at the northwest point of Johnson Bay 2.3 mi. (3.7 km) south of the village of Harkers Island 2.9 mi. (4.6 km) northwest of Barden Inlet. **Historical note** See Goulds Lump for an explanatory note.

HARGRAVES BEACH A beach in Dare County, Atlantic Township at 36°08′50″N 75°44′43″W and located but not named on the Martin Point map. The name refers to a beach on Currituck Banks on both the ocean and sound sides and is located just north of Southern Shores, 5.8 mi. (9.3 km) north northwest of Kitty Hawk.

HARKERS ISLAND A populated place, 7 ft. (2.1 m) high with a population of about 1,700, in Carteret County, Harkers Island Township at 34°41′40″N 76°33′30″W and located on the Harkers Island map. This community is on the south shore of Harkers Island 2.4 mi. (3.8 km) north northeast of Shackleford Banks and 5.6 mi (9 km) east southeast of the mainland town of Beaufort.

HARKERS ISLAND An island, 4.2 mi. (6.8 km) long, 1.1 mi. (1.8 km) wide and 13 ft. (4 m) high, in Carteret County, Harkers Island Township at 34°42′30″N 76°35′15″W (northwest end), 34°41′17″N 76°31′32″W (southeast end), and 34°41′45″N 76°33′15″W (center) and located on the Harkers Island map. The island is in Back Sound at the southwest end of Core Sound separated from the mainland by The Straits 3.2 mi. (5.2 km) north northeast of Shackleford Banks and 5.6 mi. (9 km) east southeast of the mainland town of Beaufort. **Other names** Crane Island, Craney Island, Crany Island, Davers Island, and Markers Islands **Historical note** The island was granted to Thomas Sparrow on March 21, 1714, then sold to Ebenezer Harker on September 15, 1750. It became known as Harkers Island in 1783 when three brothers named Harker (Zachary, James and Ebenezer) divided the island among themselves.

HARKERS ISLAND HARBOR A harbor in Carteret County, Harkers Island Township at 34°42′58″N 75°35′05″W and located but not named on the Harkers Island map. The harbor is in Brooks Creek at the west end of Harkers Island 1.8 mi. (2.9 km) northwest of the village of Harkers Island and 4.1 mi. (6.6 km) east southeast of the mainland town of Beaufort.

HARKERS POINT A point of land, 5 ft. (1.5 m) high, in Carteret County, Harkers Island Township at 34°42′43″N 76°35′15″W and located on the Harkers Island map. The point is the northwest point of Harkers Island 2 mi. (3.2 km) northwest of the village of Harkers Island and 3.9 mi. (6.2 km) east of the mainland town of Beaufort.

Hataras Banks See Pea Island

Hatarask See Pea Island

Hatorasch Inlet See Old Hatteras Inlet

Hatoras Inlet See Gunt Inlet

Hatorask See Cape Hatteras

Hatorask See Hatrask

Hatoraske See Cape Hatteras

Hatorask Inlet See Gunt Inlet

HATRASK A former region in Dare County, Kennekeet Township. It was an area referred to by the local Indians and extended from former Cape Kenrick (q.v.) to the general vicinity of Oregon Inlet. **Other names** Hatorask

Hatrask See Hatteras Island

Hattars Inlett See Old Hatteras Inlet

HATTERAS A populated place, 10 ft. (1.5 m) high with a population of about 700, in Dare County, Hatteras Township at 35°13′10″N 75°41′29″W and located on the Hatteras map. The village is on southwest Hatteras Island on a marsh peninsula extending into Pamlico Sound, 2.3 mi. (3.7 km) west southwest of Frisco and 9.6 mi. (15.4 km) southwest of Buxton. **Other names** Hatteras Village and Port of Hatteras **Historical note** The name is possibly an English corruption of an Algonquian word meaning area of sparse vegetation. During the War Between the States Hatteras was the capital of "the true and faithful State of North Carolina." The Outer Banks and some people on the coastal mainland did not agree with the secessionists who joined North Carolina with the Confederacy, and these anti-secessionists elected delegates to send to Washington, D.C. much in the same fashion as that part of Virginia that became West Virginia as a result of pressure from anti-secessionists. However, the delegates from the Outer Banks to Washington, D.C. were never seated in Congress, therefore, the government at Hatteras was never recognized. A post office was established at Hatteras in 1858, and the village was incorporated in 1931.

Hatteras Bank See Hatteras Island

Hatteras Banks See Hatteras Island

Hatteras Bar See Hatteras Island

HATTERAS BEACH A beach in Dare County, Hatteras Township at 35°13′15″N 75°31′55″W and located but not named on the Hatteras map. The beach is located at Cape Hatteras, 3.5 mi. (5.6 km) south of Buxton. **Historical note** The reference is generally to the beach in the Cape Hatteras area, but the name has been applied to varying extents of the entire shore of Hatteras Island.

HATTERAS BIGHT A bight, 6 mi. (9.7 km) long, in Dare County, Hatteras Township at 35°13′30″N 75°34′45″W and located on the Cape Hatteras map. The bight is in the Atlantic Ocean on the south shore of Hatteras Island extending from Cape Hatteras on the east to a point 0.6 mi. (1 km) south of Frisco on the west. **Other names** Bight of Hatteras, Hatteras Cove and The Bight

Hatteras Cove See Hatteras Bight

HATTERAS GROUND A former reference to an area of open sea in Dare County, Hatteras and Kennekeet townships. The area was a whaling ground in the Atlantic Ocean east and south of Cape Hatteras. **Other names** Hatteras Grounds **Historical note** This was a former area of concentration of whales and used as a hunting and cruising ground for whaling. It was discovered by whalers from New England in the 1830s and used extensively until the whales in the area were depleted. The whalers of the Outer Banks did not hunt for whales in ships as the New England whalers did, but instead sighted whales from land and captured them by using boats similar to long boats. See Cape Lookout Grounds for a further description of whaling Outer Banks style.

Hatteras Grounds See Hatteras Ground

HATTERAS INLET A water passage in Dare County, Hatteras Township and Hyde County, Ocracoke Township at 35°11′37″N 75°45′10″W and located on the Hatteras and Green Island maps. The water passage connects Pamlico Sound to the Atlantic Ocean and separates Hatteras Island and Ocracoke Island 4 mi. (6.4 km) southwest of the village of Hatteras. **Historical note** The inlet was opened in 1846 by the same hurricane that opened Oregon Inlet and should not be confused with Old Hatteras Inlet (q.v.).

Hatteras Inlet See Old Hatteras Inlet

HATTERAS INLET CHANNEL A channel, 3 mi. (4.8 km) long, in Dare County, Hatteras Township at 35°13′25″N 75°42′07″W (northeast end), 35°12′18″N 75°44′45″W (southwest end), and 35°12′58″N 75°43′30″W (center) and located but not named on the Hatteras map. The channel trends southwest-northeast and connects Hatteras Inlet to Rollinson Channel just west of the village of Hatteras. **Other names** Barney Slue and Long Slue

HATTERAS ISLAND A former island, 33 mi. (52.8 km) long, in Dare County, Kennekeet and Hatteras Townships at 35°40′30″N 75°29′15″W (north end), 35°11′38″N 75°44′38″W (south end), and 35°25′00″N 75°35′00″W (center) and located on the Pea Island, Rodanthe, Little Kinnakeet, Buxton, Cape Hatteras and Hatteras maps. This island extends northeast from Hatteras Inlet to Cape Hatteras then north to former New Inlet at the south end of former Pea Island 5.6 mi. (9.1 km) north of Rodanthe. **Other names** Cape Hatteras Banks, Cape Hatteras Island, Chicamacomico Banks, Chickonocomack Bank, Chiconomack Bank, Croatoan, Hatrask, Hatteras Bank, Hatteras Banks, Hatteras Bar, Hattorask, Hertfords Island, Kinakeet Banks, Kinnakeet Banks, and Raonack. **Historical note** Hatteras Island is made up of three historical segments of the Outer Banks, Cape Hatteras Banks (q.v.) extended from Old Hatteras Inlet (q.v.) to Cape Hatteras; Kinnakeet Banks (q.v.) extended north from Cape Hatteras to the locality known as Little Kinnakeet, or the area of former Chaneandepeco Inlet; and Chicamacomico Banks (q.v.) extended from Little Kinnakeet to former New Inlet located between Rodanthe and Oregon Inlet. Today the names Hatteras Island and Pea Island are still used even though these two former islands have been joined since the 1940s when New Inlet closed.

HATTERAS SHOALS Shoals, 2 mi. (3.2 km) long, in Dare County, Hatteras Township at 35°12′30″N 75°31′00″W and located but not shown on the Cape Hatteras map. The shoals are the inner section of Diamond Shoals extending southeast 2 mi. (3.2 km) from the tip of Cape Hatteras.

Other names Cape Hatteras Spit and The Spit

Hatteras Shoals See Diamond Shoals

HATTERAS SLOUGH A channel in Dare County, Hatteras Township at 35°11′50″N 75°30′20″W and located but not named on chart 11555. This is a natural channel between Hatteras Shoals and Inner Diamond Shoal just off Cape Hatteras.

Hatteras Slough See Diamond Slough

Hatteras Village See Hatteras

Hatteras Woods See Buxton Woods

Hattorask See Hatteras Island

Hattorask See Indian Town

HAULOVER POINT A point of land in Carteret County, Portsmouth Township at 35°04′24″N 76°03′57″W and located on the Portsmouth map. A point of Portsmouth Island 0.3 mi. (0.5 km) north of the village of Portsmouth and 8.3 mi. (13.3 km) southwest of the village of Ocracoke. **Other names** Haul Over Point **Historical note** A "haulover" is a generic or type of feature that refers to a shallow place where a boat must be actually "pulled over" from one area of deep water to another, or haulover can also refer to a narrow low isthmus where a boat may be pulled over. The term haulover is applied frequently on the Outer Banks; the haulover area is quite frequently dry.

Haul Over Point See Haulover Point

HAULOVER SLEW A water passage, 1.8 mi. (2.9 km) long, in Carteret County, Portsmouth Township at 35°04′30″N 76°04′05″W and located on the Portsmouth map. The water passage is in Pamlico Sound and separates Casey Island and Portsmouth Island 5.4 mi. (8.6 km) southwest of the village of Ocracoke. **Historical note** Slew is a generic or type of feature that can refer to a variety of features, and on the Outer Banks generally refers to a water passage, tidal stream, or a channel. There are also variations of the spelling sometimes on the same map and even the same feature on different maps. Other spellings are slough and slue. The form of spelling "slough" is in more common usage even on the Outer Banks. Use of the spelling slue historically referred specifically to a channel and most place names retain this reference. Also, see Haulover Point for a further explanatory note.

HAY POINT A point of land in Dare county, Atlantic Township at 36°03′17″N 75°42′27″W and located on the Kitty Hawk map. The point is at the northeast corner of Kitty Hawk Bay, 3.4 mi. (5.4 km) north northwest of the Wright Brothers Memorial and 0.7 mi. (1.1 km) south of Kitty Hawk.

HEAD OF THE HOLE A cove, 0.4 mi. (0.6 km) long, in Carteret County, Portsmouth Township at 34°47′45″N 76°23′00″W and located on the Davis map. The cove is in Core Sound 0.9 mi. (1.4 km) northeast of The Swash and 4.5 mi. (7.2 km) east of the mainland town of Davis.

HEADQUARTERS ISLAND An island in Dare County, Nags Head Township at 35°53′15″N 73°36′25″W and located on the Roanoke Island NE map. It is a marsh island in Roanoke Sound 4.9 mi. (7.8 km) south of Nags Head, 1 mi. (1.6 km) south of The Causeway, and 1.4 mi. (2.2 km) southwest of Whalebone Junction.

HENRY JONES CREEK A cove, 0.4 mi. (0.6 km) wide, in Carteret County, Harkers Island Township at 34°41′56″N 76°33′01″W and located on the Harkers Island map. The cove is in West Mouth Bay at the north side of Harkers Island 0.7 mi. (1.1 km) northeast of the village of Harkers Island.

HERMITAGE ISLAND A former island in Currituck County, Fruitville Township and located but not shown on the Knotts Island map. This small island was just south of Currituck Inlet at the north end of Currituck Banks. **Historical note** The name appeared on only a few early maps because the feature disappeared in the early eighteenth century.

HERRING SHOAL ISLAND An island, 0.6 mi. (1 km) long, in Dare County, Nags Head Township at 35°47′59″N 75°33′30″W and located on the Oregon Inlet map. The marsh island is in Roanoke Sound 0.7 mi. (1.1 km) southwest of Bodie Island, 2 mi. (3.2 km) east of Duck Island, and 6.5 mi. (10.4 km) southeast of Wanchese. **Historical note** A herring is a North Atlantic fish known to visit shoal areas near the shore to spawn.

Hertford Ile See Pea Island

Hertford Island See Pea Island

Hertfords Island See Hatteras Island

Hertfords Island See Pea Island

Hicks Bay See Beasley Bay

HIGH HILL A sand dune, 10 ft. (3 m) high, in Carteret County, Harkers Island Township at 34°40′37″N 76°37′09″W and located on the Harkers Island map. The dune is on Shackleford Banks 3.7 mi. (6 km) southwest of the village of Harkers Island and 1.3 mi. (2.1 km) south of Middle Marshes.

HIGH HILLS Hummocks, 0.2 mi. (0.3 km) wide, in Carteret County, Smyrna Township at 34°43′45″N 76°26′45″W and located on the Horsepen Point map. These two hummocks are marsh islands in Core Sound just east of Great Shoal 4.6 mi. (7.4 km) south of the mainland town of Davis.

High Hills Inlet See Whalebone Inlet

HIGH POINT OF HILLS A sand dune, 49 ft. (15.1 m) high, in Dare County, Hatteras Township at 35°14′40″N 75°35′14″W and located but not named on the Cape Hatteras map. The dune is a landmark on Hatteras Island just northwest of Creeds Hill, 3.4 mi. (5.4 km) northwest of Cape Point at Cape Hatteras and 4.5 mi. (7.2 km) south of Buxton.

HIGH RIDGE CREEK A stream in Dare County, Atlantic Township at 36°02′50″N 75°43′42″W and located but not named on the Kitty Hawk map. The stream heads at 36°03′12″N 75°43′36″W just east of Kitty Hawk Landing and flows south to Kitty Hawk Bay, 1.9 mi. (3 km) west southwest of Kitty Hawk and 4.2 mi. (6.7 km) south of Southern Shores.

HIGH RIDGE POINT A point of land in Dare County, Atlantic Township at 36°02′57″N 75°43′50″W and located but not named on the Kitty Hawk map. This pronounced point is 2 mi. (3.2 km) west southwest of Kitty Hawk and 4 mi. (6.4 km) south of Southern Shores.

HIGH RIDGE POND A lake in Dare County, Atlantic Township at 36°02′56″N 75°43′58″W and located but not named on the Kitty Hawk map. The Pond is located in a marsh just north of Stove Island, 2.1 mi. (3.3 km) southwest of Kitty Hawk and 4.2 mi. (6.7 km) south of Southern Shores.

Hill of the Wreck See Wreck Hill

HODGES REEF A shoal, 1 mi. (1.6 km) long, in Carteret County, Portsmouth Township at 35°00′30″N 76°11′45″W and located but not shown on the Wainwright Island map. The shoal is in Pamlico Sound 3.5 mi. (5.6 km) northeast of Chain Shot Island and 11.3 mi. (18.5 km) southwest of the village of Ocracoke.

HOG CREEK A water passage, 0.4 mi. (0.6 km) long, in Currituck County, Poplar Branch Township at 36°14′43″N 75°47′55″W and located but not named on the Jarvisburg map. The water passage connects Baums Creek to Pine Island Bay, 6.3 mi. (10.1 km) northwest of Duck and 9.4 mi. (15 km) south of Corolla.

HOG ISLAND An island, 0.5 mi. (0.8 km) wide, in Dare County, Nags Head Township at 35°02′36″N 75°37′23″W and located on the Wanchese and Oregon Inlet maps. The island is just south of Roanoke Island and 2.2 mi. (3.5 km) south of Wanchese.

HOG ISLAND An island, 0.1 mi. (0.2 km) wide, in Dare County, Atlantic Township at 36°02′46″N 75°43′27″W and located on the Kitty Hawk Map. The island is in the north portion of Kitty Hawk Bay 1.7 mi. (2.7 km) southwest of Kitty Hawk. **Other names** Little Hog Island

HOG ISLAND An island, 0.1 mi. (0.2 km) long and 0.05 mi. (0.08 km) wide, in Dare County, Kennekeet Township at 35°40′04″N 75°29′30″W and located on the Pea Island map. This island is a marsh island 0.3 mi. (0.5 km) north northwest of Cedar Hammock and 5.2 mi. (8.4 km) north northwest of Rodanthe.

HOG ISLAND CREEK A water passage, 0.7 mi. (1.1 km) long, in Dare County, Nags Head Township at 35°48′59″N 75°37′36″W (north end) and 35°48′42″N 75°37′45″W (south end) and located on the Wanchese map. The water passage trends north-south and separates an unnamed marsh island from Hog Island, 2.2 mi. (3.5 km) south southeast of Wanchese.

HOG ISLANDS Islands, approximately 1 mi. (1.6 km) long, in Currituck County, Poplar Branch Township at 36°16′45″N 75°48′47″W and located on the Mossey Islands map. The islands are a north-south series of 8-10 marsh islands in Beasley Bay just west of Currituck Banks, 2 mi. (3.2 km) south of Three Dunes, 6.8 mi. (10.9 km) south of Corolla and 9.4 mi. (15 km) north northwest of Duck.

HOGPEN BAY A cove, 0.7 mi. (1.1 km) long and 0.5 mi. (0.8 km) wide, in Carteret County, Smyrna Township at 34°40′54″N 76°29′20″W and located on the Horsepen Point map. The cove is a shallow area at the entrance to Caggs Creek 4.2 mi. (6.7 km) east of the village of Harkers Island.

HOG POINT A point of land in Dare County, Atlantic Township at 36°02′53″N 75°43′27″W and located but not named on the Kitty Hawk map. The point is just west of Grants Cove on the north shore of Kitty Hawk Bay, 1.6 mi. (2.6 km) southwest of Kitty Hawk and 4.2 mi. (6.7 km) south of Southern Shores.

HOMICKY LAND An historical reference to an area of sand dunes located on the Pea Island and Rodanthe maps. The name refers to the area in and around Rodanthe on the north portion of Hatteras Island and the south portion of Pea Island. **Historical note** The term was used earlier to refer to an area of hills or dunes and is still sometimes used as a geological or geographical reference. Sometimes homick or hommock was a variation of hummock and hammock and the name was used accordingly.

HOOKERS FIELD An area in Dare County, Nags Head Township at 35°50′32″N 75°39′07″W and located but not named on the Wanchese map. This former open area was located on southwestern Roanoke Island, 0.8 mi. (1.3 km) west of Wanchese.

HOOKERS LANDING A former landing in Dare County, Nags Head Township at 35°50′28″N 75°39′29″W and located but not named on the Wanchese map. The landing was located at the southwest part of Roanoke Island, 1.1. mi. (1.8 km) west of Wanchese.

Hoop Hole See Hoop Pole Creek

HOOP POLE CREEK A water passage, 1 mi. (1.6 km) long, at 34°42′30″N 76°45′37″W and located on the Mansfield map. The water passage is in Bogue Sound 1.3 mi. (2.1 km) west of Atlantic Beach and 3.2 mi. (5.1 km) southwest of the mainland town of Morehead City. **Other names** Hoop Pole and Hoop-pole Creek **Historical note** A hoop pole is a slender length of green sapling wood used for barrel hoops.

Hoop-pole Creek See Hoop Pole Creek

HOOP POLE LANDING A landing in Carteret County, Morehead Township at 34°42′14″N 76°48′22″W and located on the Mansfield map. The landing is on the sound side of Bogue Banks at Hoop Pole Woods 3.9 mi. (6.2 km) west of Atlantic Beach and 5.4 mi. (8.6 km) southwest of Morehead City. **Historical note** See Hoop Pole Creek for an explanatory note.

HOPE POLE WOODS Woods, 2.3 mi. (3.7 km) long, in Carteret County, Morehead Township at 34°42′00″N 76°48′30″W and located on the Mansfield map. This wooded area is on Bogue Banks, 4 mi. (6.4 km) west of Atlantic Beach and 5.6 mi. (9 km) southwest of the mainland town of Morehead City. **Other names** Hoop-pole Woods **Historical note** See Hoop Pole Creek for an explanatory note.

Hoop-pole Woods See Hoop Pole Woods

HORSEBONE A water passage, 0.4 mi. (0.6 km) long, in Currituck County, Poplar Branch Township at 36°14′40″N 75°48′34″W and located on the Jarvisburg map. This is a small water passage between two unnamed marsh islands just southeast of Goat Island Bay, 1.7 mi. (2.7 km) west of Currituck Banks, 6.5 mi. (10.4 km) northwest of Duck and 9.3 mi. (14.9 km) south of Corolla. **Other names** Horse Island

HORSE ISLAND An island, 0.2 mi. (0.3 km) long, in Carteret County, Atlantic Township at 34°53′27″N 76°16′14″W and located on the Atlantic map. The island is in Core Sound 0.2 mi. (0.3 km) west of Core Banks and 3.6 mi. (5.8 km) east of the mainland village of Atlantic.

HORSE ISLAND An island, 1 mi. (1.6 km) long and 0.6 mi. (1 km) wide, in Carteret County, Davis Township at 34°47′07″N 76°23′57″W and located on the Davis map. The marsh island is in Core Sound and separated from Core Banks by Horse Island Creek, 3.6 mi. (5.8 km) east of the mainland village of Davis.

HORSE ISLAND An island, 0.05 mi. (0.08 km) long, in Carteret County, Harkers Island Township at 34°39′59″N 76°30′37″W and located on the Harkers Island map. The island is in Core Sound 3.5 mi. (5.6 km) southeast of the village of Harkers Island and 2.5 mi. (4 km) north northeast of Barden Inlet.

HORSE ISLAND An island, 0.4 mi. (0.6 km) long, in Carteret County, Smyrna Township at 34°42′54″N 76°27′59″W and located on the Horsepen Point map. This irregularly shaped marsh island is in Core Sound and is separated from Core Banks by Lewis Creek 5.3 mi. (8.5 km) east of the village of Harkers Island.

HORSE ISLAND An island, 0.8 mi. (1.3 km) long, in Carteret County, Beaufort Township at 34°42′15″N 76°38′37″W and located on the Beaufort map. The marsh island is in Back Sound, 1.6 mi. (2.6 km) southeast of the mainland town of Beaufort and 4.6 mi. (7.4 km) east of the village of Harkers Island.

Horse Island See Horsebone

Horse Island See House Island

Horse Island Bay See The Swash

HORSE ISLAND CHANNEL A former channel, about 2 mi. (3.2 km) long in Carteret County, Portsmouth Township at 35°04′30″N 76°03′20″W and located but not shown on the Portsmouth map. The channel was in Ocracoke Inlet just east of the village of Portsmouth and 4.2 mi. (6.7 km) southwest of the village of Ocracoke. **Other names** Brant Shoal Channel

HORSE ISLAND COVE A cove, 0.1 mi. (0.2 km) long and 0.05 mi. (0.08 km) wide, in Carteret County, Davis Township at 34°47′09″N 76°24′10″W and located on the Davis map. The cove is in Core Sound at the northwest portion of Horse Island 3.4 mi. (5.4 km) east of the mainland village of Davis.

HORSE ISLAND CREEK A water passage, 0.5 mi. (0.8 km) long, in Carteret County, Davis Township at 34°46′45″N 76°23′53″W and located on the Davis map. The water passage is in Core Sound and trends northeast-southwest separating Horse Island from Core Banks and connecting The Swash and Great Island Creek, 4.7 mi. (7.5 km) east southeast of the mainland village of Davis.

HORSE ISLAND CREEK A water passage, 1 mi. (1.6 km) long, in Carteret County, Beaufort Township at 34°42′11″N 76°38′02″W (east end), 34°42′25″N 76°38′55″W (west end), and 34°42′15″N 76°38′28″W (center) and located but not named on the Beaufort map. The water passage separates Horse Island from Carrot Island, 1.7 mi. (2.7 km) southeast of the mainland town of Beaufort and 4.6 mi. (7.4 km) east of the village of Harkers Island.

HORSE ISLAND POINT A point of land in Carteret County, Davis Township at 34°47′34″N 76°23′57″W and located on the Davis map. It is the north point of Horse Island and is located 3.6 mi. (5.8 km) east of the mainland village of Davis.

HORSE ISLANDS Former islands in Dare County, Nags Head Township at 35°54′15″N 75°36′30″W and located but not shown on the Roanoke Island NE map. The islands were in Roanoke Sound just west of Whalebone Junction, 4 mi. (6.4 km) south of Nags Head. **Historical note** There were originally four or five islands here that are now joined into one island which is now known as Cedar Island (q.v.).

Horse Islands See Cedar Island (35°54′15″N 75°36′29″W)

HORSE MARSH Islands, 0.4 mi. (0.6 km) wide, in Carteret County, Harkers Island Township at 34°43′10″N 76°35′09″W and located on the Harkers Island map. These islands are at the junction of North River and The Straits 2.3 mi. (3.7 km) northwest of the village of Harkers Island and 4.1 mi. (6.6 km) east northeast of the mainland town of Beaufort.

HORSEPEN CREEK A cove, 0.2 mi. (0.3 km) long, in Carteret County, Atlantic Township at 34°50′23″N 76°20′10″W and located on the Styron Bay map. The Cove is in Core Sound 2.9 mi. (4.6 km) south of the mainland village of Atlantic.

HORSEPEN CREEK A water passage, 0.9 mi. (1.4 km) long, in Carteret County, Smyrna Township at 34°43′29″N 76°26′44″W and located on the Horsepen Point map. The water passage separates Core Banks from an unnamed marsh area in Core Sound 4.8 mi. (7.7 km) south of the mainland village of Davis.

HORSEPEN POINT A point of land in Carteret County, Smyrna Township at 34°43′29″N 76°27′20″W and located on the Horsepen Point map. The point of land is on a marsh area of Core Banks opposite Great Shoal and located 5 mi. (8 km) south of the mainland village of Davis.

HORSEPEN POINT A point of land in Hyde County, Ocracoke Township at 35°07′01″N 75°58′36″W and located on the Ocracoke map. The point is on Ocracoke Island 1.1 mi. (1.8 km) west of The Plains and 0.8 mi. (1.3 km) northeast of the village of Ocracoke.

HORSE POINT A point of land in Carteret County, Harkers Island Township at 34°39′42″N 76°34′01″W and located on the Harkers Island map. The point is on Shackleford Banks at the north point of an unnamed mud flat just northwest of Johnsons Bay, 2.3 mi. (3.7 km) south of the village of Harkers Island and 3.1 mi. (5 km) northwest of Barden Inlet.

HOTEL HILL A sand dune in Dare County, Nags Head Township at 35°57′05″N 75°37′30″W and located but not named on the Manteo and Roanoke Island NE maps. The dune is in Nags Head 3.7 mi. (5.9 km) northeast of Manteo. **Historical note** The feature was named because the nineteenth century hotel was nearby. The sand dune is part of the Seven Sisters (q.v.) complex and is of historical significance only. The name is rarely used today.

HOUSE ISLAND An island, 0.4 mi. (0.6 km) long and 0.3 mi. (0.5 km) wide, in Dare County, Nags Head Township at 35°53′30″N 75°37′09″W and located on the Roanoke Island NE map. The marsh island is in Roanoke Sound 4.5 mi. (7.2 km) south of Nags Head, and 1.5 mi. (2.4 km) west southwest of Whalebone Junction. **Other names** Horse Island **Historical note** The original name was Horse Island but a transcribing error has been continually perpetuated on maps until the name has become changed to House.

HOWARD REEF A shoal, 1.8 mi. (2.9 km) long and 0.5 mi. (0.8 km) wide, in Hyde County, Ocracoke Township at 35°08′20″N 75°58′30″W and located on the Howard Reef map. The shoal is in Pamlico Sound 2 mi. (3.2 km) north northeast of the village of Ocracoke. **Other names** Our Reef

Hunting Quarter Inlet See Cedar Inlet

HUNTING QUARTER An historical area. This is a general term referring to most of Core Banks and an extensive portion of the mainland in and around the present area of Cedar Island and the mainland village of Atlantic. The name is an English translation of the Indian name for the area. In the fifteenth century it was common practice to name large undefined areas based on the four quarters of the compass and later the term quarter came to be a reference to a specific region or place.

HUNTING QUARTER SOUND An historical section of a lagoon in Carteret County; Portsmouth, Cedar Island and Atlantic townships at 34°54′00″N 76°16′30″W and located but not shown on the Wainwright Island and Atlantic maps. It was formerly the northeast portion of Core Sound (q.v.) and was separated from Pamlico Sound by Chain Shot, Harbor, Wainwright, and Shell Islands. The southern boundary of Hunting Quarter Sound was in the general vicinity of the mainland village of Atlantic.

HYDE COUNTY A civil division, 613 sq. mi. (980.8 sq. km) with a population of 5,765, that includes Ocracoke, Swan Quarter, Currituck, Fairfield, and Lake Landing townships at 35°26′00″N 76°11′30″W. The county is bounded by Dare, Carteret, Tyrrell, Beaufort, and Pamlico Counties, and Ocracoke Island is the only part of the county on the Outer Banks. **Historical note** The county was originally formed as Wickham Precinct of Bath County in 1705 and changed to Hyde in 1712 when it was re-named for Governor Edward Hyde.

I

Iland of Saint John See Currituck Banks

Ile Goade See Currituck Banks

Ile Raonoake See Roanoke Island

INDIAN BEACH A populated place in Carteret County, Morehead Township at 34°41′14″N 76°53′33″W and located but not shown on the Salter Path map. The community is just west of Salter Path 9.1 mi. (14.6 km) west of Atlantic Beach.

INDIAN CREEK A stream, 0.2 mi. (0.3 km) long, in Currituck County, Fruitville Township at 36°29′30″N 75°56′15″W and located on the Barco map. The stream's source is at 36°30′15″N 75°56′14″W in the southeast portion of Great Marsh and it flows south through Indian Pond to Currituck Sound, 9.2 mi. (14.7 km) northwest of Corolla.

INDIAN GAP A water passage in Currituck County, Poplar Branch Township at 36°15′45″N 75°49′13″W and located on the Mossey Islands map. The water passage is located in Currituck Sound just south of Indian Gap Island, 7 mi. (11.2 km) south of Corolla and 9 mi. (14.4 km) northwest of Duck.

INDIAN GAP ISLAND An island, 0.8 mi. (1.3 km) long, in Currituck County, Poplar Branch Township at 36°15′55″N 75°49′17″W and located on the Mossey Islands map. This is an elongated island trending northeast-southwest in Currituck Sound just north of Indian Gap, 7.1 mi. (11.4 km) south of Corolla and 9.1 mi. (14.6 km) northwest of Duck.

INDIAN PEAK A former rock in Currituck County, Fruitville Township and located but not shown on the Knotts Island map. It was formerly a very large mound of conch shells in Currituck Sound near Currituck Inlet. The mound was built by the Indians after centuries of gathering and

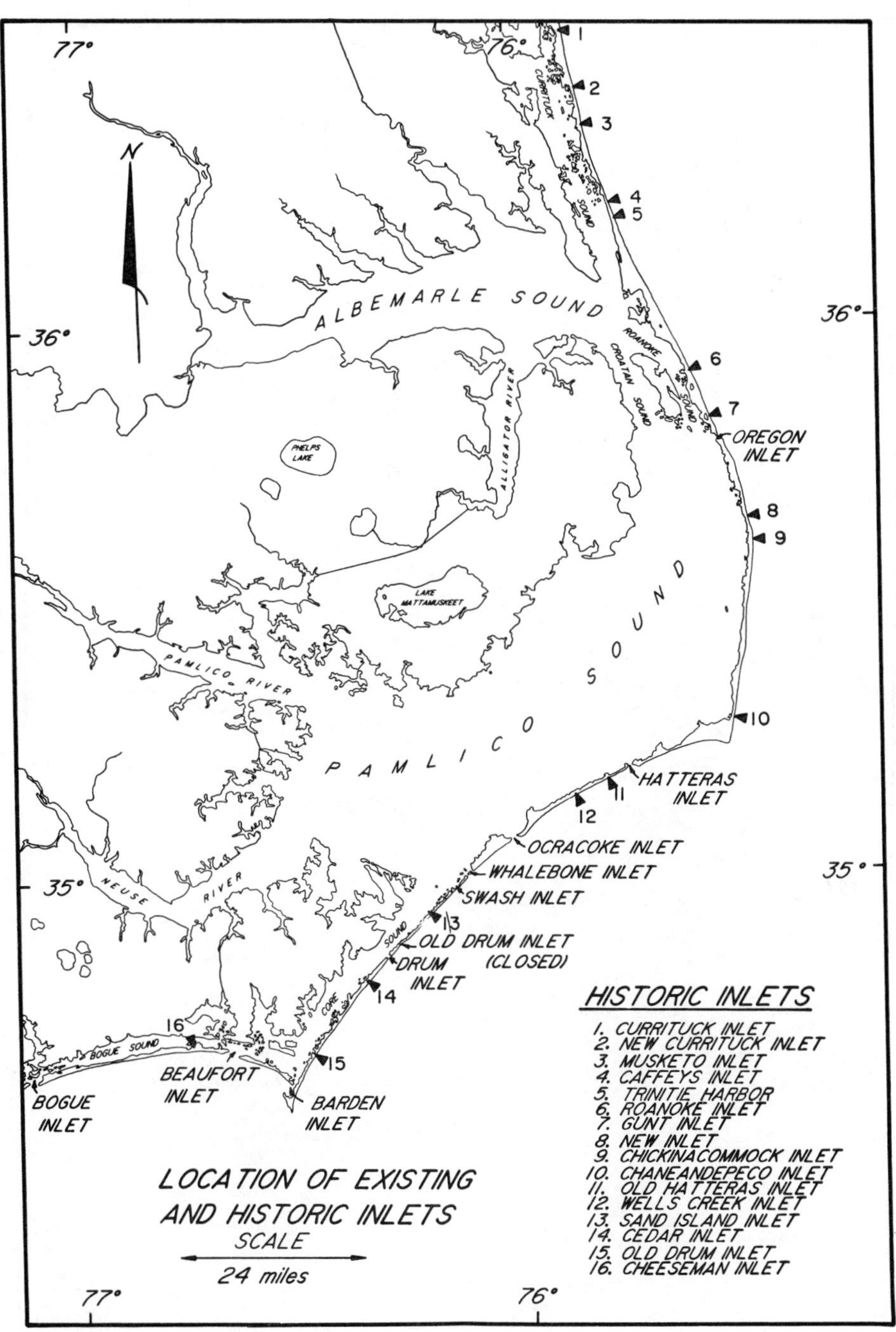
77°
76°
36°
35°
N
CURRITUCK SOUND
ALBEMARLE SOUND
ROANOKE SOUND
CROATAN SOUND
ALLIGATOR RIVER
PHELPS LAKE
LAKE MATTAMUSKEET
PAMLICO RIVER
PAMLICO SOUND
NEUSE RIVER
CORE SOUND
BOGUE SOUND
OREGON INLET
HATTERAS INLET
OCRACOKE INLET
WHALEBONE INLET
SWASH INLET
OLD DRUM INLET (CLOSED)
DRUM INLET
BEAUFORT INLET
BOGUE INLET
BARDEN INLET
HISTORIC INLETS
1. CURRITUCK INLET
2. NEW CURRITUCK INLET
3. MUSKETO INLET
4. CAFFEYS INLET
5. TRINITIE HARBOR
6. ROANOKE INLET
7. GUNT INLET
8. NEW INLET
9. CHICKINACOMMOCK INLET
10. CHANEANDEPECO INLET
11. OLD HATTERAS INLET
12. WELLS CREEK INLET
13. SAND ISLAND INLET
14. CEDAR INLET
15. OLD DRUM INLET
16. CHEESEMAN INLET
LOCATION OF EXISTING AND HISTORIC INLETS
SCALE
24 miles

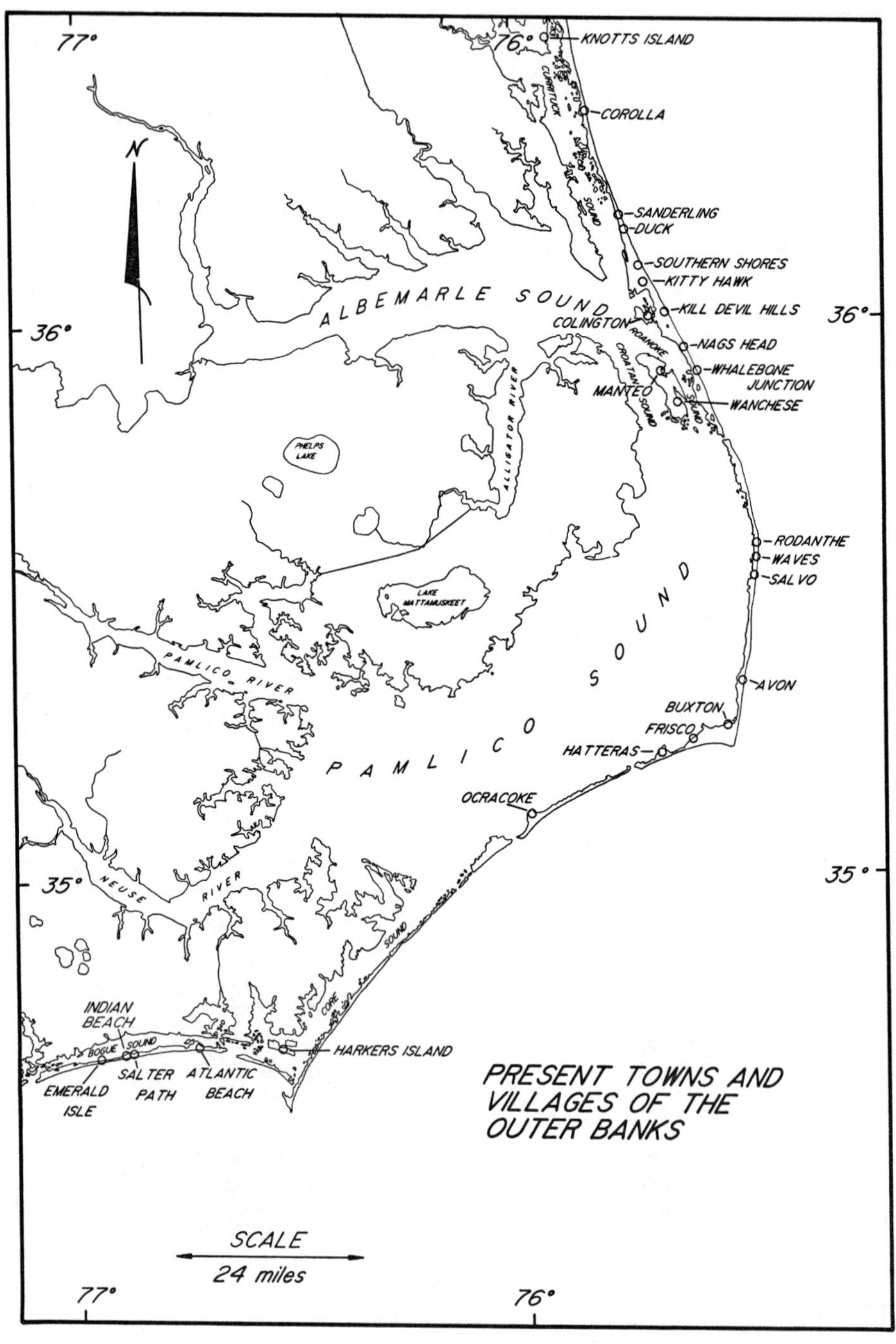
77°
76°
KNOTTS ISLAND
COROLLA
CURRITUCK
SOUND
SANDERLING
DUCK
SOUTHERN SHORES
KITTY HAWK
KILL DEVIL HILLS
36°
ALBEMARLE SOUND
COLINGTON
ROANOKE
NAGS HEAD
CROATAN SOUND
WHALEBONE JUNCTION
MANTEO
WANCHESE
N
PHELPS LAKE
ALLIGATOR RIVER
RODANTHE
WAVES
SALVO
LAKE MATTAMUSKEET
PAMLICO RIVER
PAMLICO SOUND
AVON
BUXTON
FRISCO
HATTERAS
OCRACOKE
35°
NEUSE RIVER
CORE SOUND
INDIAN BEACH
BOGUE SOUND
HARKERS ISLAND
EMERALD ISLE
SALTER PATH
ATLANTIC BEACH
PRESENT TOWNS AND VILLAGES OF THE OUTER BANKS
SCALE
24 miles

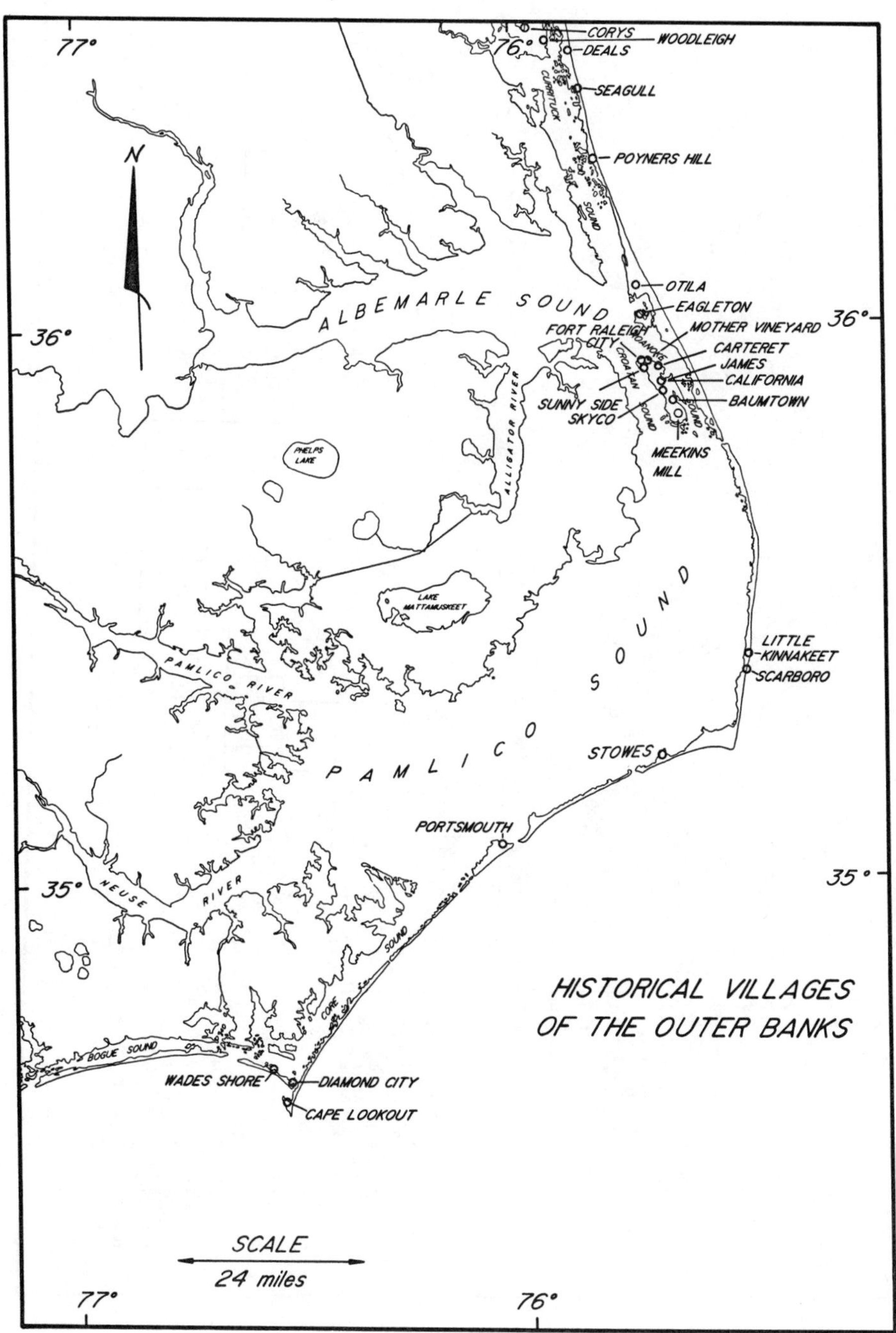
CORYS
WOODLEIGH
DEALS
SEAGULL
POYNERS HILL
CURRITUCK
SOUND
OTILA
EAGLETON
ALBEMARLE SOUND
FORT RALEIGH CITY
MOTHER VINEYARD
CARTERET
JAMES
CALIFORNIA
BAUMTOWN
SUNNY SIDE
SKYCO
ROANOKE
CROATAN
SOUND
MEEKINS MILL
PHELPS LAKE
ALLIGATOR RIVER
LAKE MATTAMUSKEET
PAMLICO RIVER
PAMLICO SOUND
LITTLE KINNAKEET
SCARBORO
STOWES
PORTSMOUTH
NEUSE RIVER
CORE SOUND
BOGUE SOUND
WADES SHORE
DIAMOND CITY
CAPE LOOKOUT
HISTORICAL VILLAGES OF THE OUTER BANKS
SCALE
24 miles
77°
76°
36°
35°
N

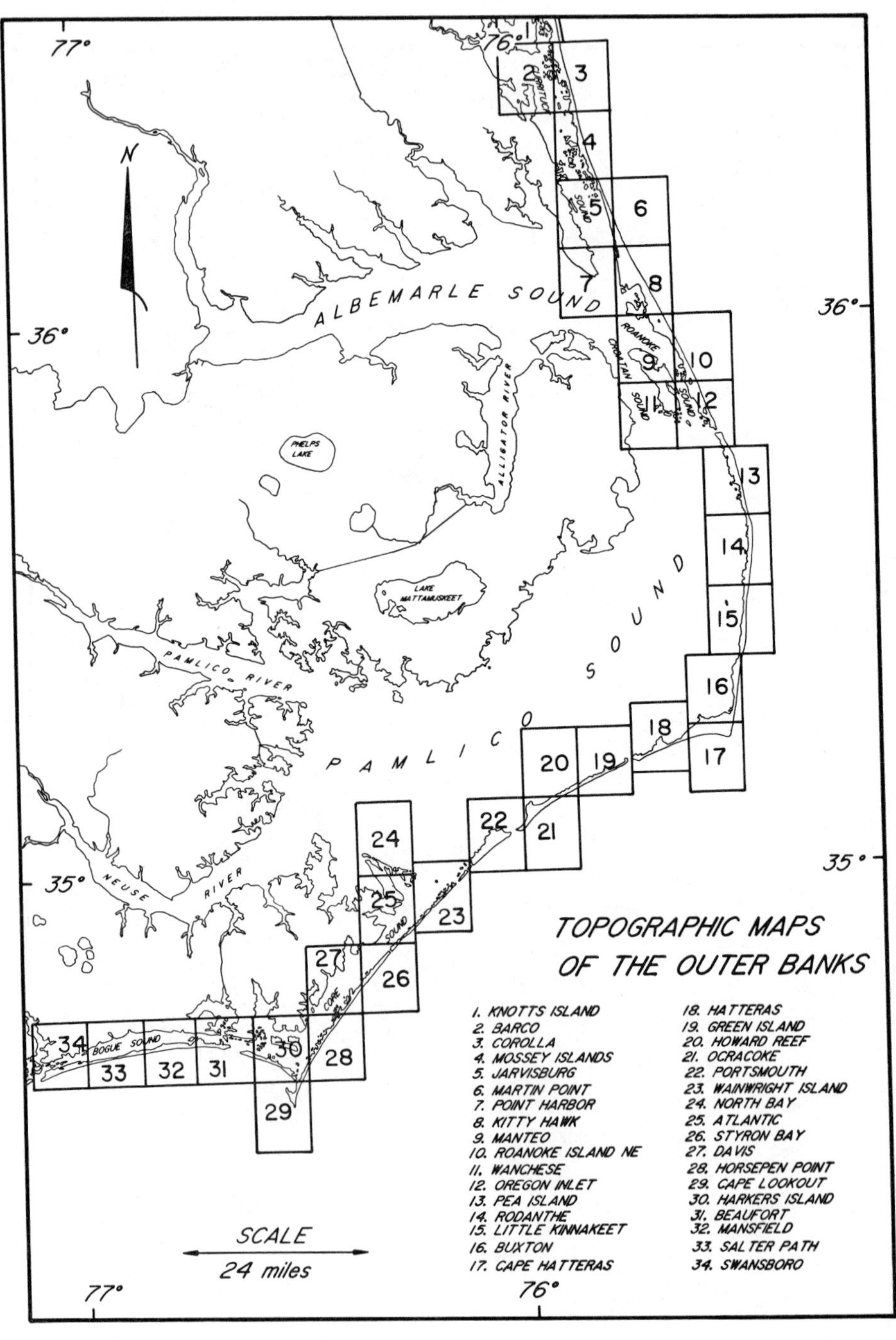

TOPOGRAPHIC MAPS
OF THE OUTER BANKS
1. KNOTTS ISLAND
2. BARCO
3. COROLLA
4. MOSSEY ISLANDS
5. JARVISBURG
6. MARTIN POINT
7. POINT HARBOR
8. KITTY HAWK
9. MANTEO
10. ROANOKE ISLAND NE
11. WANCHESE
12. OREGON INLET
13. PEA ISLAND
14. RODANTHE
15. LITTLE KINNAKEET
16. BUXTON
17. CAPE HATTERAS
18. HATTERAS
19. GREEN ISLAND
20. HOWARD REEF
21. OCRACOKE
22. PORTSMOUTH
23. WAINWRIGHT ISLAND
24. NORTH BAY
25. ATLANTIC
26. STYRON BAY
27. DAVIS
28. HORSEPEN POINT
29. CAPE LOOKOUT
30. HARKERS ISLAND
31. BEAUFORT
32. MANSFIELD
33. SALTER PATH
34. SWANSBORO
SCALE
24 miles
77°
76°
36°
35°
N
ALBEMARLE SOUND
PAMLICO SOUND
PAMLICO RIVER
NEUSE RIVER
ALLIGATOR RIVER
PHELPS LAKE
LAKE MATTAMUSKEET
ROANOKE
CROATAN
BOGUE SOUND
CORE SOUND

discarding shells. The feature no longer exists, but was a prominent landmark in the early colonial period.

INDIAN POND A lake, 0.3 mi. (0.5 km) long and 0.1 mi. (0.2 km) wide, in Currituck County, Fruitville Township at 36°29′51″N 75°56′14″W and located on the Barco map. The lake is a wide swampy area of Indian Creek and located in the southeast portion of Great Marsh, 1.9 mi. (3 km) southeast of the village of Knotts Island and 10.2 mi. (16.3 km) northwest of Corolla.

INDIAN SHELL BANKS Islands and marsh, about 1 mi. (1.6 km) long in Dare County, Nags Head Township at 35°48′45″N 75°37′00″W and located but not named on the Oregon Inlet map. The marsh island complex is in Roanoke Sound at the southeast end of Roanoke Island, 2.4 mi. (3.8 km) southeast of Wanchese and 5.5 mi. (8.8 km) northwest of Oregon Inlet.

INDIAN TOWN A former Indian village in Dare County, Hatteras Township and located but not shown on either the Buxton or Cape Hatteras maps. The village was formerly on Hatteras Island near the present village of Buxton. **Other names** Cape Hatteras Indian Town, Croatan, Hattorask and Indian Towne **Historical note** The population was probably never more than approximately 80, and in fact it was probably a semi-permanent fishing village used by Indians from the mainland.

Indian Towne See Indian Town

Inland Waterway See Intracoastal Waterway

Inlet of Roanoke See Roanoke Inlet

Inlet of 1849 See Oregon Inlet

Inlet Island See Radio Island

INLET PENINSULA A peninsula, 1.5 mi. (2.4 km) long and 5 ft (1.5 m) high, in Dare County, Hatteras Township at 35°11′45″N 75°44′17″W and located on the Hatteras map. The peninsula is the southwest tip of Hatteras Island which is at the northeast shore of Hatteras Inlet 3.4 mi. (5.4 km) southwest of the village of Hatteras.

Inner Diamonds See Inner Diamond Shoal

INNER DIAMOND SHOAL A shoal in Dare County, Hatteras Township at 35°11′15″N 75°29′18″W and located but not named on chart number 11555. This shoal area represents the middle section of Diamond Shoals and is located 3 mi. (4.8 km) southeast of Cape Hatteras. **Other names** Diamond Shoal, Inner Diamonds, The Diamond Shoals, and The Spit

INNER GRASS LUMP An island, 0.3 mi. (0.5 km) wide, in Carteret County, Stacy Township at 34°48′49″N 76°22′20″W and located on the Styron Bay map. The island is in Core Sound 0.7 mi. (1.1 km) north of Core Banks, 0.3 mi. (0.5 km) south of Outer Grass Lump, and separated from Core Banks by Old Channel 3.4 mi. (5.4 km) south of the mainland village of Sea Level. **Historical note** See Goulds Lump for an explanatory note.

Inner Green Island See Green Island (Dare County, Kennekeet Township)

INNER MIDDLE A shoal, 2.2 mi. (3.5 km) long, in Hyde County, Ocracoke Township at 35°14′35″N 76°17′35″W and located but not named on chart number 11555. The shoal is on the central part of Middle Ground 17.6 mi.

(28 km) northwest of Ocracoke Inlet and 17.8 mi. (28.3 km) northwest of the village of Ocracoke.

Inner Middle See Middle Ground (35°15′20″N 76°18′00″W)

INSHORE SLEW A former channel in Hyde County, Ocracoke Township and located but not shown on the Portsmouth map. The channel was the north approach to Ocracoke Inlet about 3 mi. (4.8 km) southwest of the village of Ocracoke. **Historical note** This approach was very close to Ocracoke Island hence the name. There is no trace of this channel since Ocracoke Island has extended into this part of the historic inlet at Ocracoke.

INTRACOASTAL WATERWAY A canal in Currituck, Dare, Hyde, and Carteret counties. The waterway is a network of inland waterways that extends from Boston, Massachusetts to Brownsville, Texas. **Other names** Inland Waterway **Historical note** Since the canal is a system of inland waterways, very little of the system is related to the Outer Banks. From North to South the waterway crosses Currituck Sound 0.1 mi. (0.2 km) southwest of Mackay Island and crosses Albemarle Sound 12 mi. (19.2 km) west of Kitty Hawk. The waterway does not appear near the Outer Banks again until it emerges from the Adams Creek Canal into Bogue Sound at the mainland town of Morehead City where it follows the coast approximately 0.5 mi. (0.8 km) from Bogue Banks until it leaves the Outer Banks area at the mainland town of Swansboro.

IRA LUMP An island, 0.1 mi. (0.2 km) long and 0.05 mi. (0.08 km) wide, in Dare County, Kennekeet Township at 35°39′32″N 75°29′24″W and located on the Pea Island map. The marsh island is in Pamlico Sound just south of Goulds Lump 4.5 mi. (7.2 km) north northwest of Rodanthe. **Historical note** See Goulds Lump for an explanatory note.

IRA MORRIS CAMP A camp, 5 ft. (1.5 m) high, in Carteret County, Portsmouth Township at 34°53′52″N 76°15′23″W and located on the Atlantic map. The campsite is on Core Banks 5 mi. (8 km) east of the mainland village of Atlantic and 1.8 mi. (2.8 km) northeast of Drum Inlet. **Historical note** The use of temporary "camps" on the Outer Banks has been a practice of people who live on the mainland and they are used for a variety of purposes.

IRON CREEK A cove, 0.4 mi. (0.6 km) long, in Carteret County, Harkers Island Township at 34°40′07″N 76°29′45″W and located on the Horsepen Point map. The cove is in Core Sound just southeast of Gunning Hammock Island and 4.3 mi. (6.9 km) southeast of the village of Harkers Island.

ISAAC POND A lake, 0.2 mi. (0.3 km) long, in Dare County, Hatteras Township at 35°12′42″N 75°41′49″W and located on the Hatteras map. The lake is on Hatteras Island 0.7 mi. (1.1 km) south southwest of the village of Hatteras.

ISLAND CREEK A cove, 0.2 mi. (0.3 km) wide, in Hyde County, Ocracoke Township at 35°07′45″N 75°55′45″W and located on the Howard Reef map. The cove is in Pamlico Sound just north of Hammock Oaks, 9.8 mi. (15.7 km) southwest of Hatteras Inlet, and 3.5 mi. (5.6 km) northeast of the village of Ocracoke.

ISLAND CREEK HILLS Sand dunes, 26 ft. (7.9 m) high, in Hyde County, Ocracoke Township at 35°07′42″N 75°55′53″W and located on the Howard Reef map. These dunes are on Ocracoke Island 4.2 mi. (6.5 km) northeast of the village of Ocracoke.

Isle of Pines See Pine Knoll Shores

J

Jackey Ridge See Jockeys Ridge

JACKS ISLAND An island, 0.2 mi. (0.3 km) long, in Carteret County, Harkers Island Township at 34°40′23″N 76°34′37″W and located on the Harkers Island map. The island is in Back Sound at the entrance to Bald Hill Bay, 1.8 mi. (2.9 km) south southwest of the village of Harkers Island and 4.3 mi. (6.9 km) northwest of Barden Inlet. **Other names** Jades Island

JACK SHOAL An island, 0.4 mi. (0.6 km) long and 0.3 mi. (0.5 km) wide, in Dare County, Kennekeet Township at 35°41′05″N 75°30′15″W and located on the Pea Island map. The island is in Pamlico Sound 0.3 mi. (0.5 km) southwest of Jesse Shoal Point and 6.7 mi. (10.8 km) north northwest of Rodanthe. **Other names** Jacks Shoal

Jacks Shoal See Jack Shoal

Jades Island See Jacks Island

JAMES A former area in Dare County, Nags Head Township and located but not shown on the Manteo map. The area was located somewhere on the north portion of Roanoke Island. **Other names** James Settlement **Historical note** This settlement was actually land given to freed Negroes who had come to Roanoke Island for the purpose of homesteading, and the community was named for Horace James the superintendant of Blacks for the District of North Carolina. Almost all of these freed Negroes eventually left Roanoke Island and today there is apparently no trace of the former settlement. Actually, the feature was probably never very permanant nor was it probably intended to be more than a collection area for resettling the freed Negroes. Also, it was never formerly named, but for purposes of record was referred to as James after its perpertrator. It may have been in the southern part of present day Manteo or the area referred to as California (q.v.) although no documented evidence can support this location over another.

James Creek See Janes Creek

James Settlement See James

Jane Gute Creek See Jeanguite Creek

JANES CREEK A cove, 0.4 mi. (0.6 km) wide, in Carteret County, Harkers Island Township at 34°42′37″N 76°34′32″W and located on the Harkers Island map. The cove is located at the northwest end of Harkers Island and connected to The Straits by a narrow water passage, 1.4 mi. (2.2 km) northwest of the village of Harkers Island and 4.7 mi. (7.5 km) east of the mainland town of Beaufort. **Other names** James Creek

JARVIS CHANNEL A water passage, 1.8 mi. (2.8 km) long, in Currituck County, Poplar Branch Township at 36°16′22″N 75°49′47″W and located on the Mossey Islands map. The water passage is in Currituck Sound 2 mi. (3.2 km) west of Currituck Banks and separates South Burris Island, Long

Island, and Indian Gap Island 7.6 mi. (12.3 km) south of Corolla, and 9.8 mi. (15.7 km) northwest of Duck.

Jeanette Sedge See Jennette Sedge

Jeangite Creek See Jeanguite Creek

Jeanguite See Southern Shores

JEANGUITE CREEK A bay, 2 mi. (3.2 km) long and 0.2 mi. (0.3 km) wide, in Dare County, Atlantic Township at 36°06′57″N 75°44′42″W and located on the Kitty Hawk and Martin Point maps. The bay is in Currituck Sound between the main portion of Currituck Banks and Martin Point just west of Southern Shores and 3.7 mi. (5.9 km) northwest of Kitty Hawk. **Other names** Gingite Creek, Ginguite Creek, Guingite Bay, Guinguys Creek, Jane Gute Creek, Jeangite Creek, Jean Guite Creek, Jean Gute Creek and Martins Point Creek. **Historical note** The name is of Algonquian origin and was originally Chincoteague which means large stream or inlet, and Jeanguite is merely an anglicized corruption of the Indian name. Acutally, the feature is a swale between two ridges and flooded by Currituck Sound, and it is not likely that the feature is the remnant of a former inlet as some authors hypothesize. The official name is Jeanguite Creek, but local usage seems to apply Martins Point Creek almost as often as the official name. Historically, the name has been applied only to the flooded swale north of the Wright Memorial Bridge, but lately the name has also been applied to a canalized extension of the original feature southward to Kitty Hawk Bay. The extenstion of Jeanguite Creek increases the length of the feature by an additional 4 mi. (6.4 km) through a ridge and swale system to a point near Hog Island at 36°02′43″N 75°43′40″W in Kitty Hawk Bay.

Jean Guite Creek See Jeanguite Creek

Jean Gute Creek See Jeanguite Creek

JENKINS COVE A cove in Currituck County, Fruitville Township at 35°24′30″N 75°50′49″W and located on the Corolla map. The cove is in Currituck Sound just west of Currituck Banks, 2.1 mi. (3.3 km) northwest of Corolla.

JENNETTE SEDGE A marsh, 2.5 mi. (4 km) long, in Dare County, Hatteras Township at 35°15′07″N 75°32′34″W and located on the Buxton map. The marsh is an area of sedge grass 1 mi. (1.6 km) south of Buxton Woods, 0.9 mi. (1.4 km) northwest of Cape Hatteras, and 1.1 mi. (1.8 km) south of Buxton. **Other names** Jeanette Sedge **Historical note** Sedge normally refers to any of various types of coarse grass found growing in marsh areas.

JESSE SHOAL POINT A point of land in Dare County, Kennekeet Township at 35°41′20″N 75°30′01″W and located on the Pea Island map. This marsh point is 0.3 mi. (0.5 km) northeast of Jack Shoal and 6.8 mi. (11 km) north northwest of Rodanthe.

Jockey Ridge See Jockeys Ridge

Jockeys Hill See Jockeys Ridge

JOCKEYS RIDGE A sand dune, 1.1 mi. (1.8 km) long and 138 ft. (45.5 m) high, in Dare County, Nags Head Township at 35°53′13″N 75°38′34″W and located on the Manteo map. This large sand dune trends north northwest-south southeast on Currituck Banks just east of Nags Head

Woods and 1.3 mi. (2.1 km) northwest of Nags Head. **Other names** Jackey Ridge, Jockey Ridge, Jockeys Hill, and Nags Head Hill **Historical note** Local stories indicate that the sand dune acquired its name from the fact that the top of the dune afforded an excellent view of a racetrack for horses in the flats just southwest of the dune. This explanation of the name may be true, but early maps indicate the surname Jackey or Jacock in this area. A cartographic practice in the seventeenth and eighteenth centuries was to include the surname of the land owners. Since Jackey or Jacock appears in this vicinity, the original name may have been Jackey Ridge which was portrayed on the Manteo map until 1953.

JOCKEYS RIDGE SAND DUNES Sand dunes in Dare County, Nags Head Township and located but not named on the Manteo map. The name is a general term that has recently been applied to Jockeys Ridge and other dunes in the immediate vicinity because of the prominence of Jockeys Ridge and the popularity of the state park established in this area.

JOE SAUR CREEK A cove, 0.2 mi. (0.3 km) wide, in Dare County, Hatteras Township at 35°13′42″N 75°38′23″W and located on the Hatteras map. The cove is 0.8 mi. (1.3 km) southwest of Frisco and 2.9 mi. (4.7 km) northeast of the village of Hatteras.

JOES CREEK A water passage, 0.6 mi. (1 km) long, in Currituck County, Poplar Branch Township at 36°14′22″N 75°47′16″W and located but not named on the Jarvisburg map. The water passage connects Doxeys Salthouse and Beach Creek, 5.9 mi. (9.4 km) north northwest of Duck and 9.8 mi. (15.7 km) southeast of Corolla.

John Mann Point See Northwest Point

John Manns Point See Northwest Point

JOHNS CREEK A cove, 0.4 mi. (0.6 km) long and 0.1 mi. (0.2 km) wide, in Dare County, Nags Head Township at 35°52′23″N 75°38′02″W and located on the Hatteras map. The cove is in Roanoke Sound 2.5 mi. (4 km) southeast of Manteo and 3.4 mi. (5.4 km) north of Wanchese.

JOHNSON CREEK A cove, 0.9 mi. (1.4 km) long, in Carteret County, Smyrna Township at 34°45′01″N 76°26′01″W and located on the Davis and Horsepen Point maps. The cove is in Core Sound 0.4 mi. (0.6 km) south of Goose Island and 3.8 mi. (5.1 km) southeast of the mainland village of Davis.

JOHNSON ISLAND An island, 0.5 mi. (0.8 km) wide, in Currituck County, Fruitville Township at 35°27′45″N 75°53′20″W and located on the Barco map. This marsh island is in Currituck Sound just north of South Channel 0.4 mi. (0.6 km) southeast of Swan Island, and 6.5 mi. (10.4 km) north northwest of Corolla. **Other names** Johnsons Island

JOHNSONS BAY A cove, 0.7 mi. (1.1 km) wide, in Carteret County, Harkers Island Township at 34°39′17″N 76°33′39″W and located on the Harkers Island map. This embayment is in the Back Sound just north of Shackleford Banks, 2.7 mi. (4.3 km) south of the village of Harkers Island and 2.4 mi. (3.8 km) northwest of Barden Inlet.

Johnsons Island See Johnson Island

JOHN STYRONS CREEK A cove, 0.05 mi. (0.08 km) wide, in Carteret County, Portsmouth Township at 35°03′45″N 76°04′15″W and located on the Portsmouth map. The cove is at Baymarsh Thorofare 0.9 mi. (1.4 km)

west southwest of the village of Portsmouth and 7.3 mi. (11 km) southwest of the village of Ocracoke.

JONES CREEK A cove, 0.4 mi. (0.6 km) wide, in Carteret County, Harkers Island Township at 34°42′37″N 76°34′32″W and located on the Harkers Island map. The cove is in The Straits at the northwest end of Harkers Island, 1.4 mi. (2.2 km) northwest of the village of Harkers Island and 4.7 mi. (7.5 km) east of the mainland town of Beaufort.

JONES HILL A sand dune, 33.8 ft. (11 m) high, in Currituck County, Fruitville Township at 36°23′10″N 75°49′57″W and located but not named on the Corolla map. The dune is on Currituck Banks just north of Corolla and 9.7 mi. (15.6 km) southeast of the village of Knotts Island.

JONES POINT A point of land in Currituck County, Fruitville Township at 36°22′47″N 75°50′57″W and located but not named on the Corolla map. The marsh point is on an unnamed marsh island in Currituck Sound, 1.2 mi. (1.9 km) west of Corolla and 9.8 mi. (15.7 km) southeast of the village of Knotts Island.

JUDGEMENT BEACH A beach, 0.5 mi. (0.8 km) long, in Carteret County, Morehead Township at 34°41′02″N 76°53′00″W and located but not named on the Salter Path map. **Historical note** The name is the whimsical result of a legal ruling regarding the land around Salter Path. Various claims to the estate of the owner of the land led to a legal ruling. The "Bankers" argued that while they held no deeds they had occupied the land for centuries. The ruling allowed the people of Salter Path to "live and fish inperpetuum" at this site provided that they remove no trees and do not build on the ocean side.

K

KATHRYNE JANE ISLANDS Islands, in Carteret County, Portsmouth Township at 35°00′37″N 76°07′45″W and located on the Wainwright Island map. This group is made up of four islands in Pamlico Sound 0.6 mi. (1 km) west of Portsmouth Island, 5.2 mi. (8.3 km) southwest of the village of Portsmouth, and 11.2 mi. (17.9 km) southwest of the village of Ocracoke.

Keeterhook See Kitty Hawk

Kendricker Mounts See Kenricks Mounts

Kendricker Ridge See Kenricks Mounts

KENECKID INLET A former water passage in Dare county, Kennekeet Township at approximately 35°30′00″N 75°28′45″W. This inlet may have been located about 3 mi (4.8 km) south of Salvo and about 6 mi. (9.6 km) south of Rodanthe. **Historical note** The inlet is only mentioned sporadically as a temporary inlet in early references and the location is very uncertain. It may be the "fret" (a breach of the island by the sea) that John White refers to as where the ship anchored when searching for the Lost Colonists. White refers to anchoring at the extreme northeast point of Croatoan which must have extended further north than the later cartographic application. White specifically states that the breach or water passage was at "35 degr. & a half." If his calculations were off by about 15 minutes of latitude then he would have been anchored at the later cartographic limits of Croatoan, and the breach he was describing was most likely former Chaneandepeco Inlet (q.v.) which was open in 1590 when White arrived. Either instance described above is possible and the exact reference meant by White may never be known. It is simply not clear as to whether White was describing Chaneandepeco Inlet or the more illusive Keneckid Inlet if in fact it ever existed.

Kennekeet Banks See Kinnakeet Banks

Kennekut See Avon

Kennekut See Little Kinnakeet

Kenrick Ridge See Kenricks Mounts

KENRICKS MOUNTS An historical reference applied to certain prominent sand dunes in Dare County, from Cape Hatteras northward to the Nags Head area. These dunes were on what is now Hatteras Island, Pea Island, Bodie Island, and Currituck Banks. **Other names** Kendricker Mounts, Kendricker Ridge, Kendrickers Mounts, Kenrick Ridge and Mount Kenrick. **Historical note** The use of this name is historical only and was originally descriptive as was most of the the very early names applied by the English. Ken Rick was most likely a reference to any of the large or prominent dunes or ridges first sighted and used as landmarks. The word is a combination of obsolete terms. Ken or kenning referred to the distance that land is discernable from a ship or about 20 mi. (32 km). The use of ken as a place name generic was applied in parts of England and Wales and is from the Gaelic word *Ceann* meaning head or top. A rick is specifically a pile of something such as sand. The reference then was to the large dunes first visible from a ship.

Ketterhock See Kitty Hawk

Kettyhauk See Kitty Hawk

KIB GUTHRIES LUMP A former populated place in Carteret County, Harkers Island Township and located but not shown on the Harkers Island map. The small community of a few families was located on the western end of Shackleford Banks.

Killdeer Hills See Kill Devil Hill

Killdevil Hill See Kill Devil Hill

KILL DEVIL HILL A hill, 88.6 ft. (27 m) high, in Dare County, Atlantic and Nags Head townships at 36°00′52″N 75°40′10″W and located on the Kitty Hawk map. The hill is on south Currituck Banks, just south of the village of Kill Devil Hills, 3.7 mi. (5.9 km) southeast of Kitty Hawk and 4.3 mi. (6.9 km) northwest of Nags Head. **Other names** Big Hill, Big Kill Devil Hill, Killdeer Hills, Killdevil Hill, Kill Devil Hills, Killdevil Hills, Little Hill, Roesepock Hill, Roespock Hill, Rowspock Hill and West Hill **Historical note** It was from this sand dune that the Wright Brothers made the first heavier than air flight in 1903. The dune was successfully stabilized in 1927 with different varieties of grass, and today a national monument is atop this stabilized dune commemorating the first heavier than air flight by the Wright Brothers. There are a number of legends concering the origin of the name. It is said that sailors stated that this portion of the sound was enough "to kill the devil to navigate." William Byrd of Virginia in 1728 reportedly referred to the rum in the area as being so bad that it would kill the devil. Also, a ship carrying a cargo of this "kill devil rum" wrecked on a nearby beach. While guarding the cargo of the wrecked ship, the guards reported that portions of the cargo would mysteriously disappear at night. A local resident named "devil Ike" stated that he would guard the cargo, and while standing guard he discovered that another local person was tying a rope around the cargo and pulling it away by using a horse. Ike succeeded in frightening away the would-be culprit and not wanting to implicate a neighbor Ike stated that the devil was stealing the cargo and that he (Ike) had killed the devil. Another legend states that a local resident made a pact with the devil - the man's soul for a bag of gold - and the exchange was to be made on top of what is now Kill Devil Hill. The day before the exchange was to take place, the local resident dug a hole from the top of the sand dune to the bottom of the sand dune. When the "banker" and the devil met for the exchange, the devil was coaxed into the hole and was quickly covered with sand. The term "kill" is a Dutch generic term meaning stream or channel and the term "devil" is used to refer to a sand spout or whirling dervish. While the combination of these two terms in this area utilizing their meanings is plausible it is not likely because there was no Dutch influence in the area. A more acceptable explanation of the name origin is that the area was once the home of many Killdee or Killdeer, a common shore bird, and the name evolved from Killdeer Hill to Kill Devil Hill.

Killdevil Hills See Kill Devil Hill

Killdevil Hills See Kill Devil Hills (sand dunes)

KILL DEVIL HILLS Sand dunes in Dare County, Atlantic Township at 36°01′45″N 75°40′30″W and located on the Kitty Hawk and Manteo maps. The hills are a series of sand dunes extending from just northeast of Kitty Hawk south for approximately 5 mi. (8 km) of which Kill Devil Hill is the largest. **Other names** Killdevil Hills, Roesepock Hills, Roespock, Rosypock, Rowsypock (these four variants are various spellings of the Indian name for the area), The Kill Devil Hills **Hisotorical note** See Kill Devil Hill for an explanatory note.

KILL DEVIL HILLS A populated place, with a population of about 400 (5000 summer), in Dare County, Atlantic Township at 36°01′45″N 75°40′30″W and located on the Kitty Hawk map. The community is on Currituck Banks 2.3 mi. (3.7 km) southeast of Kitty Hawk and 6.3 mi. (10.1 km) north northwest of Nags Head. **Other names** Croatan Shores **Historical note** A post office was established here in 1938, and the community was incorporated in 1953.

Kill Devil Hills See Kill Devil Hill

Killy Hawk See Kitty Hawk

Kinakeet Banks See Hatteras Island

Kindrickers Mounts See Kenricks Mounts

Kinekeet See Avon

KINGFISH SHOAL A shoal, 1.1 mi. (1.8 km) long, in Carteret County, Cedar Island Township at 35°00′45″N 76°13′15″W and located but not shown on the Wainwright Island map. The shoal is in Pamlico Sound 1.5 mi. (2.4 km) north northeast of Chain Shot Island and 13.2 mi. (21.1 km) southwest of the village of Ocracoke. **Other names** King Fish Shoal **Historical note** Kingfish is a term that refers to any fish having a large size, but the term was in more frequent use in the nineteenth century. The original spelling of the name was the two word form, but as with many place names and words in English the one word form seems preferable today.

King Fish Shoal See Kingfish Shoal

KINGS CHANNEL A channel, 4 mi. (6.4 km) long, in Dare County, Hatteras Township at 35°17′12″N 75°33′17″W (east end), 35°15′42″N 75°39′08″W (west end), and 35°16′27″N 75°37′13″W (center) and located but not shown on the Buxton and Hatteras maps. The channel is in Pamlico Sound and extends northeast from old Rollinson Channel and is 3.1 mi. (5 km) northwest of Buxton.

KINGS ISLAND An island, 0.1 mi. (0.2 km) long and 0.05 mi. (0.08 km) wide, in Dare County, Hatteras Township at 35°16′10″N 75°36′07″W and located on the Buxton map. This marsh island is in Pamlico Sound 0.3 mi. (0.5 km) northwest of Kings Point, 7.3 mi. (11.8 km) north northeast of the village of Hatteras, and 4.5 mi. (7.2 km) west of Buxton.

KINGS POINT A point of land in Dare County, Hatteras Township at 35°15′59″N 75°35′53″W and located on the Buxton map. The point is on the west side of Hatteras Island at the south entrance to Brooks Creek 7.1 mi. (11.5 km) north northeast of the village of Hatteras, 4.2 mi. (6.7 km) west northwest of Cape Hatteras, and 3.2 mi. (5.1 km) west of Buxton.

Kinnakeet See Avon

Kinnakeet See Rodanthe

KINNAKEET BANKS A former barrier island in Dare County, Kennekeet and Hatteras townships at 35°24′23″N 75°29′30″W (north end), 35°13′10″N 75°31′53″W (south end), and 35°18′30″N 75°32′30″W (center) and located but not named on the Little Kinnakeet, Buxton, and Cape Hatteras maps. This historical barrier island is now the section of Hatteras Island which extends north from Buxton Woods to the historical southern boundary of Chicamacomico Banks (q.v.) at Chaneandepeco Inlet in the general vicinity of the locality of Little Kinnakeet. **Other names** Kennekeet Banks

Kinnakeet Banks See Hatteras Island

Kinnekeet See Rodanthe

Kitty Hauk See Kitty Hawk

Kitty-hauk See Kitty Hawk

KITTY HAWK A populated place, 9 ft. (2.7 m) high with a population of about 600 (2500 summer), in Dare County, Atlantic Township at 36°03′57″N 75°42′27″W and located on the Kitty Hawk map. The community is on Currituck Banks 3.9 mi. (6.3 km) north northwest of the Wright Brothers Memorial and 8 mi. (12.8 km) north northwest of Nags Head. **Other names** Chicahauk, Chickahauk, Chickahawk, Chickehauk, Keeterhook, Ketterhock, Kettyhauk, Killy Hawk, Kitty Hauk, Kitty-hauk, Kittyhawk, Kitty-hawk, Kitty Hawk Village, Kittyhuk, Kittyhuke, and Skeeter Hawk **Historical note** A number of legends and theories exist to describe the origin of the name Kitty hawk. It is suggested that the early settlers observed that there were a large number of mosquito hawks (very large mosquitos) in the area and they were referred to as "skeeter hawks" which eventually evolved to Kitty Hawk. Night Hawks are also known regionally as mosquito hawks. It has been reported that the name may have stemmed from the earlier Indian reference to their conception of the white man's year, that is, from "kill a hauk to kill a hauk" or the killing of the first goose of the year to the killing of the first goose of the following year. It is also known that "hauk" is an Indian reference to the local wildfowl and probably represents an immitation of the sound made by wildfowl. The name bears a resemblance to Kittywake which is the name of a gull-like bird of the Atlantic Coast; however, there is little evidence to support any relationship since the Kittywake is not generally known south of Chesapeake Bay. There is a Delaware Indian reference that translates Kitt to big and hakki to land which could be related to the name. The name is most likely an Anglicized corruption of an Algonquian Indian term Chickehauk which referred to an Indian settlement in the area. It is also possible that the name is a corruption of Etacrewac another Indian name for this general vicinity. A post office was established here in 1878.

Kittyhawk See Kitty Hawk

Kitty-hawk See Kitty Hawk

KITTY HAWK BAY A bay, 2.7 mi. (4.3 km) long and 1.7 mi. (2.7 km) wide, in Dare County, Atlantic Township at 36°02′15″N 75°43′00″W and located on the Kitty Hawk map. This shallow bay is at the east end of Albemarle Sound just north of Colington island 1.6 mi. (2.6 km) southwest of Kitty Hawk, 3.1 mi. (5 km) northwest of the Wright Brothers Memorial, and 7.9 mi. (12.6 km) northwest of Nags Head. **Other names** Bay of Kitty Hawk and Kittyhawk Bay **Historical note** It has been suggested that Kitty Hawk Bay is the remnant of the former inlet Trinitie Harbor (q.v.) or some other inlet. This in not likely because Trinitie Harbor was further north, and if there was an inlet in the area of Kitty Hawk it had to exist prior to 1600. There is little historical evidence, culturally or physically, to indicate an inlet at Kitty Hawk Bay. See Kitty Hawk for a further note of explanation.

Kittyhawk Bay See Kitty Hawk Bay

KITTY HAWK BEACH A populated place in Dare County, Atlantic Township at 36°05′45″N 75°42′29″W and located on the Kitty Hawk map. The community is on Currituck Banks 5.9 mi. (9.6 km) north northwest of the Wright Brothers Memorial and 2.1 mi. (3.4 km) north of Kitty Hawk. **Historical note** See Kitty Hawk for an explanatory note.

KITTY HAWK LANDING A landing in Dare County, Atlantic Township at 36°03′43″N 75°44′10″W and located on the Kitty Hawk map. This is a protected landing for small watercraft on the sound side of Currituck Banks 2 mi. (3.2 km) north of the entrance to Kitty Hawk Bay, 2.2 mi. (3.5 km) west of Kitty Hawk and 9 mi. (15.7 km) northwest of Nags Head.

Kitty Hawk Village See Kitty Hawk

KITTY HAWK WOODS Woods, about 3.5 mi. (5.6 km) in extent, in Dare County, Atlantic Township at 36°05′15″N 75°43′45″W and located but not named on the Kitty Hawk map. The wooded area is on Currituck Banks and extends from Kitty Hawk Bay north to Southern Shores. It is located 10 mi. (16.9 km) northwest of Nags Head.

Kittyhuk See Kitty Hawk

Kittyhuke See Kitty Hawk

KNOLL CEDARS Former woods, 10 ft. (3 m) high, in Hyde County, Ocracoke Township at 35°08′17″N 75°53′37″W and located on the Howard Reef map. This wooded area was on Ocracoke Island 0.4 mi. (0.6 km) east of Parkers Hill, 7.6 mi. (12.2 km) southwest of Hatteras Inlet, and 7 mi.

(11.2 km) northeast of the village of Ocracoke. **Other names** Knoll Woods

KNOLL CREEK A cove, 0.1 mi. (0.2 km) wide, in Hyde County, Ocracoke Township at 35°09′14″N 75°52′29″W and located on the Green Island map. The cove is in Pamlico Sound just southwest of Knoll Island and 7.6 mi. (12.2 km) northeast of the village of Ocracoke.

KNOLL HOUSE CREEK A cove. 0.1 mi. (0.2 km) wide, in Hyde County, Ocracoke Township at 35°08′43″N 75°53′20″W and located on the Howard Reef map. The cove is in Pamlico Sound 7.2 mi. (11.5 km) southwest of Hatteras Inlet and 6.5 mi. (10.4 km) northeast of the village of Ocracoke.

KNOLL ISLAND A peninsula, 0.3 mi. (0.5 km) long, in Hyde County, Ocracoke Township at 35°09′11″N 75°52′04″W and located on the Green Island map. The marsh peninsula is just southwest of the Great Swash and 7.8 mi. (12.5 km) northeast of the village of Ocracoke.

Knoll Woods See Knoll Cedars

Knot Island See Knotts Island (former island)

Knot Isle See Knotts Island (former island)

Knots Island See Knotts Island (former island)

Knott Island See Knotts Island (populated place)

Knott Island See Knotts Island (former island)

Knott Island Bay See Knotts Island Bay

Knott Island Channel See Knotts Island Channel

Knott Landing See Knotts Landing

KNOTTS ISLAND A populated place, 15 ft. (4.6 m) high with a population of about 400, in Currituck County, Fruitville Township at 36°30′43″N 75°55′32″W and located on the Knotts Island map. The community is on Knotts Island 2.7 mi. (4.3 km) west of Currituck Banks, 9.1 mi. (14.6 km) north northeast of the mainland village of Waterlily, and 9.8 mi. (15.7 km) east southeast of the mainland village of Creeds. **Other names** Knott Island **Historical note** The village of Knotts Island, settled in 1642, is generally considered to be the oldest continuous settlement in North Carolina.

KNOTTS ISLAND A former island, 5.8 mi. (9.4 km) long, 1.7 mi. (2.7 km) wide and 20 ft. (6.1 m) high, in Currituck County, Fruitville Township at 36°34′05″N 75°55′30″W (north end), 36°29′00″N 75°55′30″W (south end), and 36°31′28″N 75°55′25″W (center) and located on the Knotts Island and Barco maps. The feature was formerly an island but in now separated from the mainland by The Great Marsh and is situated between Currituck Sound and Back Bay 2.4 mi. (5.4 km) west of Currituck Banks and 8.9 mi. (14.1 km) north of the mainland village of Waterlily. **Other names** Knot Island, Knot Isle, Knots Island, Knott Island, Mackeys Island, Mackys Island, Netsiland, Nots Island, Nott Island, and Notts Island **Historical note** The feature was named for James Knott who held land on the island as early as 1642. The variant listing Netsiland was a misrepresentation on the earlier maps and records. It should have been two words and Nets is a misspelling of Nots a form of Knotts. Iland is a sixteenth century English spelling of the word island.

KNOTTS ISLAND BAY A lagoon, 1.7 mi. (2.7 km) wide, in Currituck

County, Fruitville Township at 36°30'00"N 75°53'43"W and located on the Knotts Island and Barco maps. The lagoon separates Currituck Banks and Knotts Island and is located 2 mi. (3.2 km) east southeast of the village of Knotts Island. **Other names** Knott Island Bay

KNOTTS ISLAND CHANNEL A water passage, 2 mi. (3.2 km) long, in Currituck County, Fruitville Township at 36°32'30"N 75°54'15"W (north end), 36°30'42"N 75°54'27"W (south end), and 36°31'30"N 75°54'27"W (center) and located on the Knotts Island map. The water passage connects Knotts Island Bay with Back Sound and separates Knotts Island from Currituck Banks. It is 1.6 mi. (2.6 km) northeast of the village of Knotts Island. **Other names** Knott Island Channel

KNOTTS LANDING A landing in Currituck County, Fruitville Township at 36°29'02"N 75°55'09"W and located on the Barco map. This landing is at the ferry dock at the south end of Knotts Island and is located 2.2 mi. (3.5 km) south of the village of Knotts Island. **Other names** Knott Landing and South End

Kwak Point See Quokes Point

Kwawk Hammock See Quork Hammock

L

LABRADOR CURRENT An ocean current formed by cold currents from Baffin Bay and the area around West Greenland. It flows south to the Grand Banks off the coast of Newfoundland where it encounters the Gulf Stream, but a portion of the current continues south as the Labrador Current Extension where it again mixes with the Gulf Stream in the vicinity of Cape Hatteras.

Lagerhead Hills See Loggerhead Hills

Laggerhead Hills See Loggerhead Hills

LAKE BURNSIDE A lake, 0.3 mi. (0.5 km) long and 0.05 mi. (0.08 km) wide, in Dare County, Nags Head Township at 35°54'43"N 75°41'42"W and located but not named on the Manteo map. This elongated lake is located on the northern part of Roanoke Island, 0.4 mi. (0.6 km) north of the site of General Burnside's Headquarters and 1.3 mi. (2.1 km) west of Manteo. **Historical note** The lake was named for General Burnside who commanded the Union troops that occupied Roanoke Island and the Outer Banks during The War Between the States.

LANDS END An historical area. This name was sometimes used for the North side of Oregon Inlet. It was mostly used for a short period of time from the 1940s when the permanent road was first built and before the Bonner Bridge was built in 1963. The name has fallen into disuse since the bridge was built.

LARGE SHOAL A shoal in Dare County, Hatteras Township at 35°17'45"N 75°33'00"W and located but not shown on the Buxton map. The shoal is in Pamlico Sound 0.8 mi. (1.3 km) north northwest of Buxton. **Historical note** The shoal was considerably more exposed historically.

LEGGED LUMP A shoal, 1 mi. (1.6 km) long, in Hyde County, Ocracoke Township at 35°11'58"N 75°50'30"W and located but not shown on the Green Island map. The shoal is in Pamlico Sound 4 mi. (6.4 km) northwest of Hatteras Inlet and 8.8 mi. (13.6 km) northeast of the village of Ocracoke. **Other names** Leggedy Lump and Two Legged Lump **Historical note** See Goulds Lump for an explanatory note.

Leggedy Lump See Legged Lump

Lewarks Hill See Luark Hill

LEWIS CREEK A water passage, 0.5 mi. (0.8 km) long, in Carteret County, Smyrna Township at 34°42′52″N 76°27′53″W and located on the Horsepen Point map. The water passage trends north-south and separates Horse Island from Core Banks. It is located 5.4 mi. (8.6 km) east of the village of Harkers Island.

LEWIS ISLAND An island, 0.4 mi. (0.6 km) long and 0.4 mi. (0.6 km) wide, in Carteret County, Smyrna Township at 34°43′14″N 76°27′42″W and located on the Horsepen Point map. This marsh island is in Core Sound, separated from Core Banks by Lewis Creek and is located 5.5 mi. (8.8 km) east of the village of Harkers Island.

Liberty Plains See Currituck Banks

Light House Bay See Lighthouse Bay (Dare County, Nags Head Township)

LIGHTHOUSE BAY A water passage, 0.8 mi. (1.3 km) long and 0.5 mi. (0.8 km) wide, in Carteret County, Harkers Island Township at 34°38′44″N 76°31′01″W and located on the Harkers Island map. The water passage is at the junction of Core Sound. It is a northeast extension of Barden Inlet that connects Barden Inlet to Core Sound 4 mi. (6.4 km) south southeast of the village of Harkers Island.

LIGHTHOUSE BAY A cove, 0.4 mi. (0.6 km) long and 0.1 mi. (0.2 km) wide, in Dare County, Nags Head Township at 35°48′57″N 75°34′10″W and located on the Oregon Inlet map. The cove is in Roanoke Sound 0.3 mi. (0.5 km) west southwest of Bodie Island Lighthouse and 4.5 mi. (7.2 km) east southeast of Wanchese. **Other names** Light House Bay

LIGHTHOUSE CHANNEL A channel, 1.3 mi. (2.1 km) long, in Carteret County, Harkers Island Township at 34°39′57″N 76°31′30″W and located on the Harkers Island map. The channel trends north-south at the junction of Core Sound and Back Sound and extends north from Lighthouse Bay between Whitehurst Island and Morgan Island to Shell Point at the southeast point of Harkers Island. It is 3 mi. (4.8 km) southeast of the village of Harkers Island and 2.2 mi. (3.5 km) north of Barden Inlet.

LIGHTHOUSE POND A lake, 0.2 mi. (0.3 km) across, in Currituck County, Fruitville Township at 36°22′40″N 75°50′15″W and located but not named on the Corolla map. The pond is just west of the Currituck Beach Lighthouse, 0.5 mi. (0.8 km) west of Corolla and 17.4 mi. (27.8 km) north northwest of Duck.

Little Avon See Little Kinnakeet

LITTLE BELLOWS BAY A bay, 0.7 mi. (1.2 km) long and 0.4 mi. (0.6 km) wide, in Currituck County, Fruitville Township at 36°29′45″N 75°57′37″W and located on the Barco map. This bay is the north arm of Bellows Bay between Mackay Island and Great Marsh 3.3 mi. (5.3 km) west southwest of the village of Knotts Island and 11.6 mi. (18.6 km) northwest of Corolla.

LITTLE CHANNEL A water passage, 0.5 mi. (0.8 km) long, in Carteret County, Portsmouth Township at 35°04′24″N 76°04′32″W and located on the Portsmouth map. The water passage is in Pamlico Sound just southwest of Casey Island, 0.6 mi. (1 km) west northwest of the village of Portsmouth and 6.6 mi. (10.6 km) southwest of the village of Ocracoke.

Little Colenton See Little Colington

LITTLE COLINGTON An Island in Dare County, Atlantic Township at 36°00′20″N 75°41′45″W and located on the Kitty Hawk map. The feature refers to the east portion of Colington Island. **Other names** Little Colenton and Little Colington Island **Historical note** See Big Colington for an explanatory note.

Little Colington Island See Little Colington

LITTLE DEEP MARSH ISLAND An island, 0.2 mi. (0.3 km) long, in Carteret County, Harkers Island Township at 34°40′45″N 76°30′02″W and located on the Harkers Island and Horsepen Point maps. The island is in Core Sound just north of Gunning Hammock Island and 3.5 mi. (5.6 km) east of the village of Harkers Island.

LITTLE GOAT ISLAND BAY A cove, 0.6 mi. (1 km) wide and 0.3 mi. (0.5 km) long, in Currituck County, Poplar Branch Township at 36°15′25″N 75°48′33″W and located on the Mossey Islands map. This cove is enclosed by marsh islands just north of Goat Island Bay 8.2 mi. (13.1 km) northwest of Duck and 8.5 mi. (13.6 km) south of Corolla.

Little Green Island See Green Island (Dare County, Kennekeet Township)

Little Grove See Frisco Woods

LITTLE HILL A sand dune, 13 ft. (4 m) high, in Dare County, Kennekeet Township at 35°25′00″N 75°29′14″W and located but not named on the Little Kinnakeet map. The dune is on north Hatteras Island, 0.8 mi. (1.3 km) north of Little Kinnakeet and 4.9 mi. (7.3 km) north of Avon.

Little Hill See Kill Devil Hill

LITTLE HOG ISLAND An island, 0.1 mi. (0.2 km) across, in Currituck County, Poplar Branch Township at 36°17′10″N 75°49′15″W and located on the Mossey Islands map. This is a small marshy shoal area in Currituck Sound just at the north end of Jarvis Channel 6.4 mi. (10.2 km) south of Corolla and 10 mi. (16 km) northwest of Duck.

Little Hog Island See Hog Island (Dare County, Atlantic Township)

LITTLE KINNAKEET A former populated place, 5 ft (1.5 m) high, in Dare County, Kennekeet Township at 35°24′23″N 75°29′30″W and located on the Little Kinnakeet map. The community was on Hatteras Island and located 4 mi. (6.6 km) north of Avon. **Other names** Kennekut and Little Avon **Historical note** See Little Kinnakeet, Dare County, Nags Head Township for an explanatory note.

LITTLE KINNAKEET An area in Dare County, Nags Head Township and located but not named on the Manteo map. The locality is located on Roanoke Island about 0.5 mi. (0.8 km) northwest of Manteo. **Historical note** This area was settled by some of the former residents of Little Kinnakeet (q.v.) on Hatteras Island when that village was abandoned. The name moved with them, but is generally known only as a local reference.

LITTLE PENGUIN ISLAND An island, 0.1 mi. (0.2 km) long and 0.05 mi. (0.08 km) wide, in Dare County, Nags Head Township at 35°54′45″N 75°36′38″W and located on the Roanoke Island NE map. This marsh island is in Roanoke Sound 3.1 mi. (5 km) south of Nags Head, 0.8 mi. (1.3 km) north of

The Causeway, and 0.8 mi. (1.3 km) northwest of Whalebone Junction. **Historical note** See Penguin Islands for an explanatory note.

Little Shell Rock See North Rock

Little Swash See Little Swash Opening

LITTLE SWASH OPENING A cove, 0.2 mi. (0.3 km) wide, in Hyde County, Ocracoke Township at 35°08′24″N 75°54′15″W and located on the Howard Reef map. The cove is in Pamlico Sound 8.1 mi. (13 km) south of Hatteras Inlet and 5.6 mi. (9 km) northeast of the village of Ocracoke. **Other names** Little Swash **Historical note** See Daniel Swash for an explanatory note.

LITTLE TIM ISLAND An island, 0.05 mi. (0.08 km) long and 0.05 mi. (0.08 km) wide, in Dare County, Nags Head Township at 35°47′37″N 75°33′50″W and located on the Oregon Inlet map. The marsh island is in Roanoke Sound 0.3 mi. (0.5 km) north of Walter Slough, 0.2 mi. (0.3 km) southwest of Big Tim Island and 5.9 mi. (9.6 km) southeast of Wanchese.

LITTLE YANKEE POND A cove, 0.1 mi. (0.6 km) long, in Currituck County, Poplar Branch Township at 36°14′47″N 75°47′35″W and located on the Jarvisburg map. The cove is just south of Big Yankee Pond, 6.2 mi. (9.9 km) northwest of Duck and 9.2 mi. (14.8 km) south of Corolla. **Other names** Yankee Pond **Historical note** The origin of the name is unknown.

LIVE OAK POINT A point of land in Currituck County, Fruitville Township at 36°29′34″N 75°59′20″W and located on the Barco map. It is the southwest point of Mackay Island 1 mi. (1.6 km) northwest of Halfway Point and 11.6 mi. (18.6 km) northwest of Corolla.

LIZA LUMPS Islands, 0.3 mi. (0.5 km) long and 0.1 mi. (0.2 km) wide, in Dare County, Kennekeet Township at 35°40′20″N 75°29′50″W and located on the Pea Island map. There are four islands located in Pamlico Sound 1.1 mi. (1.8 km) southeast of Jack Shoal and 5.6 mi. (9 km) northwest of Rodanthe. **Historical note** See Goulds Lump for an explanatory note.

LOG CHANNEL ROCK A former rock in Carteret County, Portsmouth Township at approximately 35°04′15″N 76°05′50″W and located but not shown on the Portsmouth map. The rock was in Pamlico Sound about 1.75 mi. (2.8 km) west of the village of Portsmouth and about 6 mi. (9.6 km) west of the village of Ocracoke.

Logerhead Shoal See Cat Island (35°38′17″N 75°28′57″W)

LOGGERHEAD HILLS Sand dunes, 0.3 mi. (0.5 km) long, in Dare County, Kennekeet Township at 35°38′37″N 75°28′56″W and located on the Pea Island map. These hills are on Hatteras Island 3.5 mi. (5.3 km) north northwest of Rodanthe. **Other names** Lagerhead Hills and Laggerhead Hills **Historical note** The name probably refers to the Loggerhead turtles at one time abundant in the area or possibly to the Loggerhead Shrike, a bird sometimes found in the area.

LOGGERHEAD INLET A former water passage in Dare County, Kennekeet Township at 35°38′25″N 75°28′25″W and located but not shown on the Pea island map. This inlet connected Pamlico Sound to the Atlantic Ocean through present Hatteras Island just north of Rodanthe. **Historical note** The inlet was apparently opened from 1650 to 1680 and reopened from 1843 to 1870. Loggerhead Inlet has periodically opened for very brief intervals since its last closing. See Loggerhead Hills for an additional explanatory note.

Loggerhead Shoal See Cat Island (35°38′17″N 75°28′57″W)

LOG SHOAL A shoal, 0.6 mi. (1 km) long, in Dare County, Hatteras Township at 35°06′57″N 75°42′00″W and located on the Hatteras map. The shoal is in Pamlico Sound just east of Clam Shoal and 3.7 mi. (5.9 km) north of the village of Hatteras.

LOG TOWN A former populated place in Dare County, Nags Head Township and located but not shown on the Manteo map. The feature was located in the general vicinity of the intersection of U.S. Route 64 and the Manteo Airport Road about 2 mi. (3.2 km) northwest of Manteo. **Historical note** The name was a general reference and is remembered only by local residents of the area.

LONE OAK CHANNEL A water passage, 1.3 mi. (2.1 km) long, in Currituck County, Poplar Branch Township at 36°17′35″N 75°50′10″W and located on the Corolla map. The water passage is in Currituck Sound just north of Big Narrows and separates Mossey Islands from North Burris Island. It is 6 mi. (9.7 km) south of Corolla and 11.2 mi. (17.9 km) north northwest of Duck.

Long Deep Marsh Island See Big Deep Marsh Island

LONG ISLAND An island, 0.5 mi. (0.8 km) long, in Carteret County, White Oak Township at 34°40′54″N 76°58′52″W and located on the Salter Path map. The island is in Bogue Sound 6.2 mi. (9.9 km) west of Salter Path. **Other names** Snake Island

LONG ISLAND An island, 0.3 mi. (0.5 km) long and less than 0.1 mi. (0.2 km) wide, in Currituck County, Poplar Branch Township at 36°16′05″N 75°49′45″W and located on the Mossey Islands map. This is an elongated island in Jarvis Channel at Currituck Sound between south Burris Island and Indian Gap Island 7.7 mi. (12.3 km) South of Corolla and 9.5 mi. (15.2 km) northwest of Duck.

LONG MARSH An island, 0.5 mi. (0.8 km) long, in Carteret County, White Oak Township at 34°40′37″N 77°00′20″W and located on the Swansboro map. The Island is in Bogue Sound 7 mi. (11.2 km) east southeast of the mainland town of Swansboro.

LONG POINT A point of land in Carteret County, Atlantic Township at 34°53′56″N 76°15′54″W and located on the Atlantic map. It is a marsh point on Core Banks 0.5 mi. (0.8 km) west of Ira Morris Camp and 4.5 mi. (7.2 km) east of the mainland village of Atlantic.

LONG POINT A point of land in Dare County, Atlantic Township at 36°02′27″N 75°44′20″W and located on the Kitty Hawk map. It is at the north entrance to Kitty Hawk Bay on the southwest point of Stove island 4.2 mi. (6.7 km) northwest of the Wright Brothers Memorial and 2.6 mi. (4.2 km) southwest of Kitty Hawk. **Other names** Long Point of Marsh

LONG POINT A point of land in Currituck County, Poplar Branch Township at 36°18′20″N 75°51′16″W and located but not named on the Mossey Islands map. The Point is the northwest point of a marsh island at the northwest entrance to Fosters Channel 12 mi. (19.2 km) northwest of Duck.

LONG POINT A point of land in Dare County, Kennekeet Township at 35°18′54″N 75°30′57″W and located on the Buxton map. It is a marsh point on an unnamed island in Pamlico Sound just west of Hatteras Island 4.7 mi. (7.5 km) north of Cape Hatteras and 2.4 mi. (3.8 km) south of Avon.

LONG POINT CREEK A cove, 0.1 mi. (0.2 km) wide, in Dare County, Kennekeet Township at 35°18′57″N 75°30′53″W and located on the Buxton map. The cove is in Pamlico Sound 4.6 mi. (7.4 km) north of Cape Hatteras and 2.3 mi. (3.7 km) south of Avon.

LONG POINT MARSH A marsh in Dare County, Atlantic Township at 36°02′37″N 75°44′13″W and located but not named on the Kitty Hawk map. This area of swamp is located on Stove Island at Long Point at the north entrance to Kitty Hawk Bay, 2.7 mi. (4.3 km) southwest of Kitty Hawk and 4.8 mi. (7.7 km) south southwest of Southern Shores.

Long Point of Marsh See Long Point (Dare County, Atlantic Township)

LONG POINT POND A lake, 0.2 mi. (0.3 km) across, in Currituck County, Poplar Branch Township at 36°18′11″N 75°51′10″W and located on the Mossey Islands map. The lake is located on the northwest part of an unnamed marsh area just south of Wells Bay, 1.2 mi. (1.9 km) north of Big Narrows, 2.4 mi. (3.8 km) west of Three Dunes, 3.2 mi. (8.3 km) south southwest of Corolla and 12.2 mi. (19.5 km) north of Duck. **Other names** Long Pond

LONG POND A lake, 0.2 mi. (0.3 km) long, in Currituck County, Poplar Branch Township at 36°19′25″N 75°50′57″W and located on the Mossey Islands map. The lake is in an unnamed marsh area just east of Brant Island, 4 mi. (6.4 km) south southwest of Corolla and 12.9 mi. (20.1 km) north northwest of Duck.

Long Pond See Long Point Pond

Long Slue See Hatteras Inlet Channel

LOOKOUT BIGHT A bight, 2.3 mi. (3.7 km) wide, in Carteret County, Harkers Island Township at 34°37′29″N 76°32′30″W and located on the Harkers Island and Cape Lookout maps. This embayment is in the Atlantic Ocean and is formed by Cape Lookout at the south end of Core Banks and the east end of Shackleford Banks at Onslow Bay. **Other names** Cape Harbour, Cape Lookout Bay, Cape Lookout Bight, Cape Lookout Harbor, and Point Lookout Bay **Historical note** The bight was a popular place in the nineteenth century for ships with a small enough drought to safely "ride out" a storm, but the bight never developed as a commercial harbor. Use of the variant name Cape Harbour is further evidence of the feature's use as a harbor and is an authentic name reflecting the original English spelling. Some recently applied names reflect this spelling in a fanciful commercial manner.

Lookout Bight Channel See Barden Inlet

LOOKOUT BREAKERS Breakers in Carteret County, Harkers Island Township at 34°29′30″N 76°29′30″W and located on Chart number 11545. This is an area of "shoal water" in the Atlantic Ocean creating breakers at Cape Lookout Shoals 4 mi. (6.4 km) southeast of Cape Lookout and covered with only about 2 ft. (0.6 m) of water.

Lookout Hill See Wreck Hill

LOOKOUT WOODS Former woods in Carteret County, Harkers Island Township at 34°38′22″N 76°32′22″W and located but not shown on the Harkers Island map. The feature was a former wooded area on Shackleford Banks in the vicinity of the former community of Diamond City (q.v.)

Lookout Woods See Diamond City

Look Shack Hill See Loop Shack Hill

LOOP SHACK HILL A sand dune, 13 ft. (3.7 m) high, in Hyde County, Ocracoke Township at 35°06′25″N 75°58′07″W and located on the Ocracoke map. The dune is on Ocracoke Island 1 mi. (1.6 km) southeast of the village of Ocracoke. **Other names** Look Shack Hill **Historical note** The feature is named for the Loop Road from a former U.S. government facility to a shack near the hill.

LOVETT ISLAND An island, 0.2 mi. (0.3 km) long, in Carteret County, White Oak Township at 34°41′28″N 76°59′37″W and located on the Salter Path map. The island is in Bogue Sound 6.9 mi. (11 km) west of Salter Path. **Historical note** The feature was named for a family who lived in the area. The spelling may be a variation of the original name.

Lower End See Wanchese

LOWER MIDDLE A shoal, 2.2 mi. (3.5 km) long, in Hyde County, Ocracoke Township at 35°14′15″N 76°13′50″W and located but not named on Chart number 11555. The shoal is on southwest Middle Ground, a large shoal in Pamlico Sound, 14.1 mi. (22.4 km) northwest of Ocracoke Inlet and 14.3 mi. (22.7 km) northwest of the village of Ocracoke.

Lower Middle See Middle Ground (35°15′20″N 76°18′00″W)

Lower Roads See Beacon Island Roads

LUARK HILL A sand dune, 68.9 ft. (21 m) high, in Currituck County, Fruitville Township at 36°25′50″N 75°50′30″W and located on the Corolla map. This is a pronounced sand dune on Currituck Banks 3.6 mi. (6.3 km) north northwest of Corolla and 1.9 mi. (3.2 km) south southeast of the remnants of New Currituck Inlet (labeled Old Currituck Inlet on the Corolla map). **Other names** Dunton Hill and Lewarks Hill

Lucke Island See Lucks Island

LUCKS ISLAND A former island in Currituck and Dare counties. It was in the general vicinity of Currituck Banks, and may have included a portion of Bodie Island. It extended north from the vicinity of Roanoke Inlet to Musketo Inlet or possibly even to Currituck Inlet. **Other names** Croatamung, Currituck Banks, and Lucke Island **Historical note** Lucks Island was the north limit of Carolina as stated in the Charter granting Carolina to the eight lords proprietors.

Lucks Island See Cow Island

Lucks Island See Croatamung

Lucks Island See Currituck Banks

M

MACKAY ISLAND An island, 1.7 mi. (2.7 km) long, in Currituck County, Fruitville Township at 36°30′17″N 75°58′17″W and located on the Knotts Island and Barco maps. The island is separated from Knotts Island by a portion of The Great Marsh 2.5 mi. (4 km) west of Knotts Island and 2.6 mi. (4.2 km) west of the village of Knotts Island. **Other names** Mackays Island, Mackees Island, Mackey Island, Mackeys Island, Mackies Island, Mackys Island and Notts Island

Mackays Island See Mackay Island

Mackees Island See Mackay Island

Mackey Island See Mackay Island

Mackeys Island See Knotts Island (former island)

Mackeys Island See Mackay Island

Mackies Island See Mackay Island

Mackys Island See Knotts Island (former island)

Mackys Island See Mackay Island

MAIDEN PAPS Islands in Dare County, Kennekeet Township and located but not shown on either the Rodanthe or Pea Island maps. The islands were located in Pamlico Sound just northwest of Chickinacommock Inlet about 10 mi. (16 km) southeast of Roanoke Island. **Other names** The Barn **Historical note** The term "pap" was used frequently by seamen in the late sixteenth and seventeenth centuries for hills or islands protruding upwards out of the water or marsh. Pap is an archaic English word referring to the teats or nipples of a woman's breast.

MAIN CHANNEL A channel in Carteret County, White Oak Township and Onslow County, Swansboro Township at 34°40′00″N 77°05′47″W and located on the Swansboro map. The channel is in Bogue Sound and trends north-south connecting Bogue Inlet and the Intracoastal Waterway. It is 1.9 mi. (3 km) southeast of the mainland town of Swansboro.

MALLARD POND A cove, 0.2 mi. (0.3 km) across, in Currituck County, Poplar Branch Township at 36°15′11″N 75°48′14″W and located on the Mossey Islands map. The cove is located at an unnamed marsh in the far northeast corner of Goat Island Bay, 7.9 mi. (12.6 km) northwest of Duck and 8.5 mi. (13.6 km) south of Corolla. **Historical note** The name indicates the large amount of ducks that stay in this area of Currituck Banks along the Atlantic Flyway.

MANN POINT A point of land in Dare County, Nags Head Township at 35°58′21″N 75°40′09″W and located on the Manteo map. This marsh point is 0.6 mi. (1 km) north of Nags Head Woods at the junction of Albemarle Sound and Roanoke Sound, 2.6 mi. (4.2 km) west northwest of Nags Head. **Other names** Manns Point

MANNS ISLANDS Islands, 1.5 mi. (2.4 km) wide, in Currituck County, Fruitville Township at 36°31′37″N 75°53′37″W and located but not named on the Knotts Island map. This is an area of marsh islands in the north part of Knotts Island Bay between Currituck Banks and Knotts Island, 1.6 mi. (2.6 km) south of the North Carolina-Virginia boundary, 2 mi. (3.2 km) northeast of the village of Knotts Island.

Manns Point See Mann Point

MANTEO A populated place, 12 ft. (3.7 m) high with a population of about 600 in Dare County, Nags Head Township at 35°54′34″N 75°40′17″W and located on the Manteo map. It is located on the north end of Roanoke Island just east of Shallowbag Bay 4.3 mi. (6.9 km) southwest of Nags Head. **Other names** Roanoak, Shallowbag Bay, Shallow Bag Bay, and Upper End **Historical note** Originally the name of the community was Shallowbag Bay, but as with many other Outer Banks communities, as well as communities throughout the country, when the Post office was established in 1873 and named Manteo, the community gradually lost the original name of Shallowbag Bay and became known as Manteo. The name is that of one of the Indians from Roanoke Island taken to England in 1584 by the explorers Amadas and Barlowe. Manteo was granted the title "Lord of Roanoke" by Queen Elizabeth I for his assistance to the colonists (not the Lost Colony) which was the first English title to be granted in the "New World." For a time the community was referred to as the Upper End and Wanchese as the Lower End because of their relative locations on Roanoke Island, but this reference was not popular and over the years the reference gradually fell into disuse.

Manteo Bay See Shallowbag Bay

Manteo Harbor See Shallowbag Bay

Manteo-Oregon Inlet Channel See Roanoke Sound Channel

Markers Island See Harkers Island

MARSH LANDING A former landing in Dare County, Nags Head Township at 35°58′10″N 75°39′23″W and located but not shown on the Manteo map. The landing was located just south of Nags Head Woods 2 mi. (3.2 km) northwest of Nags Head.

Martens Point See Martin Point

MARTIN POINT A point of land in Dare County, Atlantic Township at 36°07′34″N 75°45′00″W and located on the Jarvisburg, Martin Point, Point Harbor, and Kitty Hawk maps. The point is at the tip of a peninsula often referred to as Martin Point and located just west of Southern Shores and 5 mi. (8 km) west northwest of Kitty Hawk. **Other names** Martens Point, Martins Pint, and Martins Point **Historical note** The variant reference Martins Pint is likely a misspelling in transcribing the name; however, pint is also a reference used by the British to refer to the Laughing Gull which frequents the Outer Banks during the summer.

Martins Pint See Martin Point

Martins Point See Martin Point

Martins Point Creek See Jeanguite Creek

MARY ANNS POND A cove, 0.1 mi. (0.2 km) wide, in Hyde County, Ocracoke Township at 35°07′10″N 75°59′04″W and located on the Ocracoke map. The cove is in Pamlico Sound just west of Northern Pond and 0.3 mi. (0.5 km) north northwest of the village of Ocracoke.

MARY ISLAND An island in Currituck County, Fruitville Township at 36°23′24″N 75°51′45″W and located on the Corolla map. It is an elongated marsh island in Currituck Sound 1.7 mi. (2.7 km) west northwest of Corolla and 3.3 mi. (5.3 km) east of the mainland village of Waterlily.

MARY TILLETT PLACE An area in Dare County, Atlantic Township at 36°04′45″N 75°44′27″W and located but not named on the Kitty Hawk map. The area is situated on the east shore of Currituck Sound, 2 mi. (3.2 km) southwest of Southern Shores and 2.5 mi. (4 km) northwest of Kitty Hawk. **Historical note** The feature is of historical significance primarily and lingers today basically as a reference point. The origin of the name seems obvious, but is somewhat obscure today.

McKnights Creek See Dykes Creek

MEEKINS MILL A former populated place in Dare County, Nags Head Township at approximately 35°50′30″N 75°38′25″W and located but not shown on the Wanchese map. The mill was in Wanchese about 5.3 mi. (8.5 km) south of Manteo. **Historical note** Historically, the settlement at the southern part of Roanoke Island was scattered and there were several focal points of activity.

MERKLE HAMMOCK A tidal flat, 1.5 mi. (2.4 km) long and 0.3 mi. (0.5 km) wide, in Carteret County, Portsmouth Township at 34°59′44″N 76°08′30″W and located on the Wainwright Island map. The tidal flat is a frequently inundated mud flat between Portsmouth Island and unnamed marsh islands, 6.3 mi. (10.1 km) southwest of the village of Portsmouth and 12.3 mi. (17.7 km) southwest of the village of Ocracoke. **Other names** Great Hammock Swash **Historical note** "Merkle" is the local pronunciation of myrtle which refers to a small shrub-like tree native to the Outer Banks. See Black Hammock for an explanation of the term hammock.

METER POINT A point of land in Dare County, Atlantic Township at 36°01′28″N 75°41′30″W and located on the Kitty Hawk map. The point is located on north Colington Island extending into Colington Creek just north of Colington 3 mi. (4.8 km) south of Kitty Hawk and 6 mi. (9.6 km) northwest of Nags Head.

Michards Island See Bodie Island

MIDDLE GROUND A shoal, 6.6 mi. (10.6 km) long, in Hyde County, Ocracoke Township at 35°15′20″N 76°18′00″W and located on Chart number 11548. The shoal is in Pamlico Sound 17.6 mi. (28 km) northwest of Ocracoke Inlet and 17.8 mi. (28.3 km) northwest of the village of Ocracoke. It is made up of three sections referred to as Upper Middle, Inner Middle, and Lower Middle. **Other names** Inner Middle, Lower Middle, and Upper Middle

MIDDLE GROUND A shoal, 2.5 mi. (4 km) across, in Hyde County, Ocracoke Township at 35°06′10″N 76°00′45″W and located but not shown on the Ocracoke and Portsmouth maps. The extensive shoal area is in Pamlico Sound between Blair Channel and Teaches Hole Channel, 1.4 mi. (2.2 km) west of the village of Ocracoke. **Historical note** The name is descriptive and is often applied to shoal areas between channels.

MIDDLE GROUND A former shoal in Carteret County, Beaufort and Morehead townships at 34°41′53″N 76°40′00″W and located but not shown on the Beaufort map. The shoal was in Beaufort Inlet 1.3 mi. (2.1 km) south of the mainland town of Beaufort.

MIDDLE MARSHES Islands, 1.7 mi. (2.7 km) long and 0.7 mi. (1.1 km) wide, in Carteret County, Harkers Island Township at 34°41′37″N 76°36′30″W and located on the Harkers Island map. The islands represent a tidal marsh in northwest Back Sound 1.4 mi. (2.2 km) north of Shackleford Banks, 1.9 mi. (3 km) south southwest of the mouth of North River, and 2.6 mi. (4.2 km) west southwest of the village of Harkers Island.

MIDDLE SLEW A former channel in Carteret County, Portsmouth Township and Hyde County, Ocracoke Township and located but not named on the Portsmouth map. The channel was the center approach to Ocracoke Inlet about 3.5 mi. (5.3 km) southwest of the village of Ocracoke.

MIDGETT COVE A cove, 0.4 mi. (0.6 km) long, in Dare County, Kennekeet Township at 35°32′56″N 75°28′25″W and located on the Rodanthe map. The cove is in Pamlico Sound 0.6 mi. (1 km) north of Salvo and 1.3 mi. (2.1 km) south of Waves. **Historical note** Midgett is an old and prominent family name on the Outer Banks.

MIDGETT ISLAND An island, 0.05 mi. (0.08 km) long and 0.02 mi. (0.03 km) wide, in Dare County, Kennekeet Township at 35°33′17″N 75°28′37″W and located on the Rodanthe map. This marsh island is in Pamlico Sound near Midgett Cove, 1.1 mi. (1.8 km) north northwest of Salvo and 1 mi. (1.6 km) south southwest of Waves. **Historical note** See Midgett Cove for an explanatory note.

MIDGETTS DITCH A canal, 0.4 mi. (0.6 km) long, in Dare County, Nags Head Township at 35°53′58″N 75°38′37″W and located but not named on the Manteo map. The ditch is a canalized tidal stream on the east shore of north Roanoke Island at Midgetts Hammock 1.7 mi. (2.7 km) east southeast of Manteo. **Other names** Hammocks Ditch **Historical note** See Midgett Cove for an explanatory note.

MIDGETTS HAMMOCK A hummock in Dare County, Nags Head Township at 35°53′52″N 75°38′53″W and located but not named on the Manteo map. The hummock is on Roanoke Island 0.9 mi. (1.4 km) south of Ballast Point and 1.6 mi. (2 km) southeast of Manteo. **Historical note** See Midgett Cove and Black Hammock for explanatory notes.

Midgett Town See Rodanthe

Miesquetaugh Inlet See Musketo Inlet

MILL COVE A cove, 0.2 mi. (0.3 km) wide, in Currituck County, Fruitville Township at 36°30′52″N 75°54′45″W and located on the Knotts Island map. The cove is on Knotts Island 0.9 mi. (1.4 km) east of the village of Knotts Island.

MILL CREEK A cove in Dare County, Kennekeet Township at 35°21′53″N 75°30′29″W and located on the Buxton map. The cove is in Pamlico Sound just south of Big Island and 1.1 mi. (1.8 km) north of Avon.

Mill Creek See Mill Landing Creek

MILL LANDING A landing in Dare County, Nags Head Township at 35°50′25″N 75°37′15″W and located on the Oregon Inlet map. The landing is on a small marsh island 1.3 mi. (2.1 km) east of Wanchese and at the mouth of Mill Landing Creek. **Other names** Pughs Landing **Historical note** Mill Landing is the location of the primary fish processing facility on the Outer Banks with larger facilities near the lower portion of the Outer Banks on the mainland at Morehead City and Beaufort.

MILL LANDING CREEK A cove, 0.5 mi. (0.8 km) long, in Dare County, Nags Head Township at 35°50′52″N 75°37′02″W and located on the Oregon Inlet map. The cove is in Roanoke Sound 1.3 mi. (2.1 km) east of Wanchese and 5.8 mi. (9.3 km) southeast of Manteo. **Other names** Mill Creek **Historical note** Mill Landing Creek is an important harbor for the fishing industry of Wanchese and Roanoke Island. The catch is unloaded and processed here for shipment.

Mingers Gut See Mingoes Ridge Gut

Mingers Ridge Gut See Mingoes Ridge Gut

Mingoes Gut See Mingoes Ridge Gut

MINGOES RIDGE GUT A tidal stream, 0.6 mi. (0.8 km) long, in Dare County, Atlantic Township at 36°03′38″N 75°42′23″W and located but not named on the Kitty Hawk map. The stream is in Kitty Hawk at North

Cove 8.5 mi. (13.6 km) northwest of Nags Head. **Other names** Mingers Gut, Mingers Ridge Gut, and Mingoes Gut

Misher Island See Bodie Island

Money Bay See Money Island Bay

MONEY ISLAND An island, 0.2 mi. (0.3 km) long, in Carteret County, Morehead Township at 34°42′08″N 76°43′53″W and located but not shown on the Beaufort map. The island is at the south end of Money Island Bay and separated from Bogue Banks at Atlantic Beach by Money Island Slough. It is 1.5 mi. (2.4 km) south of the mainland town of Morehead City.

MONEY ISLAND BAY A cove, 0.6 mi. (1 km) wide, in Carteret County, Morehead Township at 34°42′18″N 76°43′13″W and located but not shown on the Beaufort map. The cove is in Bogue Sound at Atlantic Beach 1.3 mi. (2 km) south of the mainland town of Morehead City. **Other names** Money Bay

MONEY ISLAND BEACH A beach in Carteret County, Morehead Township at 34°41′54″N 76°43′23″W and located on the Beaufort map. The beach is on the east part of Bogue Banks, 1.6 mi. (2.6 km) south of the mainland town of Morehead City and 0.9 mi. (1.4 km) east of Atlantic Beach.

MONEY ISLAND SLOUGH A water passage, 0.3 mi. (0.5 km) long, at 34°42′05″N 76°43′54″W and located but not shown on the Beaufort map. The water passage is in Money Island Bay at Atlantic Beach 1.5 mi. (2.4 km) south southwest of Morehead City.

MON ISLAND An island, 0.7 mi. (1.1 km) long, in Currituck County, Fruitville Township at 36°32′45″N 75°54′23″W and located on the Knotts Island map. This marsh island is at the north end of Knotts Island Channel 2.4 mi. (3.9 km) north northeast of the village of Knotts Island. **Other names** Buckle Island and Buckle Islands **Historical note** The origin is not known but Mon is a dialectical derivation of Man or Mann which is prevalent in the local place names.

MONKEY ISLAND An island, 0.2 mi. (0.3 km) long, in Currituck County, Fruitville Township at 36°24′25″N 75°52′23″W and located on the Corolla map. The island is in Currituck Sound 2.7 mi. (4.3 km) northwest of Corolla. **Historical note** The name is probably a corruption of Pumonkey the name of the Indians that inhabited the area.

Moore Shore See More Shore

Moores Shore See Avalon Beach

Moores Shore See More Shore

MOREHEAD CITY CHANNEL A channel, 2.2 mi. (3.5 km) long, in Carteret County, Beaufort and Morehead townships at 34°42′30″N 76°41′20″W (northwest end), 34°41′30″N 76°40′06″W (southeast end), and 34°42′00″N 76°40′43″W (center) and located but not shown on the Beaufort map. The channel trends northeast-southwest and connects Beaufort Inlet and the Newport River at the Morehead Port facility. It is 2.1 mi. (3.3 km) east southeast of the mainland town of Morehead City. **Historical note** This channel is the approach channel to the port and docking facilities at Morehead City used for transporting phosphate and in support of the Menhaden fishing industry.

MORE SHORE A section of shore, 0.7 mi. (1.1 km) long, in Dare County,

Atlantic Township at 36°03′15″N 75°41′39″W and located but not named on the Kitty Hawk map. This shore is at the east end of Kitty Hawk Bay just south of Kitty Hawk and 7.4 mi. (11.8 km) north northwest of Nags Head. **Other names** Moore Shore and Moores Shore **Historical note** The original application of the name is meant to be descriptive because of the extremely shallow depth of Kitty Hawk Bay here which is no more than 1 or 2 ft. (.3 or .7 m) deep for a considerable distance from the shore. Cartographers have mislabeled maps with the surname Moore but the descriptive place name is correct.

MORGAN ISLAND An island, 0.5 mi. (0.8 km) long, in Carteret County, Harkers Island Township at 34°39′36″N 76°31′30″W and located on the Harkers Island map. The island is an irregularly shaped marsh island at the junction of Core Sound and Back Sound 3.1 mi. (5 km) south southeast of the village of Harkers Island and 2 mi. (3.2 km) north of Barden Inlet.

MORRISON GROVE An area in Dare County, Nags Head Township at 35°56′07″N 75°42′02″W and located but not named on the Manteo map. The feature is on north Roanoke Island just east of Fort Raleigh National Historic site, 2.3 mi. (3.7 km) northwest of Manteo.

Morses Point See Halfway Point

MORSES SLUE A former channel in Carteret County, Beaufort Township at 34°42′00″N 76°38′00″W and located but not named on the Beaufort map. This small channel trended north-south from Horse Island Creek at Carrot Island to Shackleford Slue, 2.2 mi. (3.5 km) southeast of the mainland town of Beaufort. **Historical note** The feature has almost disappeared and is of little practical use today. See Shackleford Slue for an explanatory note about the generic slue.

Mossey Island See Mossey Islands

MOSSEY ISLANDS Islands, 3 mi. (4.8 km) long and 1 mi. (1.6 km) wide, in Currituck County, Fruitville Township at 36°18′30″N 75°50′00″W and located on the Mossey Islands map. They are a series of marsh islands in Currituck Sound 1.2 mi. (1.9 km) west of Currituck Banks, 4.7 mi. (7.5 km) south of Corolla and 11.6 mi. (18.6 km) north northwest of Duck. **Other names** Mossey Island **Historical note** These marsh islands are a major stopover and feeding area for migrating birds along the Atlantic Flyway, and is one of the few areas still open to hunters.

MOSSEY POND A lake, 0.1 mi. (0.2 km) across, in Currituck County, Poplar Branch Township at 36°18′25″N 75°50′11″W and located on the Mossey Islands map. The lake is located at the approximate center of Mossey Islands, 4.8 mi. (7.7 km) south southwest of Corolla and 11.6 (18.6 km) north northwest of Duck. **Other names** Mossy Pond

Mossy Pond See Mossey Pond

MOTHER VINEYARD A populated place, 15 ft. (4.6 m) high with a population of about 120, in Dare County, Nags Head Township at 35°55′29″N 75°40′05″W and located on the Manteo map. It is located on the northeast shore of Roanoke Island 1 mi. (1.6 km) north of Manteo. **Historical note** The feature is named for a very old and large scuppernong grape vine which was first discovered by Amadas and Barlowe while exploring the area for Sir Walter Raleigh. The exact age of the vine is not known but is at least 500 years old. The name is a reference to the great age and stamina of the vine.

MOTTS CREEK A cove, 0.3 mi. (0.5 km) long and 0.4 mi. (0.6 km) wide, in Dare County, Nags Head Township at 35°47′37″N 75°32′59″W and located on the Atlantic map. The cove is located in Roanoke Sound 1.2 mi. (1.9 km) north northwest of Oregon Inlet and 6.1 mi. (9.9 km) southeast of Wanchese.

Mount Kenrick See Kenricks Mount

Mount Vernon See Mount Vernon Rock

MOUNT VERNON ROCK A former rock in Carteret County, Portsmouth Township at approximately 35°04′45″N 76°05′50″W and located but not shown on the Portsmouth map. The rock was located in Pamlico Sound about 1.5 mi. (2.4 km) west northwest of the village of Portsmouth and about 6 mi. (9.6 km) southwest of the village of Ocracoke. **Other names** Mount Vernon **Historical note** The origin of the name is unknown.

Muddy Slue See Buxton Harbon Channel

MUD ISLAND An island, 0.2 mi. (0.3 km) wide, in Carteret County, Portsmouth Township at 34°57′59″N 76°11′09″W and located on the Wainwright Island map. The island is in Core Sound 0.3 mi. (0.5 km) southwest of Cowpen Point, 9.5 mi. (15.2 km) southwest of the village of Portsmouth, and 15.5 mi. (23.2 km) southwest of the village of Ocracoke.

MUD POINT A point of land in Carteret County, White Oak Township at 34°39′52″N 77°03′53″W and located but not named on the Swansboro map. The point is just on Bogue Banks south of the Bogue Sound Bridge and 3.5 mi. (5.3 km) southeast of the mainland town of Swansboro.

MULLET COVE A cove, 0.3 mi. (0.5 km) long and 0.1 mi. (0.2 km) wide, at 34°42′17″N 76°28′17″W and located on the Horsepen Point map. The cove is in Core Sound 1.6 mi. (2.6 km) south of Horsepen Point and 5.1 mi. (8.2 km) east of the village of Harkers Island. **Historical note** The feature is named for a small variety of fish found on the Outer Banks.

MULLET CREEK A water passage, 0.7 mi. (1.1 km) long, in Currituck County, Poplar Branch Township at 36°14′20″N 75°48′34″W and located but not named on the Jarvisburg map. The water passage is on the northwest part of Pine Island, 6.2 mi. (9.9 km) northwest of Duck and 9.9 mi. (15.8 km) south of Corolla. **Historical note** See Mullet Cove for an explanatory note.

MULLET POND A lake, 0.1 mi. (0.2 km) wide, in Carteret County, Harkers Island Township at 34°41′04″N 76°38′34″W and located on the Beaufort map. The lake is a fresh water pond located on the southwest tip of Shackleford Banks, 1.5 mi. (2.4 km) east of Beaufort Inlet and 2.6 mi. (4.2 km) south southeast of the mainland town of Beaufort. **Historical note** The Pond was formed as a result of enclosure by the westward migration of the sand spit or hook at the west end of Shackleford Banks. A spit or hook forms by the process of longshore drift or the movement of sand and materials by the oblique or angular action of waves. The depositional activity can be noted on the Beaufort map. See Mullet Cove for an additional explanatory note.

Mullet Pond See Wades Shore

MULLET SHOAL A shoal, 2 mi. (3.2 km) long, in Carteret County, Portsmouth Township at 34°59′42″N 76°09′35″W and located but not shown on the Wainwright Island map. The shoal is located in Core Sound near its junction with Pamlico Sound just west of Merkle Hammock 10.5 mi. (16.8 km) southwest of the village of Ocracoke. **Historical note** See Mullet Cove for an explanatory note.

MULLET SHOAL A shoal in Carteret County, Harkers Island Township at 34°43′32″N 76°29′28″W and located on the Horsepen Point map. The shoal is located in Core Sound 2 mi. (3.2 km) east of Horsepen Point and 5.6 mi. (9 km) north northeast of the village of Harkers Island. **Historical note** See Mullet Cove for an explanatory note.

Mullet Shore See Shackleford Banks

Mullet Shore See Wades Shore

MUSKETO INLET A former water passage in Currituck County, Fruitville Township at 36°23′30″N 75°49′45″W and located but not shown on the Corolla map. The inlet formerly connected Currrituck Sound through Currituck Banks to the Atlantic Ocean at a point just north of Corolla. **Other names** Bay of Muskito, Miesquetaugh Inlet, and New Inlet **Historical note** This inlet was apparently open for the period of time from just before 1585 until the 1670's. Musketo is a variation in the spelling of mosquito but may also refer to moskity which is Algonquian for grassland.

MYRTLE BAY A cove, 0.3 mi. (0.5 km) across, in Currituck County, Poplar Branch Township at 36°15′41″N 75°48′46″W and located on the Mossey Islands map. It is a small cove located in an unnamed marsh area just north of Little Goat Island Bay, 8.3 mi. (13.3 km) south of Corolla and 8.6 mi. (13.8 km) northwest of Duck.

N

Naghead See Nags Head

Nag Head See Nags Head

NAGS HEAD A populated place, 10 ft. (3 m) high with a population of about 450 (summer 5000), in Dare County, Nags Head Township at 35°57′30″N 75°37′30″W and located on the Manteo map. The community is 4.4 mi. (7 km) east northeast of Manteo. **Other names** Etacrewac, Griffin, Naghead, Nag Head, Nagshead, and The Nags Head **Historical note** There are a number of legends concerning the origin of the name Nags Head. It was reported by sailors that when this part of the beach was viewed from a ship it resembled a horse's head or neck. One story states that certain unscupulous "bankers" (a term sometimes used for residents of the Outer Banks especially in an historical context) would hang a lantern around a horse's neck and walk him along the beach, thereby giving the impression of the lights of a ship. This illusion would then sometimes lure ships dangerously close to the shoals and the beach where they would wreck or run aground. The ship could then be plundered by these certain unscupulous individuals. There is no historical evidence to support this story, and hanging a smoking lantern around a horse's neck is not a task easily accomplished. Another recount of the name comes from the fact that a horse was discovered in the area with his head lodged fast among the gnarled branches of a tree. It has also been suggested that the area was so named because horses grazed there. Also, head is a generic for a piece of land protruding into the sea. The most plausible explanation of the origin of the name is that an Englishman who had moved to The Albemarle area of North Carolina purchased a sizeable tract of land in 1832 in this area. Since it reminded him of an area in England named Nags Head he named his purchase Nags Head. Also, Nags Head is commonly used in England as a place name. A post office was established here in 1884 and the name was changed to Griffin in 1909, but was changed back to Nags Head shortly thereafter. This is one of the few instances where the original name of an Outer Banks community prevailed over the post office name. The community was originally incorporated in 1923.

Nagshead See Nags Head

Nags Head Banks See Currituck Banks

NAGS HEAD BEACH A beach in Dare County, Nags Head Township at 35°57′20″N 75°37′17″W and located but not named on the Manteo and Roanoke Island NE maps. The beach is the area of ocean shore at Nags Head, 4.3 mi. (6.9 km) east of Manteo.

Nags Head Dunes See Dunes of Dare

Nags Head Hill See Jockeys Ridge

Nags Head Inlet See Roanoke Inlet

NAGS HEAD ISLAND An island, 0.3 mi. (0.5 km) long and 0.1 mi. (0.2 km) wide, in Dare County, Nags Head Township at 35°55′01″N 75°36′49″W and located on the Roanoke Island NE map. The marsh island is in Roanoke Sound, 2.8 mi. (4.5 km) south of Nags Head, 1.1 mi. (1.8 km) north of The Causeway, and 1.1 mi. (1.8 km) northwest of Whalebone Junction.

NAGS HEAD WOODS Woods, 15 ft. (1.4 m) high and 0.9 mi. (1.4 km) wide, in Dare County, Nags Head Township at 35°58′47″N 75°39′45″W and located on the Manteo map. This wooded area is located on South Currituck Banks just west of Jockeys Ridge and 2.5 mi. (4 km) northwest of Nags Head.

NAUSEGOC A former Indian Camp in Dare County, Kennekeet Township. The name was applied on a number of early maps in the vicinity of Pea Island and the north part of Hatteras Island. **Historical note** The meaning is not clear, but could have been a reference to a temporary place used by indians for camping while on fishing and foraging trips.

NEGRO BAY A cove, 0.5 mi. (0.8 km) wide, in Currituck County, Fruitville Township at 36°28′03″N 75°53′15″W and located on the Barco map. The cove is located in Currituck Sound, 0.9 mi. (1.5 km) north of South Channel with Swan Island and Johnson Island at the entrance 6.8 mi. (10.9 km) north northwest of Corolla. **Other names** Nigger Bay **Historical note** The original name is that listed here in the category "other names" but has become officially changed because in 1968 the Federal government adopted a policy of not using the word nigger on Federal maps or in other publications.

NEGRO CREEK A cove, 0.05 mi. (0.08 km) wide, in Carteret County, Atlantic Township at 34°51′02″N 76°19′40″W and located on the Styron Bay map. The cove is in Core Sound 2.3 mi. (3.7 km) south southeast of the mainland village of Atlantic. **Other names** Nigger Creek **Historical note** See Negro Bay for an explanatory note.

NEGRO HAMMOCK A hummock in Hyde County, Ocracoke Township at 35°06′58″N 75°58′15″W and located but not named on the Ocracoke map. The hummock is on Ocracoke Island, 0.8 mi. (1.3 km) east of the village of Ocracoke. **Historical note** See Black Hammock for an explanatory note about the generic hammock.

NEGRO HAMMOCKS Former islands in Hyde County, Ocracoke Township at approximately 35°07′15″N 75°58′00″W and located but not shown on the Ocracoke map. These islands were formerly in Pamlico Sound just northeast of southern Ocracoke Island and about 1 mi. (1.6 km) northeast of the village of Ocracoke. **Historical note** See Black Hammock for an explanatory note.

NEGRO ISLAND A former island in Hyde County, Ocracoke Township at 35°06′30″N 76°00′02″W and located but not shown on the Ocracoke and Portsmouth maps. The island was in Pamlico Sound about 1 mi. (1.6 km) west of the village of Ocracoke. **Historical note** The former island is a higher area of shoal on Middle Ground (q.v.) which occasionally bares at low water.

Netsiland See Knotts Island (former island)

NEUNSIOOK An historical reference. The reference is an Indian word generally applied to the southern part of Core Banks just north of Cape Lookout.

New Brittaine See Outer Banks

NEW CURRITUCK INLET A former water passage in Currituck County, Fruitville Township at 36°27′30″N 75°51′00″W and the remnants are located on the Corolla map. It formerly connected Currituck Sound to the Atlantic Ocean through Currituck Banks at the eastern end of South Channel, 5.8 mi. (9.3 km) north of Corolla and 6 mi. (9.7 km) south of the North Carolina-Virginia boundary. **Other names** Caratuk Inlet, Crow Inlet, Currchuck Inlet, Currituck Inlet, New Inlet, and Old Currituck Inlet **Historical note** The inlet opened in 1713 and closed in 1828 which for all intents and purposes ended any thoughts of economic development using Currituck Sound as a shipping lane. Re-opening of the inlet was considered, but no work was actually done. Today remnants of the inlet are still present and during storms and periods of high water the former inlet contains water for short periods of time. The remnants of the inlet are approximately 2 mi. (3.2 km) long, and are named Old Currituck Inlet on the Corolla topographic map. Since these topographic maps are supposed to reflect local preference and usage, the application of the name Old Currituck Inlet to the feature originally known as New Currituck Inlet may indicate an evolution of usage from the adjective new to the use of the adjective old because the inlet has been closed for more than 150 years. There is no doubt that when the original Currituck Inlet at the North Carolina-Virginia boundary closed and this inlet opened, the name New Inlet was applied to the new feature. Later, the name New Currituck Inlet was applied to the newly opened inlet while the site of former Currituck Inlet retained its original name. Application of the term "new" was and still is a practice on the Outer Banks because new inlets are often created during storms but quickly closed again. New inlets acquire names if there is indication that they will remain open for some time. Since the originnal Currituck Inlet at the North Carolina-Virginia boundary had closed and this new inlet remained opened, Currituck was applied to the newly opened inlet because of its close proximity (6 mi. (9.6 km) south) to the original Currituck Inlet and the adjective new was retained to indicate subsequent opening and to avoid confusion with the location of the original Currituck Inlet. While there is evidence that New Currituck Inlet has at times been referred to as simply Currituck Inlet, the application of the name Old Currituck Inlet here is very recent. In fact, Old Currituck Inlet usually is a secondary name for the site of the original Currituck Inlet at the North Carolina-Virginia boundary. For purposes of clarity and historical correctness, the former inlet at the North Carolina-Virginia boundary will be referred to as Currituck Inlet, and the remnants of the inlet, 6 mi. (9.6 km) south of the North Carolina-Virginia boundary, will be referred to as New Currituck Inlet.

New Drum Inlet See Drum Inlet

New Fort in Virginia See Fort Raleigh

NEW INLET A former water passage, 1.3 mi. (2.1 km) long, in Dare County, Kennekeet Township at 35°40′15″N 75°28′47″W and located on the Pea Island map. The former inlet connected Pamlico Sound to the Atlantic Ocean and separated Pea Island from Hatteras Island 5.6 mi. (9.1 km) north of Rodanthe. **Other names** Chick Inlet, Chickinacommack Inlet, Chickina-commock Inlet, Chickinockcominok Inlet, Chickinocominock Inlet, and Gunt Inlet **Historical note** The inlet has opened and closed periodically since the 1650's with the last closing in 1945. Today remnants of the inlet are still visible as are the ruins of wooden bridges that spanned the inlet in the 1930's. There was one attempt to re-open and maintain the inlet in 1922 by the North Carolina Fisheries Commission in order to stimulate the fishing industry on the Outer Banks, but the attempt failed. Many inlets on the Outer Banks have been referred to at one time or another as "New Inlet" because of an established practice to refer to any newly opened inlet as New Inlet for a period of time or until a newer inlet opened. Apparently this inlet opened and closed so frequently that the name New Inlet was always applicable.

New Inlet See Drum Inlet

New Inlet See Gunt Inlet

New Inlet See Musketo Inlet

New Inlet See New Currituck Inlet

New Inlet See Old Drum Inlet (Carteret County, Portsmouth and Atlantic townships)

New Inlet See Roanoke Inlet

New Inlet See Trinitie Harbor

NEWTONS POINT A point of land in Carteret County, Portsmouth Township at 35°04′05″N 76°04′14″W and located on the Portsmouth map. The point is located on northwest Portsmouth Island, 0.4 mi. (0.6 km) west of the village of Portsmouth and 6.8 mi. (10.2 km) southwest of the village of Ocracoke.

Nigger Bay See Negro Bay

Nigger Creek See Negro Creek

NINE FOOT SHOAL CHANNEL A channel in Hyde County, Ocracoke Township at 35°07′45″N 76°02′55″W and located on Chart number 11555. The channel is located in Pamlico Sound and trends northwest-southeast just west of Big Foot Slough Channel 1.8 mi. (2.9 km) northwest of the village of Ocracoke.

NO ACHE A marsh, 1.2 mi. (1.9 km) long and 0.5 mi. (0.8 km) wide, in Dare County, Kennekeet Township at 35°31′25″N 75°28′57″W and located on the Rodanthe map. The marsh juts west into Pamlico Sound from Hatteras Island and is situated between Clarks Bay and No Ache Bay 1.5 mi. (2.4 km) south of Salvo. **Other names** No Egg Point **Historical note** Legend indicates that the origin of the name is a whimsical response to a place name on the mainland. It seems that a family, near Stumpy Point across Pamlico Sound on the mainland, named Payne referred to a small bay at the mouth of Long Shoal River by the family name — Paynes Bay. Over the years the spelling of the name changed to Pains Bay. Some bankers near Salvo decided to name a feature No Ache revealing typical Outer Banks humor. While this explanation is only known by some bankers, it is the only known explanation that explains the name and seems to be further substantiated by the curious lack of a generic as part of the name.

Actually, a more plausible explanation may be offered. The very early maps of the area list the name of this marsh as No Egg Point and through pronunciation and transcribing errors the name No Ache was labeled on later maps. No Egg Point was important as a descriptive place name because egg gathering from wild birds nests was an important activity supplementing the diet of early Bankers. The name was also applied to a nearby bay, island and slough.

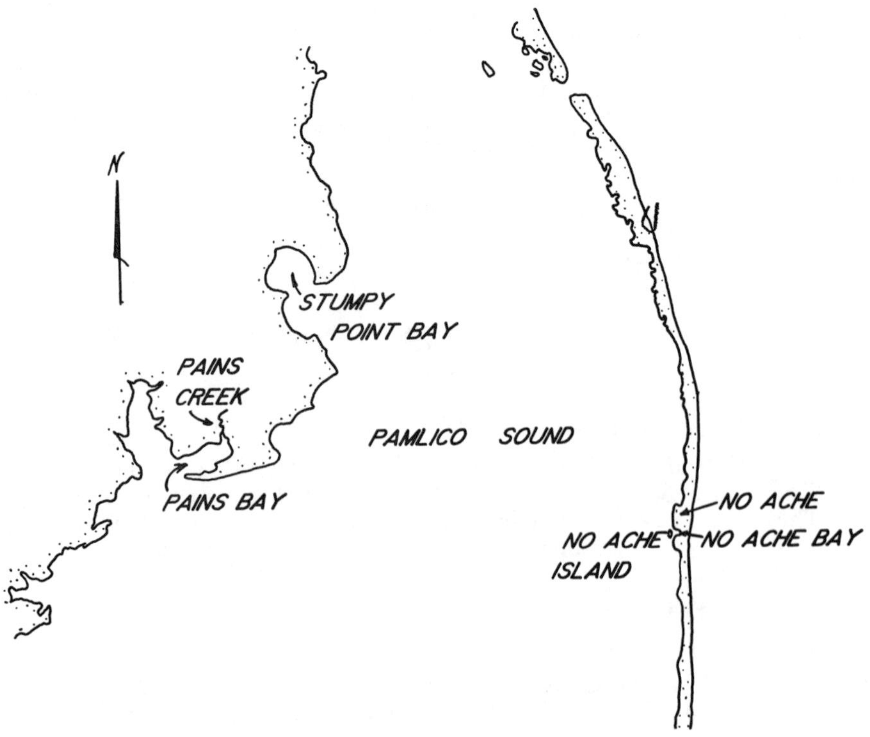

NO ACHE BAY A cove, 0.4 mi. (0.6 km) long and 0.3 mi. (0.5 km) wide, in Dare county, Kennekeet Township at 35°30′45″N 75°29′02″W and located on the Rodanthe map. The cove is located in Pamlico Sound and is bordered by a marsh area with No Ache Island at the entrance 1.9 mi. (3.1 km) south of Salvo. **Other names** No Ache Creek **Historical note** See No Ache for an explanatory note regarding the origin of the name.

No Ache Creek See No Ache Bay

NO ACHE ISLAND An island, 0.3 mi. (0.5 km) long and 0.2 mi. (0.3 km) wide, in Dare County, Kennekeet Township at 35°30′42″N 75°29′15″W and located on the Rodanthe map. The island is located in Pamlico Sound at the entrance to No Ache Bay 2.2 mi. (3.5 km) south of Salvo. **Other names** Cedar Hammock Island **Historical note** See No Ache for an explanatory note regarding the origin of the name.

NO ACHE SLOUGH A canalized tidal stream, 1.4 mi. (2.3 km) long in Dare County, Kennekeet Township at 35°30′29″N 75°28′07″W and located but not named on the Rodanthe map. The slough is in the marsh named No Ache just south of Clarks Bay and is 1 mi. (1.6 km) south of Salvo. **Historical note** See No Ache for an explanatory note.

No Egg Point See No Ache

Normans Inlet See Cedar Inlet

North Bank See Currituck Banks

North Banks See Currituck Banks

North Banks See Pea Island

North Banks of Currituck See Currituck Banks

NORTH BAR A former shoal in Hyde County, Ocracoke Township and located but not shown on the Portsmouth and Ocracoke maps. The shoal is located about 2.7 mi. (4.3 km) south of the village of Ocracoke. **Historical note** This was the shoal area at the north entrance to Ocracoke Inlet before deposition closed it off.

NORTH BITTERSWASH CREEK A cove, 0.05 mi. (0.08 km) wide, in Hyde County, Ocracoke Township at 35°10′02″N 75°50′06″W and located on the Green Island map. The cove is located in Pamlico Sound, 0.4 mi. (0.6 km) northeast of South Bitterswash Creek, and 9.9 mi. (15.8 km) northeast of the village of Ocracoke.

NORTH BREAKERS An area of breakers in Dare County, Hatteras Township at 35°11′30″N 75°43′30″W and located but not shown on the Hatteras map. The breakers are at the northern approach to Hatteras Inlet, 2.8 mi. (4.4 km) southwest of the village of Hatteras.

NORTH BREAKERS A former area of breakers in Hyde County, Ocracoke Township and located but not shown on the Portsmouth and Ocracoke maps. The area of breakers was at North Bar on the north side of Ocracoke Inlet (before deposition filled it in) and about 2.7 mi. (4.3 km) south of the village of Ocracoke.

NORTH BURRIS ISLAND An island, 0.8 mi. (1.3 km) long and 0.3 mi. (0.5 km) wide, in Currituck County, Poplar Branch Township at 36°17′23″N 75°50′23″W and located on the Mossey Islands map. It is located in Currituck Sound at Big Narrows and separated from South Burris Island by Burris Bay, 7.1 mi. (11.4 km) south of Corolla and 10.9 mi. (17.4 km) northwest of Duck.

NORTH CAROLINA, STATE OF A civil division at 35°30′00″N 80°00′00″W. The state is one of the original thirteen states and was the twelfth state to ratify the Constitution after agreeing to give up claims to its western lands. It is bounded on the east by the Atlantic Ocean, the south by South Carolina and Georgia, the west by Tennessee, and the north by Virginia. The state contains 57,712 square miles of which 3,645 are water.

North Carolina at Hatteras See Outer Banks

North Carolina Banks See Outer Banks

NORTH CAROLINA SOUND Lagoons in Currituck, Dare, Hyde, and Carteret counties at 35°30′00″N 75°45′00″W. This is an historical term that referred to the sound or lagoon system of coastal North Carolina which is now composed of Currituck, Albemarle, Croatan, Roanoke, Pamlico, Core and Bogue Sounds. **Historical note** This historical term is used to collectively refer to all of the major lagoons in the coastal system, and primarily used only as a written reference.

North Chicamacomico See Rodanthe

NORTH COVE A cove, 0.6 mi. (1 km) wide, in Dare County, Atlantic Township at 36°03′25″N 75°42′00″W and located but not named on the Kitty Hawk map. The cove is in the northeast corner of Kitty Hawk Bay just south of Kitty Hawk and 8.2 mi. (13 km) northwest of Nags Head.

NORTH DRAIN A cove in Dare County, Kennekeet Township at 35°34′49″N 75°28′09″W and located on the Rodanthe map. The cove is located in Pamlico Sound 0.2 mi. (0.3 km) north of Aunt Phoebes Marsh and 1.1 mi. (1.8 km) south of Rodanthe.

NORTHEAST POND A lake, 0.1 mi. (0.2 km) across, in Currituck County, Poplar Branch Township at 36°19′52″N 75°50′30″W and located on the Mossey Islands map. The lake is located on the northeast part of Brant Island just northwest of Mossey Islands, 3.3 mi. (5.3 km) south southwest of Corolla and 13 mi. (20.8 km) northwest of Duck.

NORTHERN POND A cove in Hyde County, Ocracoke Township at 35°07′14″N 75°58′56″W and located on the Ocracoke map. The cove is located in Pamlico Sound at Gap Point 0.3 mi. (0.5 km) north of the village of Ocracoke.

Northern Woods See Rodanthe

NORTH POINT A point of land in Dare County, Nags Head Township at 35°46′30″N 75°32′28″W and located on the Oregon Inlet map. The point is the southernmost point of Bodie Island at Oregon Inlet 6.5 mi. (10.4 km) southeast of Wanchese.

NORTH POINT A former point of land in Dare County, Hatteras Township at 35°18′30″N 75°39′00″W and located but not shown on Chart 11555. The point was at the north shore of Clam Shoal, 5.2 mi. (8.3 km) north northeast of the village of Hatteras. **Historical note** The point was prominent in the nineteenth century but was often covered at high tide. Today, the feature is completely inundated.

North Point See Eagleton Point

North Point of Roanoke Island See Ethridges Point

NORTH RIVER CHANNEL A channel, 1.5 mi. (2.4 km) long, in Carteret County, Harkers Island Township at 34°42′15″N 76°35′53″W (northeast end), 34°42′00″N 76°37′30″W (southwest end) and 34°42′07″N 76°36′35″W (center) and located on the Harkers Island map. The channel separates Middle Marshes from Carrot Island 2.8 mi. (3.5 km) southeast of the mainland town of Beaufort.

NORTH ROCK A rock, 0.3 mi. (0.5 km) long, in Carteret County, Portsmouth Township at 35°06′23″N 76°04′15″W and located on the Portsmouth map. The rock is in Pamlico Sound at the west end of Ocracoke Inlet, 2.5 mi. (4 km) north of the village of Portsmouth and 5.1 mi. (8.2 km) west southwest of the village of Ocracoke. **Other names** Great Shell Rock and Little Shell Rock **Historical note** In the late eighteenth centur: he middle section of the feature was submerged and the west end was called Great Shell Rock and the east end was called Little Shell Rock. The middle section of the feature periodically becomes submerged, but today this middle section is usually above water.

North Rodanthe See Rodanthe

Northwest Passage See Roanoke Inlet

NORTHWEST POINT A point of land in Dare County, Nags Head Township at 35°56′07″N 75°43′42″W and located on the Manteo map. The Point is the northwest point of Roanoke Island and is located 3.6 mi. (5.8 km) northwest of Manteo and 1.1 mi. (1.8 km) west of Fort Raleigh National Historic Site. **Other names** John Mann Point, John Manns Point, NW Point, West Point of Roanoke Island and West End

NORTHWEST POND A cove, 0.1 mi. (0.2 km) across, in Currituck County, Poplar Branch Township at 36°19′40″N 75°50′44″W and located but not named on the Mossey Islands map. The cove is just east of Brant Island and just southwest of Northeast Pond. It is located in Brant Island Pond 3.3 mi. (5.3 km) south of Corolla and 13.1 mi. (21 km) northwest of Duck.

Northwest River See Currituck Sound

NORTHWEST STRADDLE A submerged point of land in Carteret County, Cedar Island Township at 35°08′50″N 76°09′40″W and located but not named on Chart 11550. The feature is an underwater point at the northwest point of Royal Shoal in Pamlico Sound, 9 mi. (14.4 km) west northwest of the village of Ocracoke. **Historical note** Straddle is a generic used to indicate the extreme points of a measurement. In this case, the point indicates the northwest extremity of the western part of Royal Shoal. The term was more extensively used historically.

Nots Island See Knotts Island (former island)

Nott Island See Knotts Island (former island)

Notts Island See Knotts Island (former island)

Notts Island See Mackay Island

NW Point See Northwest Point

O

Oacock See Ocracoke Island

Oa Cock Bar See Ocracoke Island

OAK HAMMOCK A hummock, 1 mi. (1.6 km) long and 5 ft. (1.5 m) high, in Carteret County, Harkers Island Township at 34°42′44″N 76°34′07″W and located on the Harkers Island map. The hummock is located on the northwest part of Harkers Island just west of West Mouth Bay 1.3 mi. (2.1 km) northwest of the village of Harkers Island and 4.3 mi. (6.9 km) east of the mainland town of Beaufort. **Historical note** See Black Hammock for an explanatory note.

OAK ISLAND An island, 0.2 mi. (0.3 km) long and less than 0.1 mi. (0.2 km) wide, in Dare County, Atlantic Township at 36°12′50″N 75°47′47″W and located but not named on the Jarvisburg map. The elongated marsh is in Currituck Sound, 4.6 mi. (7.4 km) northwest of Duck and 11.5 mi. (18.4 km) south of Corolla.

Oakocock See Ocracoke Island

OAK POINT A point of land in Carteret County, White oak Township at 34°40′32″N 77°01′06″W and located but not named on the Swansboro map. The point is just west of Archer Point, 5.8 mi. (9.3 km) east of the mainland town of Swansboro.

OAK POND A lake, 0.3 mi. (0.5 km) long and 0.1 mi. (0.2 km) wide, in Currituck County, Fruitville Township at 36°26′58″N 75°51′25″W and located on the Corolla map. The lake is located in a marsh area just west of Currituck Banks, 0.4 mi. (0.6 km) south of the remnants of New Currituck Inlet and 5 mi. (8 km) north northwest of Corolla.

Ocacoc See Ocracoke Island

Ocacock See Ocracoke

Ocacock Inlet See Ocracoke Inlet

Ocacock Inlett See Ocracoke Inlet

Ocacock Island See Ocracoke Island

Ocacok Channel See Ocracoke Inlet

Occacock See Ocracoke

Occacock See Ocracoke Island

Occacock Bar See Ocracoke Island

Occacock Inlet See Ocracoke Inlet

Occacock Island See Ocracoke Island

Occacode Island See Ocracoke Island

Occacoke Inlet See Ocracoke Inlet

Occacoke Island See Ocracoke Island

Occam See Croatan Sound

Occam See Currituck Sound

Occam See Pamlico Sound

Occam River See Albemarle Sound

Occam River See Pamlico Sound

Ocean River See Gulf Stream

Ocoan River See Roanoke Sound

Ocock See Ocracoke Island

Ocracock See Ocracoke

Ocracock See Ocracoke Island

Ocracocke Inlet See Ocracoke Inlet

Ocracock Inlet See Ocracoke Inlet

Ocracock Island See Core Banks

Ocracock Town See Ocracoke

Ocracok Bar See Ocracoke Swash

OCRACOKE A populated place, 3 ft. (0.8 m) high with a population of about 600, in Hyde County, Ocracoke Township at 35°06′54″N 75°59′01″W and located on the Ocracoke map. The village is located on the southwest end of Ocracoke Island 17.9 mi. (28.8 km) southwest of the village of Hatteras. **Other names** Ocacock, Occacock, Ocracock, Ocracock Town, Ocracoke Village, Okcrecock, Okerecock, Okok, Pilot Town, Port Bath, Woccock, Wococan, Wococon, and Wocokon **Historical note** An interesting tale describes one legend as to the origin of the name Ocracoke. Blackbeard the pirate, who made this part of the Outer Banks and the area of Bath on the mainland a semi-permanent home, was killed near Ocracoke by Lieutenant Maynard of Virginia. Maynard was dispatched by the governor of Virginia to subdue Blackbeard and his pirates because of their threat to commerce and shipping. Legend states that Blackbeard eager to do battle and waiting for sunrise repeatedly cursed "O cry cock" and hence the name Ocracoke. There is no foundation to support this legend.

The origin of the name could be an anglicized corruption of the Algonquian word "waxihikami" which means enclosed place, fort, or stockade. This could have become, through pronunciation and misspelling, Wococon, which is a very common term used on the early maps of the island and over the years has evolved into Ocracoke.

The early name of the village was Pilot Town because most of the Pilotmen who steered ships over the shoals through Ocracoke Inlet to the port of Portsmouth just south of Ocracoke lived at the village on Ocracoke Island. Port Bath was a secondary name for a while because most ships stopping at Ocracoke were bound for Bath on the mainland. A post office was established here in 1840; however, mail delivery was very sporadic even as late as the 1950's when mail was delivered only once a week by boat from the mainland village of Atlantic.

Ocracoke Bar See Ocracoke Island

Ocracoke Bar See Ocracoke Swash

OCRACOKE INLET A water passage, 2 mi. (3.2 km) long, in Hyde County, Ocracoke Township and Carteret County, Portsmouth Township at 35°04′00″N 76°01′07″W and located on the Portsmouth map. The water passage connects Pamlico Sound to the Atlantic Ocean and separates Ocracoke Island from Portsmouth Island 3.6 mi. (5.8 km) southwest of the village of Ocracoke. **Other names** Beacon Island Roads, Ocacock Inlet, Ocacock Inlett, Ocacok Channel, Occacock Inlet, Occacoke Inlet, Ocracock Inlet, Ocracocke Inlet, Ocracook Inlet, Okerecok Inlet, Okok Inlet, Onoconon Inlet, Port Grenvil, Port of Ocracoke, Roanok Inlet, Roanok Inlett, Wakokon Inlet, Woccock Inlet, Wococock Inlett, Wococon Inlet, Wococon Inlett, Wocoken Inlet, Wokokon Inlet, Wosoton Inlet, and Woston Inlet **Historical note** Ocracoke Inlet is one of the three Outer Banks inlets continuously open since 1585. Beaufort and Bogue inlets are the other two continuously open inlets. The inlet served as a major commercial artery serving the port of Portsmouth in the eighteenth and early nineteenth centuries, and later was responsible for the economical support of the village of Ocracoke. See Ocracoke for an explanatory note.

OCRACOKE ISLAND A barrier island, 17 mi. (27.2 km) long, in Hyde County, Ocracoke Township at 35°11′15″N 75°46′25″W (northeast end), 35°04′25″N 76°01′20″W (southwest end), and 35°07′30″N 75°53′30″W (center) and located on the Green Island, Howard Reef, Ocracoke and Portsmouth maps. The barrier island extends southwest from Hatteras Island at Hatteras Inlet to Ocracoke Inlet at Portsmouth Island. **Other names** Gordons Ile, Oacock, Oa Cock Bar, Oakocock, Ocacôc, Ocacock Island, Occacock, Occacock Bar, Occacock Island, Occacode Island, Occacoke Island, Ocock, Ocracock, Ocracoke Bar, Ocrecock, Ocrecok Island, Ocreecock, Okercock, Okerecock, Okok, Sequotan, Vokokon, Woccock, Woccocon, Wococock, Wococon, Wocokon, Wocotan, Wokokon, and Wosotan **Historical note** See Ocracoke for an explanatory note.

OCRACOKE LANDING A former landing in Hyde County, Ocracoke Township at 35°09′20″N 76°00′35″W and located but not named on Chart 11550. The landing was in Pamlico Sound, 2 mi. (3.2 km) north of the village of Ocracoke. **Historical note** The landing was actually the hulk of a sunken ship where boats anchored to transfer goods for the village of Ocracoke. The site was used for only a short period of time. Today Big Foot Slough Channel extends south from here.

OCRACOKE SWASH An area of breakers in Hyde County, Ocracoke Township and Carteret County, Portsmouth Township at 35°03′45″N 76°00′53″W and located but not shown on the Portsmouth map. The feature is an area of shoals at the entrance to Ocracoke Inlet, 4 mi. (6.4 km) southwest of the village of Ocracoke. **Other names** Ocracock Bar and Ocracoke Bar **Historical note** See Ocracoke for an explanatory note.

Ocracoke Village See Ocracoke

OCRACOKE WHARF An historical landing in Hyde County, Ocracoke Township at 35°06′50″N 76°59′02″W and shown but not named on the Ocracoke map. This former reference is to the docking facility located in Silver Lake at Ocracoke. The name was in use in the late nineteenth century but is not used today.

Ocracook Inlet See Ocracoke Inlet

Ocrecock See Ocracoke Island

Ocrecok Island See Ocracoke Island

Ocreecock See Ocracoke Island

OFF ISLAND An island, 0.4 mi. (0.6 km) long and 0.4 mi. (0.6 km) wide, in Dare County, Nags Head Township at 35°48′37″N 75°34′02″W and located on the Oregon Inlet map. This marsh island is located in Roanoke Sound and is separated from Bodie Island by Blossie Creek 0.9 mi. (1.4 km) north of Herring Shoal Island and 4.8 mi. (7.7 km) southeast of Wanchese. **Other names** Cutoff Island **Historical note** The name could be a reference to the island's proximity to The Cutoff (q.v.) which is just south of the island. The name origin could be any of several references because off has many nautical meanings. Usually, it refers to lying seaward or a ship riding at a distance from the shore. It can also mean away from the wind.

Okcrecock See Ocracoke

Okercock See Ocracoke Island

Okerecock See Ocracoke

Okerecock See Ocracoke Island

Okerecok Inlet See Ocracoke Inlet

Okok See Ocracoke

Okok See Ocracoke Island

Okok Inlet See Ocracoke Inlet

Okok Inlet See Swash Inlet

OLD CHANNEL A water passage, 0.6 mi. (1 km) long, in Carteret County, Sea Level Township at 34°48′54″N 76°22′07″W and located on the Styron Bay map. The water passage is located in Core Sound and separates Inner Grass Lump from Core Banks 4.4 mi. (7 km) south of the mainland village of Atlantic.

OLD CHANNEL POINT A point of land in Carteret County, Davis Township at 34°49′07″N 76°22′32″W and located on the Davis map. The point is located on Outer Grass Lump 1 mi. (1.6 km) northwest of Core Banks and 5.5 mi. (8.8 km) east of the mainland town of Davis.

Old Currituck Inlet See Currituck Inlet

Old Currituck Inlet See New Currituck Inlet

Old Dominion Docks See Ashbee Harbor

OLD DRUM INLET A former water passage, 0.5 mi. (0.8 km) wide, in Carteret County, Portsmouth and Atlantic townships at 34°53′00″N 76°16′53″W and formerly located on the Atlantic map. The former water passage connected Core Sound with the Atlantic Ocean through Core Banks 2.8 mi. (4.5 km) northeast of present Drum Inlet and 3.2 mi. (5.1 km) east of the mainland village of Atlantic. **Other names** Drum Inlet and New Inlet **Historical note** Old Drum Inlet opened in the early eighteenth century, closed after about 50 years, reopened in 1933, and closed again in 1971. Actually, the site of this former inlet has not officially been named Old Drum Inlet, but is used here to provide clarity between this site which closed in 1971 and the present location of Drum Inlet which is 2.8 mi. (4.5 km) southwest of this site. The application of the name Old Drum Inlet here should not be confused with the use of the name Old Drum Inlet (q.v.) with another dormant inlet that was located approximately 18 mi. (28.8 km) southwest of what is referred to here as Old Drum Inlet (former Drum Inlet) and 15.2 mi. (24.3 km) southwest of the present location of Drum Inlet. The historical inlet, that was open for a short time and referred to as Old Drum Inlet, was only open for about fifty years in the mid-eighteenth century and the name has little or no meaning today. See Drum Inlet for explanatory notes regarding the name origin.

OLD DRUM INLET A former water passage in Carteret County, Smyrna Township at 34°40′38″N 76°29′02″W and located but not shown on the Horsepen Point map. The inlet connected Core Sound and the Atlantic Ocean at what is now Hogpen Bay, 7.8 mi. (12.5 km) south of the mainland town of Davis and 18 mi. (28.8 km) southwest of what is now also known as Old Drum Inlet. **Other names** Drum Inlet **Historical note** The former inlet seems to have been open for about 50 years during the mid-eighteenth century. There is some question as to the name of this inlet. While there is no doubt that the inlet existed, the reason it is referred to as Old Drum Inlet is not known since it was supposedly opened during the same general period as what was then known as Drum Inlet and today is also known as Old Drum Inlet.

Old Drum Inlet See Drum Inlet

OLD HAMMOCK CREEK A cove, 0.05 mi. (0.08 km) wide, in Hyde County, Ocracoke Township at 35°07′59″N 75°55′14″W and located on the Howard Reef map. The cove is located in Pamlico Sound 9.2 mi. (14.7 km) southwest of Hatteras Inlet and 4.5 mi. (7.2 km) northeast of the village of Ocracoke.

OLD HATTERAS INLET A former water passage in Hyde County, Ocracoke Township at 35°09′00″N 75°51′30″W and located but not shown on the Green Island map. The inlet connected Pamlico Sound to the Atlantic Ocean and was located near the northeast end of Ocracoke Island in the vicinity of The Great Swash (q.v.). It was 8.3 mi. (12.9 km) northeast of the village of Ocracoke and 11 mi. (17.6 km) southwest of the village of Hatteras. **Other names** Greenvills Rode, Hattars Inlett, Hatteras Inlet, Hatorasch Inlett, Passage de Hattarxis, Passage de Hattaxis, Port Grenvil, and West Inlet **Historical note** The inlet opened prior to 1585 and closed in 1764.

OLD HOUSE BEACH A beach, 1.6 mi. (2.6 km) long, in Carteret County, Portsmouth Township at 34°55′34″N 76°13′14″W and located on the Wainwright Island map. The beach is located on Core Banks just southwest of Sand Inlet 12.8 mi. (20.5 km) southwest of the village of Portsmouth and 18.8 mi. (30.1 km) southwest of the village of Ocracoke. **Historical note** The exact origin of the name is not remembered but probably refers to one of the structures used at temporary campsites.

OLD HOUSE CHANNEL A channel, 5.5 mi. (8.8 km) long, in Dare County, Nags Head and Kennekeet townships at 35°46′15″N 75°34′48″W (northeast end), 35°42′55″N 75°37′45″W (southwest end), and 35°45′15″N 75°33′23″W (center) and located on the Oregon Inlet map. The channel trends northeast-southwest in Pamlico Sound from Oregon Inlet Channel 5.4 mi. (8.6 km) southeast of Wanchese. **Other names** Old House Slough

OLD HOUSE POND A lake, in Currituck County, Poplar Branch Township at 36°18′35″N 75°49′32″W and located on the Mossey Islands map. The lake is located in Mossey Islands, 4.6 mi. (7.4 km) south of Corolla and 11.4 mi. (18.2 km) north northwest of Duck. **Historical note** See Old House Beach for an explanatory note.

Old House Slough See Old House Channel

Old Inlet See Currituck Inlet

Old Inlet See Gunt Inlet

Old Inlet See Roanoke Inlet

Old Inlett See Gunt Inlet

Old Nags Head See Sound Side

Old Quork Point See Quokes Point

Old Quorks Point See Quokes Point

Old Roanoke Inlet See Roanoke Inlet

Old Rock See Shell Castle

Old Rollenson Sound See Old Rollinson Channel

OLD ROLLINSON CHANNEL A channel, 3.6 mi. (5.8 km) long, in Dare County, Hatteras Township at 35°15′42″N 75°39′08″W (east end), 35°14′44″N 75°42′48″W (west end), and 35°15′13″N 75°40′58″W (center) and located but not shown on the Hatteras map. The channel extends southeast in Pamlico Sound from Kings Channel, 2.5 mi. (4 km) north of the village of Hatteras and 3 mi. (4.8 km) southwest of Bird Islands. **Other names** Old Rollenson Sound

Old Ruins See Fort Hancock

OLD SLOUGH A cove, 0.2 mi. (0.3 km) long and 0.05 mi. (0.08 km) wide, in Hyde County, Ocracoke Township at 35°06′10″N 75°59′10″W and located on the Ocracoke map. The cove is located in Pamlico Sound 1 mi. (1.6 km) south southwest of the village of Ocracoke.

OLD SWASH CHANNEL A former channel, about 1 mi. (1.6 km) long, in Carteret County, Portsmouth Township at 35°06′00″N 76°04′10″W and located but not named on the Portsmouth map. The channel was in Pamlico Sound and was a small channel that extended from Wallace Channel to Flounder Slue in an arc between Shell Castle and North Rock, 4 mi. (6.4 km) west of the village of Ocracoke. **Historical note** Today there is no trace of the channel.

Old Topsail Inlet See Beaufort Inlet

OLIVER CHANNEL A former channel, less than 1 mi. (1.6 km) long, in Dare County, Hatteras Township at 35°14′45″N 75°45′45″W and located but not shown on Chart 11555. The channel was in Pamlico Sound just southwest of Oliver Reef, 3.1 mi. (5 km) north of Hatteras Inlet and 3.3 mi. (5.3 km) northwest of the village of Hatteras. **Other names** Olivers Channel **Historical note** The feature was prominent in the nineteenth century.

OLIVER REEF A shoal, 1 mi. (1.6 km) long, in Dare County, Hatteras Township and Hyde County, Ocracoke Township at 35°14′40″N 75°43′35″W and located but not shown on the Green Island and Hatteras maps. The shoal is located in Pamlico Sound 3.4 mi. (5.4 km) north of Hatteras Inlet and 3 mi. (4.8 km) northwest of the village of Hatteras. **Other names** Olivers Reef **Historical note** The shoal was given to the U.S. Government 1874 for use in naval target practice. It was returned to North Carolina in 1965.

Olivers Channel See Oliver Channel

Olivers Reef See Oliver Reef

Onoconon Inlet See Ocracoke Inlet

ONSLOW BAY A bight, 100 mi. (160 km) long, in Carteret, Onslow, New Hanover, and Brunswick counties at 34°30′00″N 77°15′00″W and located on the Cape Lookout, Harkers Island, Beaufort, Mansfield, Salter Path, and Swansboro maps. The bight is located in the Atlantic Ocean and trends northeast-southwest from Cape Lookout to Cape Fear.

OPENING MARSHES A marsh in Dare County, Kennekeet Township at 35°32′28″N 75°28′35″W and located but not named on the Rodanthe map. The marsh area is on upper Hatteras Island west of Salvo and 1.8 mi. (2.9 km) south of Waves.

Open Pond See Open Ponds

OPEN PONDS Lakes in Dare County, Hatteras Township at 35°15′23″N 75°32′10″W and located but not named on the Buxton map. These lakes are a series of at least seven ponds situated between Buxton Woods and Jennette Sedge, 1 mi. (1.6 km) south of Buxton and 0.7 mi. (1.1 km) north of Cape Hatteras. **Other names** Open pond

OREGON INLET A water passage, 1.5 mi. (2.4 km) long, in Dare County, Nags Head Township at 35°46′45″N 75°32′15″W and located on the Oregon Inlet map. The water passage trends north northeast-south southwest, connects Pamlico Sound to the Atlantic Ocean, separates Bodie Island from Pea Island and is spanned by the Herbert Bonner Bridge 7.3 mi. (11.7 km) southeast of Wanchese and 13.8 mi. (22.3 km) south southeast of Nags Head. **Other names** Inlet of 1849 **Historical note** The inlet opened during a hurricane in 1846 and was named for the first vessel to pass through it, the side-wheeler "Oregon." Today the channel through the inlet is constantly dredged and maintained because the inlet provides the necessary outlet to the sea that supports the fishing industry of the Outer Banks centered at Wanchese. North Point (q.v.) is migrating southward from deposition shifting the orientation of the inlet more north-south. Refer to the introduction for additional explanation. The use of the variant name Inlet of 1849 was a cartographic method of indicating new inlets that had not yet acquired a name. The practice only lasted a short time and was used primarily by map makers, and the use of 1849 was a transcribing error. Refer to the introduction for an explanation of new inlet naming.

OREGON INLET CHANNEL A channel, 3 mi. (4.8 km) long, in Dare County, Nags Head Township at 35°47′25″N 75°34′25″W (northwest end), 35°46′20″N 75°32′15″W (southeast end), and 35°47′00″N 75°33′23″W (center) and located on the Oregon Inlet map. The channel trends northwest in Pamlico Sound from Oregon Inlet to Roanoke Sound Channel 5.8 mi. (9.3 km) southeast of Wanchese.

OTILA A former populated place in Dare County, Atlantic Township at 36°04′20″N 75°43′45″W and located but not named on the Kitty Hawk map. The community was on Currituck Banks just northwest of Kitty Hawk in the general vicinity of Kitty Hawk Landing and Sound Landing 8.3 mi. (14.1 km) north northwest of Nags Head. **Other names** Botilla and Ottilla **Historical note** A post office was established in the community surrounding Sound Landing in 1905, but only operated a short time before it was discontinued in 1914. The short operating time for this post office is why the name was never applied to the community. Today the name is remembered by many local residents but is not used for any application.

Otilla See Sound Landing

OTIS COVE A cove, 0.6 mi. (1 km) long and 0.1 mi. (0.2 km) wide, in Dare County, Nags Head Township at 35°56′15″N 75°41′57″W and located on the Manteo map. The marsh cove is located at the north end of Roanoke Island and is separated from Roanoke Sound by Crab Claw Spit 1.5 mi. (2.4 km) north northwest of Manteo and 0.6 mi. (1 km) east of Fort Raleigh National Historic Site.

OTTER POND POINT A point of land in Dare County, Kennekeet Township at 35°20′23″N 75°31′04″W and located on the Buxton map. It is a marsh point just north of Black Hammock, 0.8 mi. (1.3 km) southwest of Avon and 6.4 mi. (10.3 km) north of Cape Hatteras.

Ottilla See Otila

OURDSLEYS HAMMOCK A sand dune in Dare County, Hatteras Township at 35°11′52″N 75°43′22″W and located but not named on the Hatteras map. The dune is 2 mi. (3.2 km) northeast of Hatteras Inlet and 2.3 mi. (3.7 km) southwest of the village of Hatteras. **Other names** Round Hammock **Historical note** Both names were used interchangeably in the nineteenth century when the feature was more prominent, but the names have fallen into disuse.

Our Reef See Howard Reef

OUTER BANKS A barrier complex in Currituck, Dare, Hyde, and Carteret counties at 36°42′45″N 75°55′30″W (north end), 34°38′20″N 77°06′00″W (south end), and 35°30′00″N 75°30′00″W (center). It is a narrow chain of barrier islands, barrier beaches, and barrier spits extending south from the North Carolina-Virginia boundary to Cape Hatteras then southwest to Bogue Inlet. From north to south the barriers are named Currituck Banks, Bodie Island, Pea Island, Hatteras Island, Ocracoke Island, Porthsmouth Island, Core Banks, Shackleford Banks, and Bogue Banks. Currituck Banks and Bodie Island are now joined just north of Whalebone Junction, and Pea Island and Hatteras Island are now joined at former New Inlet just north of Rodanthe. **Other names** Annunciata, Arabia, Arcadia, Carolina Banks, Carolina Outer Banks, Dare Coast, New Brittaine, North Carolina at Hatteras, North Carolina Banks, Sir Walter Raleigh Coastland, The Banks, Verazzano Isthmus, and Virginia. **Historical note** There are many divisions of the Outer Banks for a variety of reasons. The delimitation of the Outer Banks, according to this study, is based upon what is considered to be a logical physical and cultural delimitation. Refer to the introduction for more information. The first recorded European visit to the Outer Banks was made by Verazzano searching for a route to the West, and the area was referred to as Annunciata. The area was also known for a short time as Verazzano Isthmus. Subsequently, Annunciata is likely to be the first European name ever applied to the Outer Banks. It was given by Verrazzano's brother to what they hoped was an isthmus separating the western ocean from the eastern seas and the western route to China. The name means to announce especially as predicted and indicates the intense desire for finding a western water route to the East. As with other features named by Verazzano's crew, the names did not prevail because no maps or permanent settlements were made. When the English increased their activity and visits to the area, the entire region in this part of the New World was referred to briefly as New Brittaine. For a short time the area was referred to as Arcadia by people not living at the Banks because of the Outer Banks life style. The name was originally that of a place in ancient Greece where the people sustained a simplistic and rustic lifestyle and Arcadia was often applied to areas where rural people displayed this type of lifestyle. The name as applied to the Outer Banks never became popular.

Roanoke Island was the site of the now famous "Lost Colony," which was the first attempt at colonization in the New World by the English and was organized and financed by Sir Walter Raleigh. When a supply ship returned from England, the colony was completely deserted with "CROA" carved onto a tree. The carving probably indicates a hurried attempt to carve the word Croatan or Croatoan (q.v.), who were thought to be friendly Indians in the area of what is now Cape Hatteras. The secret distress signal - a patée cross (arms are wider at the extremities) was never found to be carved anywhere. Endless speculation as to the fate of these colonists has occurred but no factual trace has ever been found nor is likely to be found. In fact, the original site of this first colony has not been found and is likely inundated because of the erosion on the north part of Roanoke Island.

Eventually, the entire area was called Virginia for Queen Elizabeth I of England, the "virgin queen." During the War Between the States, the residents of the Outer Banks had little sympathy for the Southern cause nor for the Northern cause. Dissatisfied with North Carolina joining the Confederacy, the Outer Banks formed the "true and faithful" government of North Carolina with its capital at Hatteras. Representatives were elected and sent to Washington, D.C., but unlike the West Virginia situation, the Outer Banks representatives were not seated in Congress. Shortly afterwards, Union forces easily captured the hastily fortified posts of the Confederacy on the Outer Banks with only a minimum of fighting, and with the major battle occuring on Roanoke Island. During the entire occupation, the "Bankers" were quite indifferent to the affair.

During the mid-nineteenth century, many people in North Carolina referred to the Outer Banks as Arabia alluding to its inaccessability but the name was not used on the Banks. The history of the area is filled with hundreds of shipwrecks because of the dreaded Diamond Shoals of Cape Hatteras and this earned the area the infamous name of "the Graveyard of the Atlantic," but today shipwrecks are not very prevelent because of sophisticated warning equipment. Shipwrecks were at one time easily visible at many places along the Outer Banks, but only the remnants of a few are visible today.

Outer Diamonds See Outer Diamond Shoal

OUTER DIAMOND SHOAL A shoal, 4 mi. (6.4 km) long, in Dare County, Hatteras Township at 35°08′40″N 75°27′15″W and located on Chart number 11555. The shoal is the southeast most extension of Diamond Shoals in the Atlantic Ocean and is located 6.5 mi. (10.3 km) southeast of Cape Hatteras. **Other names** Full Moon Shoal (much larger in the late eighteenth century), Outer Diamonds, Outer Shoal, Outer Shoals, Outward Shoal of Cape Hatteras.

OUTER GRASS LUMP An island, 0.3 mi. (0.5 km) wide, in Carteret County, Smyrna Township at 34°49′07″N 76°22′24″W and located on the Styron Bay and Davis maps. The marsh island is located in Core Sound 0.3 mi. (0.5 km) north of Inner Grass Lump and 3.1 mi. (5 km) south of the mainland village of Sea Level. **Historical note** See Gould Lump for an explanatory note.

OUTER GREEN ISLAND An island, 0.1 mi. (0.2 km) across, in Hyde County, Ocracoke Township at 35°11′05″N 75°48′25″W and located on the Green Island map. The marsh island is in Pamlico Sound just north of Green Island, 7.2 mi. (11.5 km) southwest of the village of Hatteras and 11.7 mi. (23.7 km) northeast of the village of Ocracoke.

Outer Green Island See Green Island (Hyde County, Ocracoke Township)

Outer Shoal See Outer Diamond Shoal

Outer Shoals See Outer Diamond Shoal

Outer Slue Channel See Diamond Slough

Outward Shoal of Cape Hatteras See Outer Diamond Shoal

OVERHAUL POND A lake, 0.1 mi. (0.2 km) across, in Currituck County, Poplar Branch Township at 36°18′44″N 75°50′15″W and located on the Mossey Islands map. The lake is in Mossey Islands just east of Wells Bay, 4.6 mi. (7.4 km) south southwest of Corolla and 12 mi. (19.2 km) north northwest of Duck.

OYSTER CREEK A water passage, 0.5 mi. (0.8 km) long, in Dare County, Nags Head Township at 35°49′07″N 75°37′07″W and located on the Oregon Inlet map. The feature trends north-south in Roanoke Sound, just northeast of Hog Island, 3.2 mi. (5.1 km) south of Wanchese. **Other names** Oyster Creek Cutthrough

OYSTER CREEK A water passage, 0.5 mi. (0.8 km) long, in Dare County, Nags Head Township at 35°50′10″N 75°39′37″W and located on the Wanchese map. The water passage is located in Croatan Sound 0.7 mi. (1.1. km) south of Baum Creek and 1.4 mi. (2.3 km) west of Wanchese.

Oyster Creek Cutthrough See Oyster Creek (35°49′07″N 75°37′07″W)

OYSTER ROCKS Rocks in Carteret County, Portsmouth Township at 35°05′20″N 76°03′30″W and located but not shown on the Portsmouth map. These shoals and rocks extend from North Rock southeastward to Wallace Channel just southwest of Beacon Island, and are located in Pamlico Sound, 4 mi. (6.4 km) west of the village of Ocracoke. **Other names** Eastern Rocks and Western Rocks **Historical note** The eastern end is sometimes known as Eastern Rocks and the western end is sometimes known as Western Rocks.

P

PADDOCKS CREEK A former tidal stream in Dare County, Kennekeet Township approximately 35°46′15″N 75°31′30″W and located but not shown on the Oregon Inlet map. The tidal stream was located just south of Oregon Inlet on Pea Island near the Coast Guard Station and about 7.5 mi. (12 km) southwest of Wanchese. **Historical note** The feature no longer exists.

PADDYS HOLLOW A flat in Hyde County, Ocracoke Township at 35°06′45″N 75°58′49″W and located on the Ocracoke map. The flat is located on Ocracoke Island in the village of Ocracoke 0.3 mi. (0.5 km) east of Silver Lake. **Historical note** The use of the generic hollow is unusual on the Outer Banks. The reason is unclear and not known, but the name may have been introduced by someone originally not from the Outer Banks.

PAMLICO SOUND A lagoon, 80 mi. (120 km) long and 30 mi. (48 km) wide, in Carteret County, Cedar Island and Portsmouth townships; Dare County, Croatan, Nags Head, Kennekeet, and Hatteras townships; and Hyde County, Ocracoke Township at 35°15′00″N 76°00′00″W and located on the Wanchese, Oregon Inlet, Pea Island, Rodanthe, Little Kinnakeet, Buxton, Cape Hatteras, Hatteras, Howard Reef, Ocracoke, Portsmouth, and Wainwright Island maps. The lagoon extends from Oregon Inlet south to the south end of Portsmouth Island and separates Pea Island, Hatteras Island, Ocracoke Island, and Portsmouth Island from the mainland. It contains a combination of fresh to brackish waters from the Roanoke River (through Albemarle, Croatan, and Roanoke Sounds), Pamlico River, and the Neuse River then drains to the Atlantic Ocean through Oregon Inlet, Hatteras Inlet, and Ocracoke Inlet. **Other names** Albemarle Sound, Occam, Occam River, Pamplico Sound, Pamticoe Sound, Pamticough Sound, Pomouik, The Sound, and Verazzanos Sea **Historical note** The lagoon is named for the Pamlico or Paquiac Indians who inhabited its shores, and it is the largest inland body of water on the East Coast of the U.S.

Pamplico Sound See Pamlico Sound

Pamticoe Sound See Pamlico Sound

Pamticough Sound See Pamlico Sound

PAQUIAC A former region in Dare County, Hatteras and Kennekeet townships at 35°14′15″N 75°02′00″W and located but not shown on the Rodanthe, Little Kinnakeet, Buxton, and Cape Hatteras maps. Paquiac is a term applied by early mapmakers to what are now portions of Hatteras and Pea islands from the general vicinity of Cape Hatteras to the former location of the now submerged Cape Kenrick at Wimble Shoals near Rodanthe. **Other names** Paquiwoc and Paquiwock **Historical note** Paquiac is the Algonquian word for shallow area and actually referred to Pamlico Sound but was misapplied by early mapmakers.

Paquiwoc See Paquiac

Paquiwock See Paquiac

Parker Hills See Parkers Hill

PARKERS CREEK A tidal stream, 0.3 mi. (0.5 km) long, in Hyde County, Ocracoke Township at 35°08′18″N 75°54′09″W and located but not named on the Howard Reef map. The stream heads at 35°08′12″N 75°53′53″W in Parker Hills and trends northwest to Little Swash Opening in Pamlico Sound, 5.4 mi. (8.6 km) northeast of the village of Ocracoke and 8.1 mi. (13 km) southwest of Hatteras Inlet.

PARKERS HILL A sand dune, 14 ft. (4.3 m) high, in Hyde County, Ocracoke Township at 35°08′20″N 75°53′54″W and located on the Howard Reef map. The dune is located on Ocracoke Island between Try Yard Creek and Little Swash Opening, 7.8 mi. (12.5 km) southwest of Hatteras Inlet and 5.8 mi. (9.3 km) northeast of the village of Ocracoke. **Other names** Parker Hills **Historical note** The variant name seems to indicate that originally there was a series of hills here.

Passage de Hattarxis See Old Hatteras Inlet

Passage de Hattaxis See Old Hatteras Inlet

PATCH FENCE CREEK A cove, 0.2 mi. (0.3 km) wide, in Hyde County, Ocracoke Township at 35°10′10″N 75°49′10″W and located but not named on the Green Island map. The cove is in Pamlico Sound at Cockrel Creek, 8.3 mi. (12.9 km) southwest of the village of Hatteras and 10.8 mi. (17.3 km) northeast of the village of Ocracoke.

PAULS DITCH A cove, 0.3 mi. (0.5 km) long and 0.1 mi. (0.2 km) wide, in Dare County, Kennekeet Township at 35°36′29″N 75°28′17″W and located on the Rodanthe map. The cove is located in Pamlico Sound 0.9 mi. (1.5 km) north of Rodanthe.

PAUL GAMIELS HILL A sand dune in Dare County, Atlantic Township at 36°08′30″N 75°44′30″W and located but not named on the Martin Point map. The dune is located on south Currituck Banks, 5.8 mi. (9.3 km) north northwest of Kitty Hawk and 13.3 mi. (21.3 km) north northwest of Nags Head.

Paw Ridge Landing See Poor Ridge Landing

PEA ISLAND A former island, 8.2 mi. (13.2 km) long, 10 ft. (3 m) high, in Dare County, Kennekeet Township at 35°46′43″N 75°38′48″W (north end), 35°40′15″N 75°28′50″W (south end), and 35°43′30″N 75°30′00″W (center) and located on the Oregon Inlet and Pea Island maps. The former island was located just north of Hatteras Island and extended north from former New Inlet (q.v.) to Oregon Inlet. **Other names** Bodie Island, Chicamacomico Banks, Hataras Banks, Hatarask, Hertford Island, Hertfords Ile, Hertfords Island, and North Banks **Historical note** The name was originally applied to a small island nearby in Pamlico Sound and the name originated from the wild peas that once grew in abundance on this smaller island. Later the name was transferred to the barrier island from New Inlet (q.v.) to Oregon Inlet (q.v.). Today the area is a major stopover for many varieties of birds migrating along the Atlantic Flyway. The birds are protected and the area is designated The Pea Island National Wildlife Refuge. Even though New Inlet has closed, the last closure was in 1945 and the name is still in use today.

PEA ISLAND BAY A cove, 0.3 mi. (0.5 km) wide, in Dare County, Kennekeet Township at 35°42′35″N 75°30′37″W and located on the Pea Island map. The cove is located in Pamlico Sound 0.2 mi. (0.3 km) south of Pea Island Creek between Pea Island Point and Terrapin Creek Point, 5.3 mi. (8.6 km) south of Oregon Inlet and 8.4 mi. (13.5 km) north northwest of Rodanthe.

PEA ISLAND CREEK A cove, 0.3 mi. (0.5 km) long and 0.05 mi. (0.08 km) wide, in Dare County, Kennekeet Township at 35°42′45″N 75°30′35″W and located on the Pea Island map. The cove is located in Pamlico Sound, 5.1 mi. (8.3 km) south of Oregon Inlet and 7.5 mi. (12.3 km) north northwest of Rodanthe.

PEA ISLAND POINT A point of land in Dare County, Kennekeet Township at 35°42′43″N 75°30′45″W and located on the Pea Island map. The point is at the north point of Pea Island Bay 5.2 mi. (8.4 km) south of Oregon Inlet and 8.6 mi. (13.8 km) north northwest of Rodanthe.

PEAR PAD An area in Dare County, Nags Head Township and located but not named on the Manteo map. The name refers to an undefined area located generally north of Fort Raleigh (q.v.) **Historial note** The name is a local reference to a particular area on the north part of Roanoke Island where a cactus-like plant with pear shaped fruit grows.

PEBBLE SHOALS Shoals in Currituck County, Fruitville Township and located in the Atlantic Ocean just east of Currituck Banks near the North Carolina-Virginia boundary.

Pelican Island See Pelican Shoal

PELICAN SHOAL A shoal, 0.2 mi. (0.3 km) long and 0.5 mi. (0.8 km) wide, in Hyde County, Ocracoke Township and Dare County, Hatteras

Township at 35°11′53″N 75°45′29″W and located on the Green Island map. The shoal is in Hatteras Inlet, 3.9 mi. (6.3 km) west southwest of the village of Hatteras and 14.7 mi. (23.5 km) northeast of the village of Ocracoke. **Other names** Pelican Island

Peltatory Hill See Pilontary Islands

PENGUIN ISLANDS Islands in Dare County, Nags Head Township at approximately 35°54′53″N 75°36′45″W and located but not named on the Roanoke Island NE map. The group of several islands is in Roanoke Sound just north of the Causeway, 1 mi. (1.6 km) northwest of Whalebone Junction and 3.4 mi. (5.4 km) south southwest of Nags Head. **Historical note** The present islands of Big Penguin (q.v.), Little Penguin (q.v.), Nags Head (q.v.) and other small marsh islands were historically referred to as Penguin Islands. The name was in use on all of the early maps and the origin of the name is lost.

PENNYS HILL A sand dune in Currituck County, Fruitville Township at 36°27′30″N 75°51′00″W and located on the Barco map. The dune is on Currituck Banks approximately 5.5 mi. (8.8 km) north of Corolla near the former community of Seagull at the site of New Currituck Inlet. **Historical note** There is also some indication that another dune near (old) Currituck Inlet (q.v.) 2.5 mi. (4 km) north of the present location of Pennys Hill was also named Pennys Hill, but the feature is no longer in existence and if the name was ever applied to this dune, it is not remembered by local residents.

Pennys Hill See Seagull

PERRYS ISLAND A former island in Carteret County, Beaufort and Morehead Townships at 34°41′40″N 76°40′07″W and located but not shown on the Beaufort map. The island was located in Beaufort Inlet, 1.8 mi. (2.9 km) south of the mainland town of Beaufort. **Historical note** The feature disappeared in the early twentieth century.

Peter Quarter See Peters Quarter

PETERS DITCH A cove, 0.1 mi. (0.2 km) long and 0.05 mi. (0.08 km) wide, in Dare County, Kennekeet Township at 35°21′00″N 75°30′53″W and located on the Buxton map. The cove is located in Pamlico Sound 0.3 mi. (0.5 km) west of Avon and 7.3 mi. (11.3 km) north of Cape Hatteras. **Other names** Avon Harbor.

PETERS QUARTER An area in Currituck County, Fruitville Township at 36°20′28″N 75°49′50″W and located on the Mossey Islands map. The area is on the sound side of Currituck Banks, 2.6 mi. (4.2 km) south of Corolla and 13.4 mi. (21.4 km) north northwest of Duck. **Other names** Peter Quarter **Historical note** See Hunting Quarter for an explanatory note regarding the use of the generic quarter.

PETTYS POND A lake, 0.3 mi. (0.5 km) long and 0.05 mi. (0.08 km) wide, in Currituck County, Poplar Branch Township at 36°14′17″N 75°47′36″W and located on the Jarvisburg map. The lake is located in a marsh area between Pine Island Bay and Currituck Banks, 5.7 mi. (9.1 km) north of Duck and 9.8 mi. (15.7 km) south of Corolla. **Other names** Prettys Pond

PETTYS POND COVE A cove, 0.2 mi. (0.3 km) wide, in Currituck County, Poplar Branch Township at 36°13′55″N 75°47′37″W and located but not named on the Jarvisburg map. The cove is at Great Gap, 5.5 mi. (8.8 km)

north northwest of Duck and 10.3 mi. (16.5 km) south of Corolla.

PHIPPS COVE A cove, 0.2 mi. (0.3 km) long and 0.02 mi (0.03 km) wide, in Dare County, Kennekeet Township at 35°25′54″N 75°29′32″W and located on the Little Kinnakeet map. The cove is located in Pamlico Sound 1.8 mi. (2.9 km) north of the site of Little Kinnakeet and 5.9 mi. (9.6 km) north of Avon.

PILONTARY CREEK A cove, 0.1 mi. (0.2 km) wide, in Hyde County, Ocracoke Township at 35°10′23″N 75°48′53″W and located but not named on the Green Island map. The cove is in Pamlico Sound just east of Cockrel Island, 7.8 mi. (12.5 km) southwest of the village of Hatteras and 11.2 mi. (17.9 km) northeast of the village of Ocracoke. **Historical note** Refer to Pilontary Islands for an explanatory note.

Pilontary Hills See Pilontary Islands

PILONTARY ISLANDS Islands, 0.6 mi. (1 km) wide, in Carteret County, Portsmouth Township at 34°58′30″N 76°10′15″W and located on the Wainwright Island map. These marsh islands are located in Core Sound 8.4 mi. (13.6 km) southwest of the village of Portsmouth and 14.4 mi. (23.2 km) southwest of the village of Ocracoke. **Other names** Peltatory Hill and Pilontary Hills **Historical note** The feature's name is a corruption of the word pellitory which is an irritant and salivant from the plants in the nettle family. It actually stems from the Latin term "parietaria," meaning wall plant. This plant is native to northern Africa, and a variation of the name was applied to a similar plant found on the Outer Banks. Pellitory or pilontary is commonly found on the Outer Banks, and was used as herb medicine in the seventeenth, eighteenth, and nineteenth centuries primarily as a sedative and to induce vomiting. These islands were named for the large numbers of plants found in the area.

Pilot Town See Ocracoke

Pine Island See Pine Islands

PINE ISLAND BAY A bay, 0.5 mi. (0.8 km) across, in Currituck County, Poplar Branch Township at 36°14′15″N 75°48′05″W and located on the Jarvisburg map. The bay is located in Currituck Sound, 1.4 mi. (2.2 km) east of Currituck Banks, 5.9 mi. (9.4 km) northwest of Duck and 9.9 mi. (15.8 km) south of Corolla.

PINE ISLAND LEAD A water passage, 0.5 mi. (0.8 km) long, in Currituck County, Poplar Branch Township at 36°15′11″N 75°48′08″W and located on the Mossey Islands and Jarvisburg maps. This is a narrow passage from Currituck Sound through a thick unnamed marsh just east of Goat Island Bay at Currituck Banks, 7 mi. (11.2 km) northwest of Duck and 8.7 mi. (13.9 km) south of Corolla. **Historical note** See Buzzard Lead for an explanatory note about the generic lead.

PINE ISLANDS Islands, 0.6 mi. (1 km) across, in Currituck County, Poplar Branch Township at 36°14′30″N 75°48′24″W and located but not named on the Jarvisburg map. These marsh islands are in Currituck Sound, 6.4 mi. (10.2 km) northwest of Duck and 9.7 mi. (15.5 km) south of Corolla. **Other names** Pine Island

PINE KNOLL SHORES A populated place in Carteret County, Morehead Township at 34°41′57″N 76°47′54″W and located but not shown on the Mansfield map. The community is on Bogue Banks just east of Hoop Pole Woods 4.8 mi. (7.7 km) southwest of the mainland town of Morehead City and 3.4 mi. (5.4 km) west of Atlantic Beach. **Other names** Isle of Pines

PINEY COVE A cove, 0.3 mi. (0.5 km) long and 0.2 mi. (0.3 km) wide, in Currituck County, Poplar Branch Township at 36°17′40″N 75°48′55″W and located on the Mossey Islands map. The cove is in a marshy sound side area of Currituck Banks, 0.8 mi. (1.3 km) south southwest of Three Dunes, 5.8 mi. (9.3 km) south of Corolla and 10.2 mi. (16.3 km) north northwest of Duck.

PINEY CREEK A former cove in Carteret County, White Oak Township at 34°40′57″N 77°00′39″W and located but not shown on the Swansboro map. The cove was located in Bogue Sound at Piney Island, 6.4 mi. (10.3 km) east of the mainland town of Swansboro and 15.7 mi. (25.2 km) west of Atlantic Beach. **Historical note** The feature no longer exists.

Piney Creek See Archer Creek

PINEY ISLAND An island, 0.2 mi. (0.3 km) long, in Carteret County, White Oak Township at 34°40′55″N 77°00′37″W and located but not shown on the Swansboro map. The island is located in Bogue Sound 6.7 mi. (10.7 km) east southeast of the mainland town of Swansboro.

Piney Island See Bean Island (Carteret County, White Oak Township)

PINEY POINT A point of land in Carteret County, White Oak Township at 34°40′58″N 77°00′40″W and located but not named on the Swansboro map. The point is on Piney Island, 6.3 mi. (10.1 km) east of the mainland town of Swansboro and 15.6 mi. (25 km) west of Atlantic Beach.

Piney Point See Archer Point

PIPER HILL A sand dune in Currituck County, Poplar Branch Township at 36°26′50″N 75°47′55″W and located but not named on the Corolla map. The dune is located on south Currituck Banks 4 mi. (6.4 km) east of the mainland town of Poplar Branch near Beasley Bay, 13.5 mi. (21.6 km) north of Kitty Hawk and 6.1 mi. (9.8 km) south of Corolla. **Historical note** The dune is not nearly as prominent or stable as during the nineteenth century.

PIVERS ISLAND An island, 0.3 mi. (0.5 km) long and 0.1 mi. (0.2 km) wide, in Carteret County at 34°43′05″N 76°40′23″W and located on the Beaufort map. The island is just west of the mainland town of Beaufort and 3 mi. (4.8 km) east of the mainland town of Morehead City.

PLATT SHOALS Shoals, 5.5 mi. (8.8 km) long, in Dare County, Kennekeet Township at 35°46′45″N 75°27′20″W and located on Chart number 11555. The shoals are located in the Atlantic Ocean 3.7 mi. (5.9 km) east of Oregon Inlet and 12.6 mi. (20 km) southeast of Nags Head.

PLUM ORCHARD Woods, in Carteret County, White Oak Township at 34°40′08″N 77°02′20″W and located on the Swansboro map. The wooded area was on Bogue Banks, 1.5 mi. (2.4 km) west of Archer Point and 4.8 mi. (7.7 km) east southeast of the mainland town of Swansboro. **Historical note** The name became a reference for this part of Bogue Banks because there was an area of plum trees. The usage is mainly of historical significance.

POINT BACON A former barrier spit in Currituck County, Fruitville Township at 36°31′05″N 75°20′00″W and located but not named on the Knotts Island map. The feature formerly extended south from Cape Henry in Virginia to former Currituck Inlet and included a portion of the north part of Currituck Banks. **Historical note** The name appeared only on the Smith map of 1624 and was named for Sir Francis Bacon who Smith was trying to impress. A common practice in the seventeenth and eighteenth centuries, the "Age of Exploration," was to name features for prospective sponsors in order to gain their favor and backing. The name only lasted a short while and was never really applied on any other maps.

Point Bacon See Currituck Banks

POINT BOX A former point of land in Carteret County. The point is the middle point of three points protruding into Core Sound on a part of Core Banks referred to as Gordons Ile on Smith's 1624 map. As with many of the names on Smith's map, the duration of use was short. **Historical note** Box is a seventeenth century nautical term used as a reference for continually sailing back and forth. The name may have been descriptive representing a landmark along a course of "boxing about" or sailing routinely along the coast.

Point Lookout Bay See Lookout Bight

POINT OF BEACH A point of land in Carteret County, Atlantic Township at 34°53′07″N 76°16′45″W and located on the Atlantic map. It was formerly the southwest point of the north portion of Core Banks at the north shore of Old Drum Inlet (sound side) 3.4 mi. (5.4 km) east of the mainland village of Atlantic.

POINT OF BEACH A point of land in Hyde County, Ocracoke Township at 35°11′15″N 75°46′17″W and located on the Green Island map. The point is at the south shore of Hatteras Inlet, 5.1 mi. (8.2 km) southwest of the village of Hatteras and 13.7 mi. (21.9 km) northeast of the village of Ocracoke.

Point of Cape Hatteras See Cape Point (Dare County)

POINT OF GRASS A point of land in Carteret County, Portsmouth Township at 34°52′41″N 76°16′57″W and located on the Atlantic map. It was formerly the north point of a portion of Core Banks at the south shore of Old Drum Inlet (ocean side) 3.1 mi. (5 km) east of the mainland village of Atlantic.

POINT OF GRASS CREEK A cove, 0.1 mi. (0.2 km) wide, at 34°52′37″N 76°17′24″W and located on the Atlantic map. The cove is located in Core Sound 0.7 mi. (1.1 km) south of Old Drum Inlet and 2.7 mi. (4.3 km) east of the mainland village of Atlantic.

Point of the Cape See Cape Point (Dare County)

Point of the Creek See Baum Point (Dare County, Nags Head Township)

Point of the Diamonds See Diamond Shoals

Pomouik See Pamlico Sound

POND ISLAND An island, 0.5 mi. (0.8 km) long and 0.4 mi. (0.6 km) wide, in Dare County, Nags Head Township at 35°53′47″N 75°37′07″W and located on the Roanoke Island NE map. This marsh island is in Roanoke Sound 2.3 mi. (3.7 km) south of Nags Head and supports The Causeway 1.4 mi. (2.2 km) west southwest of Whalebone Junction. **Other names** Walter Island **Historical note** The name is descriptive because of the cove created by the irregular shape of the north part of the island.

POOR RIDGE LANDING A landing in Dare County, Atlantic Township at 36°03′00″N 75°42′51″W and located but not named on the Kitty Hawk map. This boat landing is on the north shore of Kitty Hawk Bay, 1.1 mi. (1.8 km) southwest of Kitty Hawk and 4 mi. (6.4 km) south of Southern Shores. **Other names** Paw Ridge Landing **Historical note** The name was originally Paw Ridge Landing because the area around the landing resembles a cat's paw when viewed from the air. The name has come to be known as Poor Ridge Landing.

PORK POINT A point of land in Dare County, Nags Head Township at 35°54′05″N 75°41′54″W and located on the Manteo map. The point is on west Roanoke Island 1.6 mi. (2.6 km) west of Manteo. **Historical note** The point was to be the eastern terminus for an embankment across Croatan Sound that was to be designed to divert the waters of Albemarle Sound and Currituck Sound through the Raleigh Canal (q.v.).

PORPOISE POND A lake, 0.1 mi. (0.2 km) across, in Currituck County, Poplar Branch Township at 36°17′50″N 75°49′55″W and located on the Mossey Islands map. The lake is in the south central part of Mossey Islands, 1.3 mi. (2.1 km) west southwest of Three Dunes, 5.8 mi. (9.3 km) south of Corolla and 11 mi. (17.6 km) northwest of Duck.

PORPOISE SLOUGH A water passage, 0.8 mi. (1.3 km) long, in Currituck County, Fruitville Township at 36°33′04″N 75°54′30″W (north end), 36°32′23″N 75°54′36″W (south end), and 36°32′37″N 75°54′35″W (center) and located on the Knotts Island map. The water passage separates Simpson Neck and Mon Island and connects Knotts Island Channel to Back Bay in Virginia 2.5 mi. (4 km) north northeast of the village of Knotts Island.

Port Bath See Ocracoke

Port Beaufort See Beaufort Inlet

Port Beaufort Inlet See Beaufort Inlet

Port Currituck See Currituck Inlet

Porters Inlet See Cedar Inlet

Port Ferdinando See Gunt Inlet

Port Fernando See Gunt Inlet

Port Grenvil See Ocracoke Inlet

Port Grenvil See Old Hatteras Inlet

Port Lane See Roanoke Inlet

Port of Currituck See Roanoke Inlet

Port of Hatteras See Hatteras

Port of Ocracoke See Ocracoke Inlet

Port Roanoke See Roanoke Inlet

PORTSMOUTH A populated place in Carteret County, Portsmouth Township at 35°04′10″N 76°03′52″W and located on the Portsmouth map. The former community is on Portsmouth Island 6 mi. (9.6 km) southwest of the village of Ocracoke. **Historical note** The community was named for Portsmouth, England and established by North Carolina legislative act in 1753. During the late eighteenth and early nineteenth centuries, Portsmouth was a thriving commercial port and stimulated trade between coastal North Carolina and the outside and helped to establish the village of Ocracoke on neighboring Ocracoke Island. The development of larger ships and more sophisticated shipping forced the establishment of other ports and caused the decline and importance of Portsmouth as a port. In 1950 there were only 18 residents and by 1960 only three people were living at Portsmouth. Today the former colonial port is all but abandoned and the post office established there in 1840 is discontinued. The National Park Service maintains the village which is in the Cape Lookout National Seashore, but most of the property is still privately held.

Portsmouth Bank See Core Banks

Portsmouth Bank See Portsmouth Island

Portsmouth Banks See Portsmouth Island

PORTSMOUTH ISLAND A barrier island in Carteret County, Portsmouth Township at 35°04′00″N 76°02′30″W (north end), 34°58′52″N 76°09′05″W (south end), and 35°02′00″N 76°05′40″W (center) and located on the Portsmouth and Wainwright Island maps. The island extends from Ocracoke Inlet to Swash Inlet and it lies between Ocracoke Island on the northeast and Core Banks on the southwest. It is considered by some as being part of the north part of Core Banks and is often referred to as Portsmouth Banks. **Other names** Core Beach, Croatan Island, Crotan, Portsmouth Bank, Portsmouth Banks, Salvage Ile, and Wococon

Potty Pond See Dotty Pond

POWELLS ISLAND A former island in Dare County, Croatan Township at approximately 35°48′35″N 75°42′05″W and located but not shown on the Wanchese map. This island was the largest island in the Roanoke Marshes complex, about 1.5 mi. (2.4 km) east of the mainland and about 4 mi. (6.4 km) southwest of Wanchese. **Historical note** The island began to disappear in the 1680s and was complete inundated by the early eighteenth century.

POWER SQUADRON SPIT A point of land in Carteret County, Harkers Island Township at 34°37′00″N 76°33′10″W and located on the Cape Lookout map. It is located at Cape Lookout 2.5 mi. (4 km) north northwest of Cape Point and 4 mi. (6.4 km) south of the village of Harkers Island. **Other names** Albacore Point, Breakwater Point, and Catfish Point **Historical note** The feature was named for the U.S. Power Squadron which meets there weekly.

POYNER BAR A shoal in Currituck County, Poplar Branch Township at 36°17′30″N 75°50′10″W and located on the Mossey Islands map. The shoal is located in Lone Oak Channel 1.5 mi. (2.4 km) west of Beasley Bay and 5.8 mi. (9.3 km) south of Corolla.

Poyner Hill See Poyners Hill (former populated place)

Poyner Hill See Poyners Hill (sand dune)

POYNERS HILL A sand dune in Currituck County, Poplar Branch Township at 36°16′25″N 75°47′47″W and located but not named on the Mossey Islands map. The dune is located just east of Beasley Bay on Currituck Banks, 4.6 mi. (7.4 km) south of Corolla and 16 mi. (25.6 km) north northwest of Kitty Hawk. **Other names** Poyner Hill and Wilets Hill **Historical note** The dune is currently about four sand ridge remnants of its former size because most of the feature has eroded away.

POYNERS HILL A former populated place in Currituck County, Poplar Branch Township at 36°16′26″N 75°47′47″W and located but not shown on the Mossey Islands map. The community was just south of Poyners Hill

5.6 mi. (10 km) south of Corolla and 15 mi. (24 km) north northwest of Kitty Hawk. **Other names** Poyner Hill and Wilets Hill

Prettys Pond See Pettys Pond

Promontorium Tremendium See Cape Lookout

Providence Inlet See Caffeys Inlet

Pughs Landing See Mill Landing

Q

Quake Hammock See Quork Hammock

QUALK SHOAL A shoal, 1 mi. (1.6 km) long, in Hyde County, Ocracoke Township at 35°05′45″N 76°00′25″W and located but not shown on the Portsmouth map. The shoal is in Pamlico Sound on Middle Ground just north of Teaches Hole and 1.7 mi. (2.7 km) southwest of the village of Ocracoke. **Historical note** See Quokes Point for an explanatory note.

Quark Hammock See Quork Hammock

Quoke Hammock See Quork Hammock

Quoke Point See Quokes Point

QUOKES POINT A point of land in Hyde County, Ocracoke Township at 35°08′14″N 75°54′42″W and located on the Howard Reef map. It is a marsh point on Ocracoke Island 8.6 mi. (13.8 km) southwest of Hatteras Inlet and 5.1 mi. (8.1 km) northeast of the village of Ocracoke. **Other names** Kwak Point, Old Quork Point, Old Quorks Point, Quolk Hommock Point, and Quoke Point **Historical note** One story relating to the origin of the name states that an irreverant castaway named Old Quork disappeared near the point while trying to put to sea during a storm, but this is not supported by local evidence. Another reference indicates that the immediate area is the breeding grounds of the Black-crowned Night Heron and "kwak" and other similar spellings refers to the sound made by the birds.

Actually, the name is a derivation of the spelling of the word quaking. A low wet marsh or hummock (hammock) is sometimes referred to as a quaking hammock or a quake hammock. Some sources indicate that if the marsh contains certain species of grass whose spikelets make a rattling or quaking noise in the wind, it is known as a quaking hammock. A quaking or quake hammock may also have its origin from the Middle English term quaghe which eventually meant quag or quake and referred to wet low marshes. The term quaking bog is a common reference in fourteenth and fifteenth century England.

Quolk Hommock Point See Quokes Point

QUORKES CREEK A cove in Hyde County, Ocracoke Township at 35°08′14″N 75°54′35″W and located on the Howard Reef map. The cove is located in Pamlico Sound just northeast of Hammock Woods 5.4 mi. (8.6 km) northeast of the village of Ocracoke. **Other names** Quorks Point Creek **Historical note** Quorke is a variation in the spelling of Quoke which is a variation of Quake. See Quokes Point for an additional explanatory note.

QUORK HAMMOCK A marsh, 0.3 mi. (0.5 km) wide, in Hyde County,

Ocracoke Township at 35°09′57″N 75°49′37″W and lcoated on the Green Island map. The marsh is on Ocracoke Island between North Bitterswash Creek and Shingle Creek 4.5 mi. (7.1 km) southwest of Hatteras Inlet and 10 mi. (15.9 km) northeast of the village of Ocracoke. **Other names** Kwawk Hammock, Quake Hammock, Quark Hammock, and Quoke Hammock **Historical note** Quork is a variation in the spelling of Quoke which is a variation of Quake. See Quokes Point for an additional explanatory note.

QUORKS HILL A sand dune, 20 ft. (6 m) high, on Ocracoke Island at 35°08′04″N 75°54′23″W and located on the Howard Reef map. The dune is just northeast of Hammock Woods and 5.2 mi. (8.3 km) northeast of the village of Ocracoke. **Historical note** Quork is a variation in the spelling of Quoke which is a variation of Quake. See Quokes Point for an additional explanatory note.

Quorks Point Creek See Quorkes Creek

R

RACCOON BAY A cove, 0.7 mi. (1.1 km) wide, in Currituck County, Fruitville Township at 35°23′17″N 75°50′34″W and located on the Corolla map. The cove is in Currituck Sound 0.7 mi. (1.1 km) northwest of Corolla and 0.8 mi. (1.2 km) south of Ships Bay.

RADIO ISLAND An island, 1.4 mi. (2.2 km) long and 0.7 mi. (1.1 km) wide, in Carteret County, Beaufort Township at 34°42′53″N 76°41′05″W and located on the Beaufort map. The island is just east of Morehead City Channel, 1.3 mi. (2.1 km) west of the mainland town of Beaufort. **Other names** Inlet Island

RALEIGH BAY A bight, 75 mi. (120 km) long, in Carteret County, Portsmouth, Atlantic, Sea Level, Stacy, Davis, Smyrna, and Harkers Island townships; Dare County, Hatteras Township; and Hyde County, Ocracoke Township at 35°14′40″N 75°31′38″W (northeast end), 34°34′57″N 76°32′01″W (southwest end), and 35°00′00″N 76°00′00″W (center). The bight is in the Atlantic Ocean and extends from Cape Hatteras southwest to Cape Lookout. **Other names** Raleighs Bay **Historical note** The feature was named for the Englishman Sir Walter Raleigh who was organizer of a number of ventures in the New World including the first English colony in the New World, the now famous Lost Colony of Roanoke Island.

RALEIGH CANAL A formerly proposed canal in Dare County, Nags Head Township and located but not shown on the Manteo and Roanoke Island NE maps. The canal was to connect Roanoke Sound with the Atlantic Ocean in the vicinity of Nags Head. **Historical note** The North Carolina General Assembly incorporated the "Raleigh Canal Company" for improving navigation and commerce in the Albermarle Sound area and to construct an inlet to be known as Raleigh Canal. It was to connect Roanoke Sound with the Atlantic Ocean in the vicinity of Nags Head, probably at or near the old site of Roanoke Inlet. There was some mild interest for a few years, but the project never materialized.

Raleighs Bay See Raleigh Bay

Raonack See Croatoan Island

Raonack See Hatteras Island

Raonack Island See Roanoke Island

Raonoak See Roanoke Island

Rawlinsons Channel See Rollinson Channel

RAWSON CREEK A cove, 0.5 mi. (0.8 km) long, at 34°40′29″N 76°29′37″W and located on the Horsepen Point map. The cove is in Core Sound just east of Core Banks 0.6 mi. (1 km) south of Rush Island and 4.3 mi. (6.9 km) east southeast of the village of Harkers Island.

RAYMOND ISLAND An island, 0.3 mi. (0.5 km) long, in Currituck County, Fruitville Township at 36°26′47″N 75°53′27″W and located on the Barco map. This marsh island is in Currituck Sound just south of South Channel, 0.7 mi. (1.1 km) south of Johnsons Island and 5.5 mi. (8.8 km) north northwest of Corolla.

REIDS MARSH A former marsh in Carteret County, Beaufort Township at 34°43′04″N 76°41′05″W and located but not named on the Beaufort map. The marsh was at the junction of Bogue Sound and Beaufort Inlet, 1.1 mi. (1.8 km) west of the mainland town of Beaufort. **Historical note** Most of this feature is now the northeastern part of Radio Island (q.v.)

Rhoanoke Island See Roanoke Island

RHODOMS POINT A point of land in Dare County, Atlantic Township at 36°00′10″N 75°43′45″W and located on the Kitty Hawk map. The point is at the west end of Colington Island, 2.2 mi. (3.5 km) west southwest of the village of Colington, 4.4 mi. (7.5 km) south southwest of Kitty Hawk, and 3.6 mi. (5.8 km) west southwest of the Wright Brothers Memorial. **Other names** Roden Point

Rice Path See Rices Path

RICES PATH A populated place in Carteret County, Morehead Township at 34°40′55″N 76°55′15″W and located on the Salter Path map. The community is located on Bogue Banks 1.8 mi. (2.9 km) west of Salter Path and 11 mi. (17.6 km) west of Atlantic Beach. **Other names** Rice Path **Historical note** The use of the generic path for localities was common on the southern part of the Outer Banks. It indicates the specific area or "path" the people from the mainland would use for various activities on the barrier island. The origin of Rices Path is the result of a wrecked ship containing a cargo of rice that the people retrieved from the wreck. Until recently an abandoned or wrecked ship belonged to the finder, and many "bankers" until the middle of this century subsidized their income by salvaging ships and cargo. While the story of the origin of the name Rice here is well known, it is difficult to verify.

River San Bartolome See Currituck Sound

Roakoke Inlet See Roanoke Inlet

Roanack See Croatoan Island

ROANOAC A former Indian community in Dare County, Nags Head Township and located but not shown on the Manteo map. It was formerly the site of an Indian village now submerged off the north coast of Roanoke Island. The village was permanent but smaller than those on the mainland. **Other names** Roanoak

Roanoac Island See Roanoke Island

Roanoak See Manteo

Roanoak See Roanoac

Roanoake Inlet See Roanoke Inlet

Roanoake Island See Roanoke Island

Roanoak Iland See Roanoke Island

Roanoak Island See Roanoke Island

Roanock Inlet See Roanoke Inlet

Roanokea Inlett See Roanoke Inlet

ROANOKE BAR A former shoal in Dare County, Nags Head Township and located but not shown on the Roanoke Island NE map. The shoal was at the entrance to Roanoke Inlet (q.v.).

Roanoke Ile See Roanoke Island

ROANOKE INLET A former water passage in Dare County, Nags Head Township at 35°54′00″N 75°35′45″W and located but not shown on the Roanoke Island NE map. It connected Roanoke Sound to the Atlantic Ocean through the barrier island and formed the boundary between Currituck Banks and Bodie Island near The Causeway at Whalebone Junction just south of Nags Head. **Other names** Inlet of Roanoke, Nags Head Inlet, New Inlet, Northwest Passage, Old Inlet, Old Roanoke Inlet, Port Lane, Port of Currituck, Port Roanoke, Roakoke Inlet, Roanoake Inlet, Roanock Inlet, Roanokea Inlett, Roanoke Inlett, Rounoak Inlet, and View Passage **Historical note** The inlet opened about 1650, began to close in 1795, and by 1811 the inlet had completely shoaled up. Port Lane was a secondary name for a short time and was named for Ralph Lane one of the early explorers. Use of the word port indicates the original reference to any opening where a ship could enter from the open sea. Roanoke Inlet was always a shallow inlet, but was utililized as much as possible especially by smaller craft because of its ideal commercial location to The Albemarle (q.v.). After the inlet closed, the people of the Albemarle region wanted to reopen the inlet and a number of studies were made over a period of about 30 years as to the best way to reopen the inlet. Each study and proposal suggested the necessity of damming Croatan and/or Roanoke sounds because this would force water from Albemarle Sound to seek a new outlet through the barrier island and the waters could be funneled through the old site at Roanoke Inlet. In 1856 actual work in the form of dredging and digging was begun, but the futility and high cost of the project was realized and the reopening of the inlet was abandoned.

While open, Roanoke Inlet provided an outlet for much of the water from the Roanoke River through Albemarle Sound. When the inlet began to close, water from Albemarle Sound was diverted through Croatan Sound and over a period of years the Roanoke Marshes (q.v.) became inundated and today only a few shoal areas are remnants of the marshes. See Roanoke Marshes for an additional explanatory note. Also, see Roanoke Island for an explanation of the origin of the name Roanoke.

Roanoke Inlett See Roanoke Inlet

ROANOKE ISLAND An island, 11 mi. (16.2 km) long and 2.3 mi. (3.7 km) wide, in Dare County, Nags Head Township at 35°56′15″N 75°43′30″W (northwest end), 35°48′10″N 75°37′30″W (southeast end), and 35°52′00″N 75°40′00″W (center) and located on the Manteo, Roanoke Island NE,

Wanchese, and Oregon Inlet maps. The island is situated between Albemarle and Pamlico Sounds and is separated from the mainland by Croatan Sound and from Bodie Island by Roanoke Sound 45 mi. (72 km) northwest of Cape Hatteras. **Other names** Ile Raonoake, Raonack Island, Raonoak, Rhoanoke Island, Roanoac Island, Roanoake Island, Roanoak Iland, Roanoak Island, Roanoke Ile, Roanok Island, and Roenoque Island **Historical note** Roanoke is the only 16th century name that still refers to the same place as it did in the 16th century. The name is of Indian origin and has many variations of spellings, and the word is thought to have multiple meanings, two of which are paramount. One meaning, is that of "northern people" and refers to the Indians living on the north part of Roanoke Island or possibly to their migration to Roanoke Island from the north. A second meaning, refers to money or the Indian's use of beads made of conch shells as a form of money. The many meanings and uses of the name Roanoke are the result of the metonymic process of word subsitution for different meanings. For example, Roanoke referred to the original inhabitants, later the meaning was transferred to their objects of barter or money and then later to the place itself.

ROANOKE MARSHES Former marsh in Dare County, Nags Head and Croatan townships at 35°48′40″N 74°42′05″W and located but not shown on the Wanchese map. The marshes are originally a series of marsh islands in Croatan Sound extending west to the mainland from southwest Roanoke Island. **Other names** Daniels Marshes and The Marshes **Historical note** These marshes, in their seventeenth century form, are no longer in existence, but were a substantial barrier until the early nineteenth century. The closing of Roanoke Inlet forced a greater volume of water through Croatan Sound submerging the marshes. There are still remnants of Roanoke Marshes at the shoreline of the mainland and as shoals in Croatan Sound. See Roanoke Island for a note on the origin of the name Roanoke.

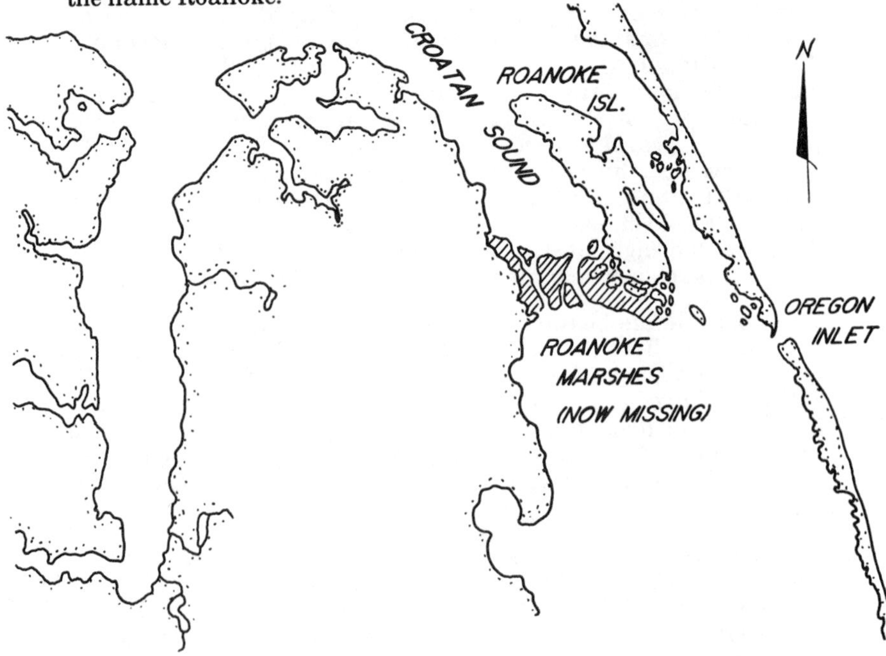

ROANOKE SOUND A strait, 17.2 mi. (27.6 km) long, in Dare County, Nags Head Township at 35°57′45″N 75°41′30″W (northwest end), 35°47′00″N 75°35′00″W (southeast end), and 35°53′00″N 75°37′00″W (center) and located on the Manteo, Roanoke Island NE, and Oregon Inlet maps. The water passage trends north northwest-south southeast from Albemarle Sound to Pamlico Sound and separates Roanoke Island from Bodie Island. **Other names** Ocoan River, Sandersons Channel and Walter Rawleigh Sound **Historical note** The water passage was named Sandersons Channel for a local landowner in the 18th century when it was smaller, but the application of the name was only temporary. See Roanoke Island for an explanatory note concerning the origin of the name Roanoke.

Roanoke Sound See Albemarle Sound

ROANOKE SOUND CHANNEL A channel, 11 mi. (17.6 km) long, at 35°56′00″N 75°39′20″W (north end), 35°47′25″N 75°34′25″W (south end), and 35°53′14″N 75°37′32″W (center) and located on the Manteo map. The channel is located in Roanoke Sound just east of Roanoke Island and extends from Oregon Inlet to a point 2 mi. (3.2 km) northeast of Manteo. **Other names** Manteo-Oregon Inlet Channel **Historical note** See Roanoke Island for an explanatory note on the origin of the name Roanoke.

Roanoke Town See Carteret

Roanok Inlet See Ocracoke Inlet

Roanok Inlett See Ocracoke Inlet

Roanok Island See Roanoke Island

ROCKHALL CREEK A cove, 0.3 mi. (0.5 km) wide, in Dare County, Nags Head Township at 35°53′17″N 75°36′42″W and located on the Roanoke Island NE map. The cove is located in Roanoke Sound at the northwest end of Headquarters Island 5 mi. (8 km) south of Nags Head.

ROCK POINT A point of land in Carteret County, Morehead Township at 34°41′27″N 76°53′45″W and located on the Salter Path map. The point is located on Bogue Banks (sound side) 9.8 mi. (15.7 km) west of Atlantic Beach. **Other names** Rocky Point

Rocky Point See Rock Point

RODANTHE A populated place, 5 ft. (1.5 m) high with a population of about 150, in Dare County, Kennekeet Township at 35°35′37″N 75°28′04″W and located on the Rodanthe map. It is on Hatteras Island 2 mi. (3.2 km) north of Waves and 27.1 mi. (43.4 km) south of Nags Head. **Other names** Big Kinnakeet, Chicamacomico, Chichinock-cominock, Chicimacomico, Chickamicomico, Chicky, Kinnakeet, Midget Town, North Chicamacomico, Northern Woods, and North Rodanthe **Historical note** Rodanthe is located at the easternmost point in North Carolina. The Post Office Department established a post office here in 1874, but refused to accept the original community name of Chicamacomico supposedly because it was too difficult to spell and pronounce, and as with many other arbitrary post office names the original meaning or choice of Rodanthe has been lost. Actually, Chicamacomico was a broad area and Rodanthe was really referred to as North Chicamacomico. Rodanthe is one of the few remaining communities in the U.S. to celebrate "Old Christmas" on January 5. In 1752, England adopted the new Gregorian calendar which was introduced by Pope Gregory XIII in 1582 to replace the Julian calendar. The change was resisted by certain isolated groups of Protestants including parts of English colonies such as those at Chicamacomico or Rodanthe. Today Rodanthe is one of the few places that celebrates Christmas according to the old calendar.

RODANTHE BEACH A beach, 1.5 mi. (2.4 km) long, at 35°35′25″N 75°27′34″W and located on the Rodanthe map. The term "the beach at Rodanthe" was originally descriptive and used to describe the ocean side beach at Rodanthe. Today the name is used more frequently as a place name.

Roden Point See Rhodoms Point

Roenoque Island See Roanoke Island

Roesepock Hill See Kill Devil Hill

Roesepock Hills See Kill Devil Hills (sand dunes)

Roespock See Kill Devil Hills (sand dunes)

Roespock Hill See Kill Devil Hill

ROLLINSON CHANNEL A channel, 2.7 mi. (4.3 km) long, in Dare County, Hatteras Township at 35° 13′50″N 75° 42′25″W and located but not shown on the Hatteras map. The channel is located in Pamlico Sound and trends north northwest into Pamlico Sound from the village of Hatteras, 4 mi. (6.4 km) northeast of Hatteras Inlet. **Other names** Rawlinsons Channel

Rosypock See Kill Devil Hills (sand dunes)

Round Hammock See Ourdsleys Hammock

ROUND HAMMOCK BAY A bay, 0.3 mi. (0.5 km) wide, in Dare County, Kennekeet Township at 35°57′30″N 75°28′30″W and located on the Pea Island and Rodanthe maps. The cove is in Pamlico Sound 1.9 mi. (3.1 km) north of Rodanthe. **Historical note** See Black Hammock for an explanatory note.

ROUND HAMMOCK POINT A point of land in Dare County, Kennekeet Township at 35° 38′10″N 75° 28′47″W and located on the Pea Island map. It is a marsh point located on Hatteras Island 2.9 mi. (4.6 km) north northwest of Rodanthe. **Historical note** See Black Hammock for an explanatory note.

Rounoak Inlet See Roanoke Inlet

Rowspock Hill See Kill Devil Hill

Rowsypock See Kill Devil Hills (sand dunes)

ROYAL POINT A point of land in Carteret County, Portsmouth Township at 35°03′06″N 76°05′17″W and located on the Portsmouth map. The point is on a small unnamed marsh island in Pamlico Sound at the north entrance to Royal Point Bay 1.8 mi. (2.9 km) southwest of the village of Portsmouth and 7.8 mi. (12.5 km) southwest of the village of Ocracoke.

ROYAL POINT BAY A cove, 0.1 mi. (0.2 km) wide, in Carteret County, Portsmouth Township at 35°03′07″N 76°05′10″W and located on the Portsmouth map. The cove is located in Pamlico Sound just southwest of The Haulover, 1.7 mi. (2.7 km) southwest of the village of Portsmouth and 7.7 mi. (12.3 km) southwest of the village of Ocracoke.

ROYAL SHOAL A shoal in Carteret County, Portsmouth Township and

Hyde County, Ocracoke Township at 35°09′10″N 76°08′45″W and located on Chart numbers 11508 and 11555. The shoal is in Pamlico Sound and forms an arc from Beacon Island 8 mi. (12.8 km) northwest of Ocracoke Inlet and 8.2 mi. (13.1 km) northwest of the village of Ocracoke. **Other names** Royal Shoal Rock, Royal Shoals, Royal Shole, and Ryals Shoal Rock

Royal Shoal Rock See Royal Shoal

Royal Shoals See Royal Shoal

Royal Shole See Royal Shoal

RUMLEYS HAMMOCK A hummock in Carteret County, Harkers Island Township at 34°41′10″N 76°29′11″W and located but not named on the Horsepen Point map. The marsh hammock is on Core Banks just south of Try Yard Creek, 4.2 mi. (6.7 km) east of the village of Harkers Island.

RUN HILL A sand dune, 78 ft. (23.5 m) high, in Dare County, Atlantic Township at 36°00′04″N 75°40′16″W and located but not named on the Kitty Hawk map. The dune is on Currituck Banks, 3.4 mi. (5.2 km) northwest of Nags Head and 4.6 mi. (7.4 km) south southeast of Kitty Hawk. **Historical note** The sand dune's name is from a stream called The Run (q.v.) that formerly extended from the Fresh Ponds to Buzzard Bay.

RUSH ISLAND An island, 0.2 mi. (0.3 km) long and 0.2 mi. (0.3 km) wide, in Carteret County, Harkers Island Township at 34°40′54″N 76°29′44″W and located on the Horsepen Point map. It is a marsh island located in Core Sound at the entrance to Hogpen Bay 3.6 mi. (5.8 km) east of the village of Harkers Island. **Historical note** The name refers to the type of "rush" plants that grow in this area.

RUSH POINT A point of land in Carteret County, Harkers Island Township at 34°42′14″N 76°35′06″W and located on the Harkers Island map. The point is on the southwest point of Harkers Island 1.6 mi. (2.6 km) west northwest of the village of Harkers Island. **Historical note** See Rush Island for an explanatory note.

Ryals Shoal Rock See Royal Shoal

S

SAINT CLAIR LUMP An island, 0.1 mi. (0.2 km) long and 0.1 mi. (0.2 km) wide, in Dare County, Kennekeet Township at 35°39′47″N 75°29′45″W and located on the Pea Island map. It is a marsh island located in Pamlico Sound just west of Goulds Lump 4.9 mi. (7.2 km) north northwest of Rodanthe. **Historical note** See Goulds Lump for an explanatory note.

SAINT CLAIR MIDGETTS CAMP A former camp in Dare County, Kennekeet Township and located but not shown on the Pea Island map. It was located near the bridge ruins across the remnants of New Inlet near St. Clair Lump and Beach Slue. **Historical note** See Ira Morris Camp for an explanatory note.

SALTER PATH A populated place, with a population of about 600, in Carteret County, Morehead Township at 34°41′20″N 76°53′07″W and located on the Salter Path map. The community is located on Bogue Banks 9.2 mi. (14.8 km) west of Atlantic Beach. **Other names** Salterpath

Historical note Salter Path developed as a temporary camp and became a permanent settlement around 1900. The generic path was frequently used in this area of the Outer Banks for temporary fishing camps, and trails to specific areas. The term path is not found in the northern part of the Outer Banks. Refer to Judgement Beach for additional information about Salter Path. See Rices Path for an additional explanatory note.

Salterpath See Salter Path

Salvage Ile See Portsmouth Island

Salvage Island See Core Banks

SALVO A populated place, 5 ft. (1.5 m) high with a population of about 150, in Dare County, Kennekeet Township at 35°32′27″N 75°28′42″W and located on the Rodanthe map. It is located on Hatteras Island 9.3 mi. (15 km) north of Little Kinnakeet and 1.9 mi. (3.1 km) south of Waves. **Other names** Cape Kenrick, Chicimacomico, Clarks, and Clarksville **Historical note** The origin of the name is interesting and seems to be substantuated. The original name of the village was Clarks, but the name apparently did not appear on maps or charts. During The War Between the States, Union forces were proceeding north after securing Forts Clark and Hatteras and the commander of one of the vessels noticed the village and inquired as to its name. He was informed that the chart had no name for the village. His remark was "give it a salvo (a simultaneous firing of cannon) anyway," and the name Salvo was arbitratily entered onto the chart. When a post office was established here in 1901, the name Salvo had been apparently perpetuated on maps and was therefore chosen by the Post Office Department as the name of the Post Office. The name of the Post Office eventually became that of the community.

Sam Windsors Lump See Sam Winsors Lump (island)

SAM WINSORS LUMP A former populated place in Dare County, Harkers Island Township and located but not shown on the Harkers Island map. This former small community of several families was located on west central Shackleford Banks in the vicinity of the island known as Sam Winsors Lump about 4.3 mi. (7.2 km) north northwest of Barden Inlet.

SAM WINSORS LUMP An island, 0.2 mi. (0.3 km) long, in Carteret County, Harkers Island Township at 34°40′37″N 76°35′15″W and located on the Harkers Island map. The island is located in Back Sound 1.9 mi. (3 km) south southwest of the village of Harkers Island and 4.5 mi. (7.2 km) northwest of Barden Inlet. **Other names** Sam Windsors Lump and Sam Winter Lump **Historical note** The feature was named for the original resident near the island on Shackleford Banks.

Sam Winter Lump See Sam Winsors Lump (island)

Sand Bank See Currituck Banks

SAND BEACH A cove, 0.2 mi. (0.3 km) wide, in Currituck County, Poplar Branch Township at 36°17′59″N 75°50′45″W and located on the Mossey Islands map. The cove is in Currituck Sound just north of Lone Oak Channel, 5.4 mi. (8.6 km) and 11.7 mi. (18.7 km) northwest of Duck.

SAND BEACH CREEK A water passage, 0.9 mi. (1.4 km) long, in Dare County, Nags Head Township at 35°53′00″N 75°37′55″W (northeast end) and 35°52′17″N 75°38′17″W (southwest end) and located on the Manteo map. The water passage trends south-north on Roanoke Island from near Broad

Creek to Johns Creek 1.3 mi. (2.1 km) north of Wanchese and 2.9 mi. (4.7 km) southeast of Manteo.

SAND COVE A cove, 0.2 mi. (0.3 km) wide in Currituck County, Poplar Branch Township at 36°17′59″N 75°50′45″W and located on the Mossey Islands map. The cove is in Currituck Sound just north of Lone Oak Channel, 5.4 mi. (8.6 km) south of Corolla and 11.7 mi. (18.7 km) northwest of Duck.

SANDERLING A populated place in Dare County, Atlantic Township at 36°12′37″N 75°45′58″W and located but not named on the Jarvisburg map. The community is on Currituck Banks about 1 mi. (1.6 km) south of the site of former Caffeys Inlet, 3.4 mi. (5.4 km) north northwest of Duck and 16.3 mi. (26 km) north northwest of Nags Head. The community is a recent resort development and is now incorporated. **Historical note** The community is reportedly named for the sanderling bird found on the Outer Banks the year round. It is very similar to a sandpiper except that it has no back toe.

SANDERS BAY A cove, 0.9 mi. (1.4 km) wide, in Currituck County, Poplar Branch Township at 36°19′40″N 75°49′50″W and located on the Mossey Islands map. The cove is in Currituck Sound and just north of Mossey Islands at Currituck Banks 3.8 mi. (6.1 km) south of Corolla and 12.7 mi. (20.3 km) north of Duck. **Other names** Brock Bay and Saunders Bay

SANDERS CREEK A water passage, 0.7 mi. (1.1 km) long, in Currituck County, Poplar Branch Township at 36°19′08″N 75°15′25″W (north end), 36°18′42″N 75°15′23″W (south end), and 36°18′52″N 75°15′24″ (center) and located on the Mossey Islands map. It is located between Mossey Islands and Currituck Banks at Three Dunes and separated from Wells Creek by Sedge Island, 4.5 mi. (7.2 km) south of Corolla and 11.7 mi. (18.7 km) north northwest of Duck.

Sandersons Channel See Roanoke Sound

SAND HOLE CREEK A cove, 0.05 mi. (0.08 km) wide, in Hyde County, Ocracoke Township at 35°07′42″N 75°56′00″W and located on the Howard Reef map. The cove is in Pamlico Sound, 3.2 mi. (4.1 km) northeast of the village of Ocracoke and 10.1 mi. (16.2 km) southwest of Hatteras Inlet. **Other names** Sandhole Creek

Sandhole Creek See Sand Hole Creek

Sand Inlet See Cedar Inlet

Sand Inlet See Sand Island Inlet

SAND ISLAND An island, 1.6 mi. (2.6 km) long, in Carteret County, Portsmouth Township at 34°56′36″N 76°11′59″W and located on the Wainwright Island map. The island is a small barrier beach between Cricket Island and Sand Island Inlet 11.2 mi. (17.9 km) southwest of the village of Portsmouth and 17.7 mi. (28.3 km) southwest of the village of Ocracoke.

SAND ISLAND INLET A water passage, 0.3 mi. (0.5 km) long, in Carteret County, Portsmouth Township at 34°56′07″N 76°12′43″W and located on the Wainwright Island map. The water passage connects Core Sound with the Atlantic Ocean and separates Sand Island from Old House Beach 12.1 mi. (19.3 km) southwest of the village of Portsmouth and 18.1 mi. (28.9 km) southwest of the village of Ocracoke. **Other names** Sand Inlet

SAND POINT A point of land in Dare County, Nags Head Township at 35°53′02″N 75°40′56″W and located on the Manteo map. It is a marsh point on southwest Roanoke Island 1.8 mi. (2.9 km) south southwest of Manteo.

SAND RIDGE Sand dunes, 4 mi. (6.4 km) long, in Currituck County, Fruitville Township at 36°31′21″N 75°51′48″W and located on the Knotts Island map. The dunes are a continuous ridge of sand dunes on Currituck Banks at the North Carolina-Virginia boundary in the vicinity of Carova 3.5 mi. (5.6 km) east of the village of Knotts Island.

SAND RIDGE Sand dunes, 0.6 mi. (1 km) long, in Dare County, Kennekeet Township at 35°37′57″N 75°28′30″W and located on the Pea Island map. These dunes are a series of sand dunes on Hatteras Island that trends northwest-southeast 0.2 mi. (0.3 km) west of Round Hammock Bay and 2.6 mi. (4.2 km) north of Rodanthe.

Sand Spit See Crab Claw Spit

SANDY BAY A bay, 1.1 mi. (1.7 km) wide, in Dare County, Hatteras Township at 35°13′29″N 75°40′30″W and located on the Hatteras map. The bay is located in Pamlico Sound 0.9 mi. (1.5 km) northeast of the village of Hatteras.

SANDY COVE A cove, 0.4 mi. (0.6 km) wide, in Currituck County, Fruitville Township at 36°29′25″N 75°56′07″W and located on the Barco map. The cove is in the extreme northeast part of Bellows Bay at the southeast part of Great Marsh, just west of the southern portion of Knotts Island, 2.2 mi. (3.5 km) south of the village of Knotts Island and 10.1 mi. (16.2 km) northwest of Corolla.

SANDY CREEK A water passage, 0.2 mi. (0.3 km) long, in Dare County, Atlantic Township at 36°13′10″N 75°47′10″W and located but not named on the Jarvisburg map. The water passage is just south of Sandy Creek Island, 4.5 mi. (7.2 km) northwest of Duck and 11.2 mi. (17.9 km) south of Corolla.

SANDY CREEK ISLAND An island, 0.2 mi. (0.3 km) long, in Dare County, Atlantic Township at 36°13′13″N 75°47′10″W and located but not named on the Jarvisburg map. This marsh island is just north of Sandy Creek, 4.6 mi. (7.4 km) northwest of Duck and 11.1 mi. (17.8 km) south of Corolla.

SANDY POINT A point of land in Carteret County, Harkers Island Township at 34°41′54″N 76°31′30″W and located on the Harkers Island map. It is the south tip of a small marsh island 0.1 mi. (0.2 km) south of Browns Island and 2.1 mi. (3.4 km) east northeast of the village of Harkers Island.

SANDY POINT A point of land in Dare County, Nags Head Township at 35°54′34″N 75°39′50″W and located on the Manteo map. It is on the northwest shore of Shallowbag Bay 0.4 mi. (0.6 km) east of Manteo.

Saunders Bay See Sanders Bay

Scabbertown See Scarboro

SCARBORO A former populated place in Dare County, Kennekeet Township at 35°21′45″N 75°30′00″W and located but not shown on the Buxton map. The community was located on Hatteras Island approximately 1.7 mi. (2.7 km) north of Avon. **Other names** Scabbertown, Scarborotown and Scarborough **Historical note** The former community was named for a family in the area but there is no trace of this former settlement today.

SCARBORO CREEK A cove, 0.3 mi. (0.5 km) wide, in Dare County, Nags Head Township at 35°54′04″N 75°39′53″W and located on the Manteo map. The cove is in Shallowbag Bay 0.7 mi. (1.1 km) south southeast of Manteo.

SCARBORO POINT A point of land in Dare County, Nags Head Township at 35°54′13″N 75°39′43″W and located but not named on the Manteo map. The feature is the north point at Scarboro Creek just south of Shallowbag Bay, 0.6 mi. (1 km) southeast of Manteo.

Scarborotown See Scarboro

Scarborough See Scarboro

Scrag Cedar Hill See Scrag Cedar Hills

SCRAG CEDAR HILLS Sand dunes, 3.6 mi. (5.6 km) long and 27 ft. (8.2 m) high, in Hyde County, Ocracoke Township at 35°09′19″N 75°51′06″W and located on the Green Island map. The dunes are on northeast Ocracoke Island 6.2 mi. (9.9 km) southwest of Hatteras Inlet and 8.8 mi. (14.1 km) northeast of the village of Ocracoke. **Other names** Scrag Cedar Hill **Historical note** The use of the term scrag in the name is a reference to the sparse vegetation here and generally prevalent throughout the Outer Banks. It should also be noted that scrag also refers to a small whale with no dorsal fin but merely protuberances on the dorsal ridge near the tale. While the reference to the specific type of whale is a possibility, the lack of vegetation is the local preference for the name origin. Also, some evidence of Outer Banks style whaling is indicated by the name of nearby Try Yard Creek (q.v.) but this activity was very early historically and most Outer Banks whaling was south of Ocracoke.

SCRAG CEDARS Former woods, 0.5 mi. (0.8 km) long and 5 ft. (1.5 m) high, in Hyde County, Ocracoke Township at 35°09′15″N 75°51′15″W and located on the Green Island map. It is an area of high dunes that was formerly wooded on northeast Ocracoke Island just south southeast of The Great Swash and 8.6 mi. (13.8 km) northeast of the village of Ocracoke. **Historical note** See Scrag Cedar Hills for an explanatory note.

SEAGULL A former populated place in Currituck County, Fruitville Township at 36°26′53″N 75°51′15″W and located but not shown on the Corolla map. It was located on Currituck Banks just south of the New Currituck Inlet site and 5 mi. (8 km) north of Corolla at Pennys Hill. **Other names** Pennys Hill **Historical note** A post office was established here at the community of Pennys Hill in 1908 and as with other communities the name of the post office was eventually adopted by the community. The reason for the name of the post office was arbitrary and for the prevalence of seagulls in the area. The post office was discontinued in 1924. As late as 1950 there were approximately 25 people at the community, but today there is virtually no trace of the former village.

Sea of Rawnocke See Albemarle Sound

Sea of Virginy See Southerne Virginia Sea

SECOND GRASS A point of land, 8 ft. (2.4 m) high, in Hyde County, Ocracoke Township at 35°05′06″N 75°59′37″W and located on the Ocracoke map. It is on Ocracoke Island 2.3 mi. (3.7 km) southwest of the village of Ocracoke. **Historical note** The same principle of naming may be applied to this name as that described in the explanatory note in the entry First Grass.

Second Hammock Hills See Hammock Oaks

SEDGE ISLAND An island, 0.3 mi. (0.5 km) long and 0.2 mi. (0.3 km) wide, in Currituck County, Poplar Branch Township at 36°18′17″N 75°49′20″W and located on the Mossey Islands map. It is at the north end of Wells Creek just west of Three Dunes, 5 mi. (8 km) south of Corolla and 10.9 mi. (17.4 km) north northwest of Duck. **Other names** Buzzard Island **Historical note** Sedge is a grass-like plant that grows throughout the Outer Banks area

Sequotan See Ocracoke Island

SEVENFOOT PATCH A shoal, 1.9 mi. (2.7 km) long, in Hyde County, Ocracoke Township at 35°15′05″N 76°05′30″W and located on Chart number 11548. The shoal is in Pamlico Sound on Bluff Shoal, 9 mi. (14.4 km) north northwest of the village of Ocracoke and 12 mi. (19.2 km) north northwest of Ocracoke Inlet. **Historical note** The feature name is descriptive of the depth of water.

SEVEN SISTERS Sand dunes, 70 ft. (21.4 m) high, in Dare County, Nags Head Township at 35°57′01″N 75°37′32″W and located on the Manteo map. The feature is a series of seven sand dunes, 0.4 mi. (0.6 km) southeast of the community of Sound Side and 0.9 mi. (1.4 km) south of Nags Head. **Other names** Seven Sisters Dunes **Historical note** The legend of the origin of the name relates the story of a very humane owner of seven very ill slave girls whom he sent to the seaside to cure their illness. The name is more than likely descriptive. This feature is not nearly as prominent as it was 100 years ago.

Seven Sisters Dunes See Seven Sisters

Shackleford See Wades Shore

Shackleford Bank See Shackleford Banks

Shackleford Bank Channel See Shackleford Slue

SHACKLEFORD BANKS A barrier island, 9.2 mi. (14.7 km) long, 0.3 mi. (0.5 km) wide and 35 ft. (10.5 m) high, in Carteret County, Harkers Island Township at 34°41′42″N 76°39′57″W (northwest end), 34°37′37″N 76°31′45″W (southeast end), and 34°40′02″N 76°35′34″W (center) and located on the Harkers Island and Beaufort maps. It trends northwest-southeast from Barden Inlet to Beaufort Inlet. **Other names** Mullet Shore, Shackeford Bank, Shacklefords Bank, Stanford Island, Stanford Islands, and Wades Shore. **Historical note** The feature is named for John Shackleford who purchased the land in 1713. The northwest tip is a spit and was deposited between 1949 and 1971.

Shackleford Banks See Wades Shore

SHACKLEFORD POINT A point of land, 7 ft. (2.1 m) high, in Carteret County, Harkers Island Township at 34°41′10″N 76°39′08″W and located on the Beaufort map. It is near the west end of Shackleford Banks 1.1 mi. (1.8 km) east of Beaufort Inlet and 2.4 mi. (3.8 km) south of the mainland town of Beaufort. **Historical note** Shackleford Point was at one time the western most point on Shackleford Banks, but as a result of deposition from longshore drift, the west most point on Shackleford Banks is 0.9 mi. (1.4 km) further west. Longshore drift refers to sand and other materials being advanced along the shore as a result of oblique or angled waves culminating in a spit or hook at the terminus of the land. See Shackleford Banks for an additional explanatory remark.

Shacklefords Bank See Shackleford Banks

Shackleford Slough See Shackleford Slue

SHACKLEFORD SLUE A channel, 3.5 mi. (5.6 km) long, in Carteret County, Harkers Island and Beaufort townships at 34°41′14″N 76°37′30″W and located on the Harkers Island and Beaufort maps. The channel trends east southeast-west northwest in Back Sound from Middle Marshes to Beaufort Inlet 2.4 mi. (4 km) southeast of the mainland town of Beaufort and it separates Horse Island, Carrot Island, and Middle Marshes from Shackleford Banks. **Other names** Shackleford Bank Channel and Shackleford Slough. **Historical note** The use of the term slue indicates a channel and is more correct than the use of slough which on the Banks indicates a tidal or stagnant area. See Shackleford Banks for an additional explanatory note.

SHAD HOLE A cove in Hyde County, Ocracoke Township at 35°07′57″N 75°55′14″W and located on the Howard Reef map. The cove is located in Pamlico Sound at Hammock Woods 4.5 mi. (7.3 km) northeast of the village of Ocracoke. **Historical note** Shad is a type of anadromous (spawns upstream) fish common to the Outer Banks.

SHAD HOLE CREEK A tidal stream, 0.5 mi. (0.8 km) long, in Hyde County, Ocracoke Township at 35°08′15″N 75°54′35″W and located but not named on the Howard Reef map. The stream heads at 35°07′52″N 75°54′35″W and trends north from unnamed sand dunes to Pamlico Sound at Quokes Point, 4.8 mi. (7.7 km) northeast of the village of Ocracoke and 8.5 mi. (13.6 km) southwest of Hatteras Inlet. **Historical note** See Shad Hole for an explanatory note.

SHALLOWBAG BAY A bay, 1.2 mi. (1.9 km) wide, in Dare County, Nags Head Township at 35°54′30″N 75°39′30″W and located on the Manteo map. The bay is in Roanoke Sound at Manteo 4.2 mi. (6.7 km) southwest of Nags Head. **Other names** Gaskins Creek, Gibs Creek, Gibson Creek, Manteo Bay, Manteo Harbor, Shallow Bag Bay, Shallowbags Bay and Town Creek **Historical note** The origin of the name is not known nor remembered but the name appears unchanged from the earliest maps to the present. The name is most likely totally descriptive. Shallow refers to the feature's overall depth and known to be a problem as evidenced by the frequent use of Ballast Point (q.v.). Bag refers to the feature's shape and was a very common feature reference in the seventeenth century. Also, bag is a common descriptive reference to the slack part in the center of a gill net frequently used in this area.

Shallowbag Bay See Manteo

Shallow Bag Bay See Manteo

Shallow Bag Bay See Shallowbag Bay

Shallowbags Bay See Shallowbag Bay

SHANNONS ISLAND An island, 0.1 mi. (0.2 km) across, in Dare County, Atlantic Township at 36°12′45″N 75°47′15″W and located on the Jarvisburg map. This marsh island is in Currituck Sound, 3.8 mi. (6.1 km) northwest of Duck and 11.9 mi. (19 km) south of Corolla.

SHARK SHOAL A shoal, 1.4 mi. (2.2 km) long, in Dare County, Hatteras Township at 35°16′35″N 75°43′10″W and located on the Hatteras map. The shoal is in Pamlico Sound 3.3 mi. (5.1 km) east of Clam Shoal and 3.4 mi. (5.4 km) north of the village of Hatteras.

SHARK SHOAL A former shoal, about 1 mi. (1.6 km) long, in Carteret County, Beaufort Township at 34°42′53″N 76°41′07″W and located but not named on the Beaufort map. The shoal was at the junction of Bogue Sound and Beaufort Inlet, 1.2 mi. (1.9 km) west of the mainland town of Beaufort. **Historical note** This feature is now the western and southern parts of Radio Island (q.v.).

SHARK SHOAL A former shoal in Carteret County, Portsmouth Township at 35°04′00″N 76°01′20″W and located but not shown on the Portsmouth map. The shoal was at the entrance to Ocracoke Inlet, 3.5 mi. (5.6 km) southwest of the village of Ocracoke. **Historical note** The shoal was actually an extension of Dry Sand Shoal (q.v.) and today is completely awash.

SHARK SHOAL CHANNEL A channel, 2 mi. (3.2 km) long, in Dare County, Hatteras Township at 35°15′30″N 75°43′30″W (south end), 35°16′45″N 75°44′10″W (north end), and 35°15′50″N 75°43′50″W (center) and located but not shown on the Hatteras map. The channel trends south southeast-north northwest in Pamlico Sound just west of Shark Shoal, 4 mi. (6.4 km) north northwest of the village of Hatteras. It is actually an extension of Rollinson Channel.

SHEEP CREEK A water passage, 0.4 mi. (0.6 km) long, in Currituck County, Poplar Branch Township at 36°14′38″N 75°47′23″W and located on the Jarvisburg map. It is a narrow water passage through unnamed marsh islands just south of Little Yankee Pond, 0.6 mi. (1 km) west of Currituck Banks, 6.1 mi. (9.8 km) northwest of Duck and 9.4 mi. (15 km) south of Corolla.

SHEEP ISLAND An island, 0.4 mi. (0.6 km) wide, in Carteret County, Portsmouth Township at 35°04′07″N 76°04′23″W and located on the Portsmouth map. The island is in Pamlico Sound just west of Portsmouth Island and separated from Portsmouth island by Baymarsh Thorofare, 0.5 mi. (0.8 km) west of the village of Portsmouth and 7 mi. (11.2 km) southwest of the village of Ocracoke.

SHEEP ISLAND An island, 0.1 mi. (0.2 km) long, in Carteret County, Harkers Island Township at 34°39′15″N 76°31′34″W and located on the Harkers Island map. It is a marsh island at the junction of Core Sound and Back Sound, 1.6 mi. (2.7 km) north of Barden Inlet and 3.4 mi. (5.4 km) south southeast of the village of Harkers Island.

SHEEP ISLANDS Islands, 0.2 mi. (0.3 km) wide, in Carteret County, Sea Level Township at 34°49′42″N 76°21′10″W and located on the Styron Bay map. The islands are in Core Sound 0.7 mi. (1.1 km) northeast of Big Marsh and 3.4 mi. (5.4 km) south of the mainland village of Atlantic.

SHEEP ISLAND SHOAL A shoal, 1.5 mi. (2.4 km) long and 0.5 mi. (0.8 km) wide, in Carteret County, Portsmouth Township at 35°04′10″N 76°05′10″W and located but not shown on the Portsmouth and Wainwright Island maps. This extensive shoal is in Pamlico sound, 1.2 mi. (1.9 km) west of the village of Portsmouth and 5.5 mi. (8.8 km) southwest of the village of Ocracoke. **Historical note** The northeastern one-third of this shoal often bares at low water.

SHEEP ISLAND SLUE A channel, 0.9 mi. (1.4 km) long, in Carteret County, Harkers Island Township at 34°49′24″N 76°31′32″W and located on the Harkers Island map. The channel is at the junction of Back Sound and Core Sound between Cedar Hammock and Morgan Island separated from Light House Channel by Morgan Island and Sheep Island, 1.8 mi. (2.7 km) north of Barden Inlet and 3.3 mi. (5.3 km) south southeast of the village of Harkers Island. **Historical note** See Shackleford Slue for an explanatory note.

SHEEP ISLAND SLUE A channel, 4 mi. (6.4 km) long, in Carteret County, Portsmouth Township at 35°04′30″N 76°02′55″W (east end), 35°04′07″N 76°06′45″W (west end), and 35°04′45″N 76°04′50″W (center) and located but not shown on the Portsmouth map. The channel trends east-west in Pamlico Sound from Wallace Channel. It is located 1 mi. (1.6 km) northwest of the village of Portsmouth and 6.2 mi. (9.9 km) southwest of the village of Ocracoke. **Historical note** See Shackelford Slue for an explanatory note.

SHEEP PEN CREEK A cove, 0.1 mi. (0.2 km) long, in Carteret County, Sea Level Township at 34°49′43″N 76°20′53″W and located on the Styron Bay map. The cove is in Core Sound 3.4. mi. (5.4 km) south of the mainland village of Atlantic. **Other names** Sheeppen Creek.

SHEEP PEN CREEK A cove, 0.6 mi. (1 km) long and 0.3 mi. (0.5 km) wide, in Carteret County, Smyrna Township at 34°41′49″N 76°28′25″W and located on the Horsepen Point map. The cove is in Core Sound 1 mi. (1.6

km) south of Cowpen Island. **Other names** Sheeppen Creek

Sheeppen Creek See Sheep Pen Creek (Carteret County, Sea Level Township)

Sheeppen Creek See Sheep Pen Creek (Carteret County, Smyrna Township)

SHELLBANK A shore area, 1 mi. (1.6 km) long, in Dare County, Atlantic Township at 36°02′55″N 75°44′23″W and located but not named on the Kitty Hawk map. The feature is situated in Currituck Sound between Shellbank Point and Long Point just north of the entrance to Kitty Hawk Bay, 2.4 mi. (3.8 km) west southwest of Kitty Hawk. **Other names** Shell Bank **Historical note** The name is descriptive for the many shells in the area.

Shellbank See Shellbank Point

Shell Bank See Shellbank

SHELLBANK POINT A point of land in Dare County, Atlantic Township at 36°03′27″N 75°44′30″W and located on the Kitty Hawk map. The point is on Currituck Banks 2.2 mi. (3.5 km) west of Kitty Hawk and 5 mi. (8 km) northwest of the Wright Brothers Memorial. **Other names** Shellbank

SHELL CASTLE An island, 0.1 mi. (0.2 km) wide, in Carteret County, Portsmouth Township at 35°05′53″N 76°04′07″W and located on the Portsmouth map. The island is in Pamlico Sound at the west end of Ocracoke Inlet 2 mi. (3.2 km) north of the village of Portsmouth and 4.9 mi. (7.8 km) west of the village of Ocracoke. **Other names** Castle, Castle Rock, Old Rock, Shell Castle Island, Shell Island, and The Castle **Historical note** The former names of Old Rock and Shell Castle Island were changed to Shell Castle by the owners John Wallace and John Gray Blount in 1789. In 1794 the federal government authorized the construction of a wooden lighthouse on Shell Castle and it was completed in 1798. The owners operated several commercial activities here. It served as a preliminary stop for Portsmouth and other inland ports serving as a "lightering" point or a place for redistributing cargo to smaller vessels for more efficient travel in the shallow sounds and estuaries. There was an area for refreshment and several warehouses available. Today there is no trace of the commercial activities of the island or of the lighthouse.

Shell Castle Island See Shell Castle

SHELL ISLAND An island in Carteret County, Cedar Island Township at 34°59′00″N 76°11′55″W and located on the Wainwright Island map. It is an elongated island in Core Sound 0.8 mi. (1.3 km) northwest of Wainwright Island, 2.5 mi. (4 km) west of Swash Inlet, 9.4 mi. (15.1 km) southwest of the village of Portsmouth and 15.4 mi. (24.7 km) southwest of the village of Ocracoke.

Shell Island See Egg Shoal

Shell Island See Shell Castle

SHELL POINT A point of land in Carteret County, Harkers Island Township at 34°40′56″N 76°31′32″W and located on the Portsmouth map. It is the southeast point of Harkers Island 2.1 mi. (3.4 km) east southeast of the village of Harkers Island. **Historical note** The feature is named for the very large mound of shells left here by Indians over a long period of time.

SHELL ROCK A rock in Currituck County, Poplar Branch Township at

36°14′32″N 75°50′36″W and located but not shown on the Jarvisburg map. The rock is in Currituck Sound 8.8 mi. (14.1 km) south southwest of Corolla and 9.1 mi. (14.5 km) northwest of Southern Shores.

SHINGLE CREEK A cove, 0.1 mi. (0.2 km) wide, in Hyde County, Ocracoke Township at 35°10′11″N 75°39′40″W and located on the Green Island map. The cove is in Pamlico Sound 4.2 mi. (6.7 km) southwest of Hatteras Inlet and 10.2 mi. (16.3 km) northeast of the village of Ocracoke. **Historical note** While the term shingle refers to a kind of beach specifically made up of varying grades of gravel, the definition does not apply here. The origin of the name is unknown.

SHINGLE LANDING A former landing in Dare County, Atlantic Township at 36°00′13″N 75°42′44″W and located but not named on the Kitty Hawk map. The landing was on the south shore of the northwest part of Colington Island, 1.3 mi. (2.1 km) southwest of the village of Colington and 4.1 mi. (6.6 km) south of Kitty Hawk.

SHINGLE POINT A point of land in Carteret County, Davis Township at 34°45′48″N 76°26′34″W and located on the Davis map. It is the west point of two unnamed marsh islands in Core Sound 0.3 mi. (0.5 km) north of Goose Island and 2.7 mi. (4.3 km) south of the mainland town of Davis. **Historical note** See Shingle Creek for an explanatory note.

SHIP CHANNEL A former channel, about 4 mi. (6.4 km) long, in Carteret County, Portsmouth Township at 35°05′30″N 76°02′30″W (southeast end), 35°06′15″N 76°05′10″W (northwest end), and 35°06′50″N 76°03′50″W (center) and located but not shown on the Portsmouth map. The channel was in Pamlico Sound and extended from Blair Channel northwestward in an arc around North Rock to what was formerly Flounder Slue, 4 mi. (6.4 km) west of the village of Ocracoke. **Historical note** The southeastern part of the channel is still partially open but the remainder of the channel has completely closed.

Ship Channel See Blair Channel

SHIPS BAY A cove, 0.5 mi. (0.8 km) wide, in Currituck County, Fruitville Township at 36°24′00″N 75°50′45″W and located on the Corolla map. The cove is in Currituck Sound, 0.7 mi. (1.1 km) north of Raccoon Bay and 1.6 mi. (2.6 km) north northwest of Corolla.

SHOAL POINT A point of land in Dare County, Hatteras Township at 35°12′10″N 75°44′34″W and located but not named on the Hatteras map. The point is just northeast of Hatteras Inlet, 3 mi. (4.8 km) southwest of the village of Hatteras. **Historical note** The feature is awash at high tide.

Shoals Bank See Core Banks

Shoe Hole See Shoehole Bay

SHOEHOLE BAY A bay, 0.3 mi. (0.5 km) across, in Currituck County, Poplar Branch Township at 36°14′08″N 75°48′30″W and located on the Jarvisburg map. It is in Currituck Sound 1.6 mi. (2.6 km) west of Currituck Banks in a small marsh area 5.8 mi. (9.3 km) north northwest of Duck and 10 mi. (16 km) south of Corolla. **Other names** Shoe Hole and The Shoehole

Sholes of Hatteras See Diamond Sholes

SHOOTING HAMMOCK An island, 0.3 mi. (0.5 km) long, in Carteret County, Harkers Island Township at 34°40′06″N 76°34′20″W and located on the Harkers Island map. It is a marsh island in Back Sound at the northeast entrance to Bald Hill Bay 2.1 mi. (3.4 km) south of the village of Harkers Island. **Historical note** The name is a reference to the hunting activity in the area. See Black Hammock for an additional explanatory note about the generic hammock.

SILVER LAKE A harbor, 0.4 mi. (0.6 km) wide, in Carteret County, Ocracoke Township at 35°06′44″N 75°59′07″W and located on the Ocracoke map. The harbor is in Pamlico Sound at the village of Ocracoke. **Other names** Cockle Creek, Cockrel Pond Creek, and Silver Lake Harbor **Historical note** The original name was Cockle Creek and it was a tidal creek at Ocracoke, but it was dredged into a harbor in 1931 and the name was changed to Silver Lake, a term descriptive of its appearance.

Silver Lake Harbor See Silver Lake

SIMPSON NECK A peninsula, 0.9 mi. (1.4 km) long, in Currituck County, Fruitville Township at 36°32′47″N 75°54′45″W and located on the Knotts Island map. The peninsula separates Capsies Creek and Porpoise Slough 2.2 mi. (3.5 km) north of the village of Knotts Island. **Historical note** The generic neck is a term applied by early settlers to interfluves (land between rivers or bodies of water) or peninsulas of land. The term is used extensively in Virginia and Maryland, but rarely used on the Outer Banks, except near the North Carolina-Virginia boundary.

Singers Point See Springers Point

Sir Walter Raleigh Coastland See Outer Banks

SIX MILE HAMMOCK A hummock in Hyde County, Ocracoke Township at 35°08′25″N 75°53′45″W and located but not named on the Howard Reef map. The hummock is an area of high ground on Ocracoke Island 6 mi. (9.7 km) northeast of the village of Ocracoke. **Historical note** The feature was named because of its distance from Ocracoke. Also, see Black Hammock for an explanation of the generic hammock.

Skeeter Hawk See Kitty Hawk

Skiko See Skyco

SKYCO A populated place in Dare County, Nags Head Township at 35°52′38″N 75°40′09″W and located on the Manteo map. It is located on southwest Roanoke Island at Ashbee Harbor 2.2 mi. (3.5 km) south of Manteo. **Other names** Ashbee Harbor, Ashbees Harbor, Ashby Harbor, Ashbys Harbor, and Skiko **Historical note** The original name of the village was Ashbees Harbor, but when the Post Office Department opened a post office here in 1892 the post office was named Skyco. The name was originally spelled Skiko and was named for the son of a chief of the Choanoke Indians who was held hostage by an early military party of English soldiers for their own protection against unfriendly Indians. The village eventually adopted the name of the Post office for the name of the village, but retained Ashbee as the name of the harbor. The decline of the steamship industry decreased the relative importance of Skyco and its post office was discontinued in 1913. Today only a few people live here.

SLOOP CREEK A water passage, 0.4 mi. (0.6 km) long, in Dare County, Atlantic Township at 36°01′17″N 75°40′40″W and located but not named on the Kitty Hawk map. This tidal passage is the northwest section of a water passage that trends southwest from Colington Creek to Dog Point Creek which connects to Blount Bay just north of the village of Colington,

3 mi. (4.8 km) south of Kitty Hawk. **Historical note** See Sloop Island for an explanatory note.

SLOOP ISLAND An island, 0.8 mi. (1.3 km) long and 0.5 mi. (0.8 km) wide, in Dare County, Atlantic Township at 36°01′45″N 75°42′20″W and located on the Kitty Hawk map. The island is in Kitty Hawk Bay just south of Burnt Island, 1.2 mi. (1.9 km) north of the village of Colington, 2.3 mi. (3.7 km) northwest of the Wright Brothers Memorial and 2.4 mi. (3.8 km) south of Kitty Hawk. **Other names** Frying Pan Island **Historical note** Sloop usually refers to a fore and aft or front and back rigged boat with a mainsail or a single mast.

SMITH CREEK A water passage, 0.3 mi. (0.5 km) long, in Dare County, Nags Head Township at 35°48′17″N 75°37′23″W and located on the Oregon Inlet map. It trends north-south in Roanoke Sound and separates Smith Island from Hog Island 3.6 mi. (5.8 km) south southeast of Wanchese.

Smith Inlet See Caffeys Inlet

SMITH ISLAND An island, 0.3 mi. (0.5 km) long, in Dare County, Nags Head Township at 35°48′15″N 75°37′15″W and located on the Oregon Inlet map. It is a marsh island in Roanoke Sound just southeast of Roanoke Island, 1.5 mi. (2.3 km) west of Duck Island and 3.6 mi. (5.8 km) south of Wanchese.

Snake Island See Long Island (Carteret County, White Oak Township)

SOUND LANDING A former landing in Dare County, Atlantic Township at 36°04′00″N 75°44′24″W and located on the Kitty Hawk map. The landing is on Currituck Banks 0.7 mi. (1.1 km) north of Shellbank Point, 2.1 mi. (3.4 km) west of Kitty Hawk and 5.6 mi. (9.1 km) northwest of the Wright Brothers Memorial. **Other names** Botilla and Otilla **Historical note** Historically, this locality was a steamboat landing for vacationers at Nags Head one of the earliest places on the Outer Banks for spending a holiday, but today the landing is rather unimportant because of modern highway access.

Sound of Weapemeoc See Albemarle Sound

Sound of Weapomeiock See Albemarle Sound

Sound of Weapomeiok See Albemarle Sound

Sound of Weopemeiok See Albemarle Sound

SOUND SIDE A former populated place in Dare County, Nags Head Township at 35°57′04″N 75°37′59″W and located on the Manteo map. The locality is now part of Nags Head 3.6 mi. (5.8 km) northeast of Manteo. **Other names** Old Nags Head **Historical note** This was the original location of the settlement around Nags Head and served as a landing area for Nags Head vacationers.

SOUTH BAR A former shoal in Carteret County, Portsmouth Township and located but not shown on the Portsmouth map. The shoal was at the southern approach to Ocracoke Inlet about 4 mi. (6.4 km) southwest of the village of Ocracoke.

SOUTH BITTERSWASH CREEK A cove, 0.1 mi. (0.2 km) long in Hyde County, Ocracoke Township at 35°09′54″N 75°50′25″W and located on the Green Island map. The cove is located in Pamlico Sound, 0.4 mi. (0.6 km) southwest of North Bitterswash Creek and 9.5 mi.(15.2 km) northeast of the village of Ocracoke.

SOUTH BREAKERS An area of breakers in Dare County, Hatteras Township and Hyde County, Ocracoke Township at 35°10′55″N 75°45′05″W and located but not shown on the Hatteras and Green Island maps. The breakers are at the entrance to Hatteras Inlet, 4.5 mi. (7.2 km) southwest of the village of Hatteras.

SOUTH BURRIS ISLAND An island, approximately 0.7 mi. (1.1 km) across, in Currituck County, Poplar Branch Township at 36°16′37″N 75°50′17″W and located on the Mossey Islands map. This is a very irregular shaped marsh island separating Currituck Sound and Burris Bay 0.7 mi. (1.1 km) south of North Burris Island, 7.2 mi. (11.5 km) south of Corolla and 10.3 mi. (16.5 km) north northwest of Duck. **Other names** South Burrus Island

South Burrus Island See South Burris Island

SOUTH CHANNEL A water passage, 1.6 mi. (2.6 km) long, in Currituck County, Fruitville Township at 36°27′20″N 75°53′05″W and located on the Corolla and Barco maps. The water passage is in Currituck Sound just west of the former location of New Currituck Inlet, 5.9 mi. (9.6 km) north northwest of Corolla. **Historical note** This channel is the remnant of the southernmost channel leading from New Currituck Inlet (q.v.). Generally, inlets exhibit two main channels while open and some channels remain in various forms for some time after an inlet closes. There is little or no trace today of the companion northern channel.

South Chicamacomico See Waves

SOUTHEAST SLEW A former channel in Carteret County, Portsmouth Township and located but not shown on the Portsmouth map. The channel was the southwest approach through the shoals at Ocracoke Inlet about 4 mi. (6.4 km) southwest of the village of Ocracoke.

South End See Knotts Landing

SOUTHERNE VIRGINIA SEA A sea. It was applied to the portion of the Atlantic Ocean between the Outer Banks and the Gulf Stream, and generally extended from Cape Hatteras north to Cape Henry in Virginia. **Other names** Sea of Virginy **Historical note** The name appeared on early maps of the New World but never became established and eventually disappeared.

Southern Plantation See South Virginia

SOUTHERN SHORES A populated place in Dare County, Atlantic Township at 36°07′09″N 75°43′45″W and located on the Kitty Hawk map. The community is on south Currituck Banks 3 mi. (4.8 km) north of Kitty Hawk. **Other names** Jeanguite **Historical note** This locality began as a real estate development in the late 1940's, but today is a well established community.

Southern Woods See Waves

South Inlet See Caffeys Inlet

SOUTH NAGS HEAD A populated place in Dare County, Nags Head Township at 35°55′20″N 75°36′20″W and located on the Roanoke Island NE map. The community is just south of Nags Head and just north of Whalebone Junction 4 mi. (6.4 km) west of Manteo.

SOUTH POINT A point of land in Dare County, Kennekeet Township at

35°46′37″N 75°31′30″W and located on the Oregon Inlet map. It is the northern most point of Pea Island at Oregon Inlet 7.8 mi. (12.5 km) southeast of Wanchese.

South Rodanthe See Waves

South Shore See Carova

SOUTH VIRGINIA An historical region. A term historically applied to The Albemarle (q.v.), but fell into disuse in the early 18th century. **Other names** Southern Plantation

SOUTHWEST SPIT A point of land in Dare County, Hatteras Township at 35°11′48″N 75°44′05″W and located but not named on the Hatteras map. The spit is at the Fort Clark ruins, 2.9 mi. (4.6 km) southwest of the village of Hatteras. **Historical note** The feature was formerly the southern tip of Hatteras Island, but today, because of deposition, the feature is 0.6 mi. (1 km) from Hatteras Inlet.

SOUTHWEST STRADDLE A submerged point of land in Carteret County, Cedar Island Township at 35°07′05″N 76°08′30″W and located but not named on Chart 11550. The feature is an underwater point at the southwest point of Royal Shoal in Pamlico Sound, 8 mi. (12.8 km) west of the village of Ocracoke. **Historical note** See Northwest Straddle for an explanatory note.

SPENCER CREEK A cove, 0.1 mi. (0.2 km) wide, in Dare County, Kennekeet Township at 35°22′14″N 75°30′07″W and located on the Ocracoke map. The point is on Ocracoke Island 0.9 mi. (1.4 km) southwest of the village of Ocracoke.

Spit House See Doxeys Salthouse

SPRINGERS POINT A point of land in Hyde County, Ocracoke Township at 35°06′14″N 75°59′24″W and located on the Ocracoke map. The point is on Ocracoke Island 0.9 mi. (1.4 km) southwest of the village of Ocracoke. **Other names** Blackbeards Point and Singers Point

Stanford Island See Shackleford Banks

Stanford Islands See Bogue Banks

Stanford Islands See Shackleford Banks

Stanley Island See Stove Island

Station Bay See Station Bay Cove

STATION BAY COVE A cove, 0.2 mi. (0.3 km) wide, in Currituck County, Poplar Branch Township and Dare County, Atlantic Township at 36°13′53″N 75°46′38″W and located but not named on the Jarvisburg map. The cove is in Currituck Sound at Currituck Banks, 5 mi. (8. km) north northwest of Duck and 10.6 mi. (17 km) southeast of Corolla. **Other names** Station Bay

STEER ISLAND An island, less than 0.1 mi. (0.2 km) across, in Currituck County, Poplar Branch Township at 36°16′50″N 75°49′15″W and located on the Mossey Islands map. It is a small marsh island in Burris Bay at the northeast end of Jarvis Channel, 6.8 mi. (10.9 km) south of Corolla and 9.7 mi. (15.5 km) north northwest of Duck.

Stone Island See Stove Island

Stone Island Point See Stove Island Point

STONE POINT A point of land in Carteret County, Davis Township at

34°45′53″N 76°25′30″W and located on the Davis map. It is located on an unnamed marsh island 0.3 mi. (0.5 km) east of Douglas Point and 3.1 mi. (5 km) south southeast of the mainland town of Davis.

STOVE ISLAND An island, 0.6 mi. (1 km) wide, in Dare County, Atlantic Township at 36°02′37″N 75°44′04″W and located on the Kitty Hawk map. This is a marsh island at the north entrance to Kitty Hawk Bay 2.5 mi. (4 km) west southwest of Kitty Hawk and 8.6 mi. (13.8 km) northwest of Nags Head. **Other names** Stanley Island and Stone Island

STOVE ISLAND POINT A point of land in Dare County, Atlantic Township at 36°02′28″N 75°43′37″W and located but not named on the Kitty Hawk map. The point is on the northeast tip of Stove Island, 2 mi. (3.2 km) west southwest of Kitty Hawk and 4.3 mi. (6.9 km) south of Southern Shores. **Other names** Stone Island Point

STOWES A former populated place in Dare County, Hatteras Township at 35°12′55″N 75°41′55″W and located but not shown on the Hatteras map. The feature was located just west of the village of Hatteras, 4 mi. (6.4 km) northeast of Hatteras Inlet. **Historical note** There was only a windmill and a general store at this small nineteenth century cluster community.

Stowes Hills See Styron Hills

Strate Creek See Straight Creek (Mossey Islands map)

STRAIGHT CREEK A tidal stream, 0.6 mi. (1 km) long, in Currituck County, Poplar Branch Township at 36°17′57″N 75°49′37″W (southeast end), 36°18′10″N 75°49′55″W (northwest end), 36°18′04″N 75°49′47″W (center) and located on the Mossey Islands map. This narrow tidal stream is in the south part of Mossey Islands 0.9 mi. (1.4 km) west of Three Dunes, 5.3 mi. (8.5 km) south of Corolla and 11.2 mi. (17.9 km) north northwest of Duck. **Other names** Strate Creek

STRAIGHT CREEK A water passage, 1 mi. (1.6 km) long, in Currituck County, Poplar Branch Township at 36°14′43″N 75°47′50″W (north end), 36°14′02″N 75°47′38″W (south end), and 36°14′23″N 75°47′43″W (center) and located on the Jarvisburg map. It is a narrow water passage through unnamed marsh islands, 0.3 mi. (0.5 km) east of Pine Island Bay, 5.8 mi. (9.3 km) northwest of Duck and 9.7 mi. (15.5 km) south of Corolla.

STUMPY COVE A cove, 0.5 mi. (0.8 km) wide, in Currituck County, Poplar Branch Township at 36°15′14″N 75°49′17″W and located on the Mossey Islands map. The cove is in Currituck Sound just south of Indian Gap at an unnamed marsh island, 8.5 mi. (13.6 km) south of Corolla and 9.1 mi. (14.6 km) north northwest of Duck.

STYRON HILLS Sand dunes, 23 ft. (7 m) high, in Hyde County, Ocracoke Township at 35°10′52″N 75°46′54″W and located on the Green Island map. The three dunes are at the northeast end of Ocracoke Island, 1.4 mi. (2.2 km) southwest of Hatteras Inlet and 13.2 mi. (21.1 km) northeast of the village of Ocracoke. **Other names** Stowes Hills, Styrons Hill, and The Three Hillocks

Styrons Hill See Styron Hills

SUES CABIN An area in Currituck County, Poplar Branch Township at 36°14′00″N 75°46′45″W and located but not named on the Jarvisburg map. The feature is 5.2 mi. (8.3 km) north northwest of Duck and 10.4 mi. (16.6 km) southeast of Corolla. **Historical note** There was a cabin here and it is reported to have been in existence as early as the eighteenth century. Today the term is still used as a reference.

SUNNY SIDE A populated place, 10 ft. (3 m) high with a population of about 50, in Dare County, Nags Head Township at 35°55′17″N 75°42′37″W and located on the Manteo map. It is located 0.8 mi. (1.3 km) northwest of the Manteo Airport on the northwest part of Roanoke Island and 2.4 mi. (3.8 km) northwest of Manteo. **Historical note** The name is descriptive. The community was predominantly one family who referred to the area as Sunny Side because it receives the afternoon sun.

SWAN ISLAND An island, 0.1 mi. (0.2 km) across, in Currituck County, Poplar Branch Township at 36°19′21″N 75°49′49″W and located on the Mossey Islands map. It is a marsh island in Sanders Bay just north of Mossey Islands, 3.9 mi. (6.2 km) south of Corolla and 12.3 mi. (19.9 km) north northwest of Duck.

SWAN ISLAND An island, 0.4 mi. (0.6 km) long and 0.3 mi. (0.5 km) wide, in Currituck County, Fruitville Township at 36°28′03″N 75°53′50″W and located on the Barco map. It is a marsh island in Currituck Sound 6.9 mi. (11.2 km) north northwest of Corolla.

SWASH CHANNEL A water passage, 0.2 mi. (0.3 km) long, in Hyde County, Ocracoke Township at 35°07′20″N 76°00′20″W and located but not shown on the Portsmouth map. It is in Pamlico Sound between Big Foot Slough Channel and Nine Foot Shoal Channel 1.3 mi. (2.1 km) northwest of the village of Ocracoke. **Historical note** See Daniel Swash for an explanatory note.

SWASH INLET A water passage, 0.8 mi. (1.3 km) long, in Carteret County, Portsmouth Township at 34°58′47″N 76°09′15″W and located on the Wainwright Island map. The water passage connects Core Sound and the Atlantic Ocean and separates Portsmouth Island from the Pilontary Islands and Core Banks 7.5 mi. (12 km) southwest of the village of Portsmouth and 13.5 mi. (21.6 km) southwest of the village of Ocracoke. **Other names** Okok Inlet, Vokokon Inlet, and Whalebone Inlet **Historical note** The inlet was open from before 1585 until the early 18th century, re-opened in 1939 and has remained open since then. The name is somewhat descriptive because the inlet has mostly "shoaled up" and is completely awash only at high tide. See Daniel Swash for an explanatory note.

T

TAR COVE MARSH A marsh, 0.5 mi. (0.8 km) wide, in Currituck County, Poplar Branch Township at 36°16′13″N 75°48′07″W and located on the Mossey Islands map. The marsh area is of recent deposition on the sound side of Currituck Banks 2.9 mi. (4.6 km) south of Three Dunes, 7.8 mi. (12.5 km) south of Corolla and 8.4 mi. (13.4 km) north northwest of Duck.

TAR HOLE BEACH A beach in Hyde County, Ocracoke Township at 35°10′42″N 75°47′07″W and located on the Green Island map. The beach is located on northeast Ocracoke Island at Tar Hole Plains 2.1 mi. (3.4 km) southwest of Hatteras Inlet and 12.9 mi. (20.7 km) northeast of the village of Ocracoke. **Historical note** The name indicates the site where local fishermen "tarred their boats and nets.

TAR HOLE INLET A cove, 0.1 mi. (0.2 km) wide, in Hyde County, Ocracoke Township at 35°11′02″N 75°47′20″W and located but not named on the Green Island map. The cove is in Pamlico Sound 1.6 mi. (2.6 km) west of Hatteras Inlet, 6.2 mi. (9.9 km) southwest of the village of Hatteras and 12.8 mi. (20.5 km) northeast of the village of Ocracoke. **Historical note** See Tar Hole Beach for an explanatory note.

Tar Hole Plain See Tar Hole Plains

TAR HOLE PLAINS A flat, 1 mi. (1.6 km) long, in Hyde County, Ocracoke Township at 35°10′45″N 75°47′10″W and located on the Green Island map. It is just behind Tar Hole Beach on Ocracoke Island near Styron Hills 1.7 mi. (2.7 km) southwest of Hatteras Inlet and 12.9 mi. (20.6 km) northeast of the village of Ocracoke. **Other names** Tar Hole Plain **Historical note** See Tar Hole Beach for an explanatory note.

TARKLE RIDGE COVE A cove, 0.1 mi. (0.2 km) wide, in Dare County, Atlantic Township at 36°03′02″N 75°43′58″W and located but not named on the Kitty Hawk map. The cove is just north of Stove Island, 1.9 mi. (3 km) west southwest of Kitty Hawk and 4 mi. (6.4 km) south southwest of Southern Shores.

TAR LANDING A landing in Carteret County, Morehead Township at 34°41′58″N 76°42′00″W and located but not named on the Beaufort map. The landing is at Tar Landing Bay on east Bogue Banks, 1.5 mi. (2.4 km) south southeast of the mainland town of Morehead City and 2 mi. (3.2 km) east of Atlantic Beach.

TAR LANDING BAY A cove, 0.4 mi. (0.6 km) long, in Carteret County, Morehead Township at 34°42′05″N 76°42′15″W and located on the Beaufort map. The cove is in Bogue Sound at the east end of Bogue Banks 1.6 mi. (2.7 km) southeast of Morehead City and 2 mi. (3.2 km) east of Atlantic Beach.

TATER PATCH COVE A cove, 0.3 mi. (0.5 km) wide, in Dare County, Atlantic Township at 36°00′56″N 75°40′54″W and located but not named on the Kitty Hawk map. The cove is in Colington Creek, 0.5 mi. (0.8 km) west northwest of the Wright Brothers Memorial and 3.2 mi. (5.2 km) south of Kitty Hawk. **Historical note** The name is descriptive, and "tater" is a southern rural colloquialism (spoken language) for potatoe.

TAYLOR CREEK A water passage, 0.4 mi. (0.6 km) long, in Currituck County, Poplar Branch Township at 36°17′53″N 75°50′50″W (east end), 36°17′55″N 75°51′13″W (west end), and 36°17′56″N 75°50′58″W (center) and located on the Mossey Islands map. The water passage is in Currituck Sound just north of Bearhead 5.6 mi. (9 km) south southwest of Corolla and 11.7 mi. (18.7 km) northwest of Duck.

TAYLOR CREEK A water passage, 2.6 mi. (4.2 km) long, in Carteret County, Beaufort Township at 34°42′27″N 76°37′05″W (east end), 34°42′45″N 76°39′30″W (west end), and 34°42′34″N 76°38′15″W (center) and located on the Beaufort and Harkers Island maps. The water passage separates Carrot Island from the mainland and is 4.4 mi. (7 km) east of the village of Harkers Island.

Teache Hole See Teaches Hole

TEACHES HOLE A channel in Hyde County, Ocracoke Township at 35°04′20″N 76°01′00″W and located but not shown on the Portsmouth map. The channel is in Pamlico Sound at the entrance to Blair Channel and Teaches Hole Channel just north of Ocracoke Inlet 3.1 mi. (5 km) southwest of the village of Ocracoke. **Other names** Teache Hole and Thatchs Hole **Historical note** The "notorious" pirate, Edward Teach or Thatch (Blackbeard), was killed off this point on November 22, 1718 by Lieutenant Robert Maynard, who had been dispatched by Governor Spotswood of Virginia, specifically to rid the Carolina coasts of Blackbeard and his pirates. The name Springers Point was an established name and Blackbeard's Point has always been a secondary name that indicates the battle. A nearby Channel is known as Teaches Hole Channel (q.v.).

TEACHES HOLE CHANNEL A channel, 1.8 mi. (2.9 km) long, in Hyde County, Ocracoke Township at 35°06′00″N 76°00′04″W and located on the Ocracoke and Portsmouth maps. The channel is in Pamlico Sound and extends from Ocracoke Inlet to Silver Lake at Ocracoke. **Historical note** See Teaches Hole for an explanatory note.

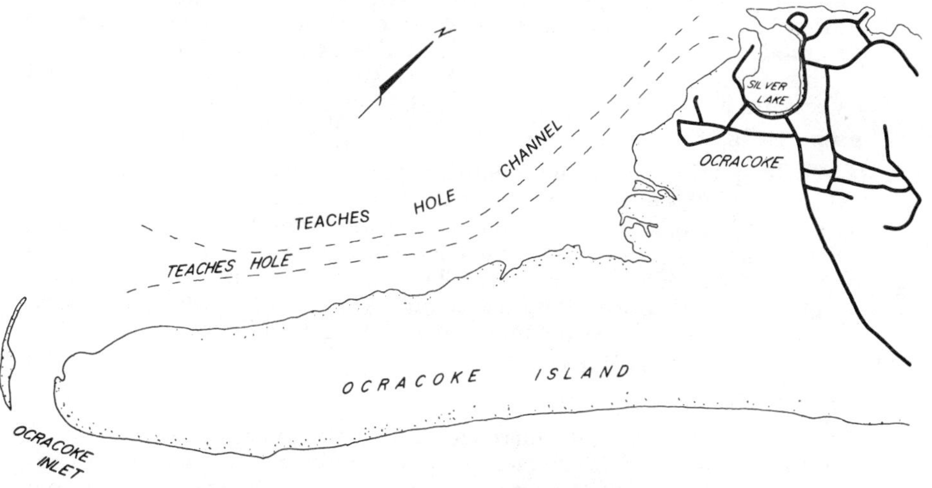

TEAL ISLAND An island, 0.2 mi. (0.3 km) long, in Carteret County, Harkers Island Township at 34°41′24″N 76°29′37″W and located on the Horsepen Point map. The island is in Core Sound 0.5 mi. (0.8 km) north of Hogpen Bay and 3.7 mi. (6 km) east of the village of Harkers Island. **Historical note** A teal is one of many surface feeding ducks common on the Outer Banks.

TERRAPIN CREEK A cove, 0.3 mi. (0.5 km) long and 0.05 mi. (0.08 km) wide, in Dare County, Kennekeet Township at 35°42′24″N 75°30′14″W and located on the Pea Island map. The cove trends east northeast-west southwest in Pamlico Sound to Terrapin Creek Bay 5.7 mi. (9.2 km) south of Oregon Inlet and 8 mi. (12.8 km) north northwest of Rodanthe. **Historical note** The term is an Anglicized version of an Algonquian Indian word that refers to any of various North American turtles inhabiting fresh or brackish waters.

TERRAPIN CREEK BAY A bay, 1.2 mi. (1.9 km) wide, in Dare County, Kennekeet Township at 35°41′54″N 75°30′15″W and located on the Pea Island map. The bay is in Pamlico Sound, 6.2 mi. (10 km) south of Oregon Inlet and 7.5 mi. (12.1 km) north of Rodanthe. **Historical note** See Terrapin Creek for an explanatory note.

TERRAPIN CREEK POINT A point of land in Dare County, Kennekeet Township at 35°42′23″N 75°30′35″W and located on the Pea Island map. It is the north point of Terrapin Creek Bay and the South point of Pea Island Bay on a marsh island 5.5 mi. (8.9 km) south of Oregon Inlet and 8.1 mi. (13 km) north northwest of Rodanthe. **Historical note** See Terrapin Creek for an explanatory note.

TERRAPIN POINT A point of land in Dare County, Kennekeet Township at 35°24′37″N 75°29′38″W and located on the Little Kinnakeet map. It is a marsh point on Hatteras Island 0.3 mi. (0.5 km) northwest of Little Kinnakeet and 4.4 mi. (7 km) north of Avon. **Historical note** See Terrapin Creek for an explanatory note.

TERRAPIN SHOAL A shoal, 0.9 mi. (1.4 km) long, in Hyde County, Ocracoke Township at 35°09′42″N 75°51′30″W and located but not shown on the Howard Reef map. The shoal is in Pamlico Sound at Ocracoke Island 6.7 mi. (8.3 km) northeast of the village of Ocracoke. **Other names** Great Swash and The Great Swash. **Historical note** Terrapin Shoal is in the vicinity of Old Hatteras Inlet (q.v.). See Terrapin Creek for an explanatory note about the word terrapin.

Thatchs Hole See Teaches Hole

THE ALBEMARLE A region; there is some controversy as to the extent of the region but it at least included the present counties of Currituck, Dare, Camden, Pasquotank, Perquimans, Chowan, Gates, Tyrrell, Washington, Bertie, and Hertford and was located at approximately 36°12′00″N 76°12′00″W. **Historical note** This term continues to have some regional significance today, especially when referring to agricultural activity. See Albemarle Sound for an additional explanatory note.

The Banks See Outer Banks

The Barn See Maiden Paps

THE BEACH An historical reference. The term was used by the residents of Hatteras and Pea islands as a general reference to the barrier islands north of Oregon Inlet. The actual limits of extent are somewhat vague, but usually extended to Kitty Hawk and sometimes to Duck and beyond.

The Bight See Hatteras Bight

The Cape See Buxton

The Cape See Cape Lookout (former populated place)

The Castle See Shell Castle

The Colonies' Gibralter See Cape Lookout

The Creek See Cockrel Creek

THE CROSSROADS An area in Carteret County, Portsmouth Township at 35°04′10″N 76°03′50″W and located but not named on the Portsmouth map. It is the main intersection in the center of Portsmouth - formerly a colonial commercial center but today the area is deserted.

THE CUTOFF A water passage in Dare County, Nags Head Township at 35°48′20″N 75°33′45″W and located on the Oregon Inlet map. The water passage is at the southeast end of Roanoke Sound just south of Off Island, 4.5 mi. (7.2 km) southeast of Wanchese.

The Diamond See Diamond Shoals

The Diamonds See Diamond Shoals

The Diamond Shoals See Inner Diamond Shoals

THE DITCH A water passage in Hyde County, Ocracoke Township at 35°06′52″N 75°59′21″W and located but not named on the Ocracoke map. It is the entrance way from Pamlico Sound to Silver Lake, the harbor at the village of Ocracoke.

THE DITCH A water passage, 0.1 mi. (0.2 km) long, in Carteret County, Harkers Island Township at 34°38′23″N 76°31′23″W and located on the Harkers Island map. It trends east-west and connects Blinds Hammock Bay to Barden Inlet 4.3 mi. (6.9 km) southeast of the village of Harkers Island.

The Dividing Creek See Colington Cut

THE DRAIN A cove, 0.3 mi. (0.5 km) long, in Dare County, Kennekeet Township at 35°24′57″N 75°29′34″W and located on the Little Kinnakeet map. The cove is in Pamlico Sound 0.7 mi. (1.1 km) north of Little Kinnakeet and 4.9 mi. (7.9 km) north of Avon.

The Drain See Barden Inlet

The Eastern End See Diamond City

THE EVERGREENS A tidal flat, 3 mi. (4.8 km) long, in Carteret County, Portsmouth Township at 35°02′15″N 76°05′10″W and located but not named on the Portsmouth map. The area is an area of Portsmouth Island that is inundated at high tide but is separated from the Atlantic Ocean by a narrow beach. It is 1.5 mi. (2.4 km) south southwest of the village of Portsmouth and 7.5 mi. (12 km) southwest of the village of Ocracoke.

THE FLATS A flat, 0.5 mi. (0.8 km) across, in Dare County, Atlantic Township at 35°59′53″N 75°39′30″W and located but not named on the Manteo and Kitty Hawk maps. This flat, sandy area is just north of the Fresh Ponds, 3.1 mi. (5 km) north of Nags Head.

The Graveyard See Diamond Shoals

The Great Fish Ponds See Fresh Ponds

The Great Fresh Ponds See Fresh Ponds

The Great River See Gulf Stream

THE GREAT SWASH A marsh, 2 mi. (3.2 km) wide, in Hyde County, Ocracoke Township at 35°09′21″N 75°51′30″W and located on the Green Island map. The marsh area is in Pamlico Sound 8.3 mi. (13.3 km) northeast of the village of Ocracoke. **Other names** Great Swash **Historical note** A swash is an area that is almost continually awash with waves or water and is rarely dry. The Great Swash is the site of Old Hatteras Inlet (q.v.).

The Great Swash See Terrapin Shoal

The Harbor See Chicamacomico Channel

THE HAULOVER A water passage, 0.5 mi. (0.8 km) long, in Carteret County, Portsmouth Township at 35°03′20″N 76°05′02″W and located on the Portsmouth map. The water passage is in Pamlico Sound southwest of Evergreen Island 1.5 mi. (2.4 km) southwest of the village of Portsmouth and 7.5 mi. (12 km) southwest of the village of Ocracoke. **Historical note** See Haulover Point for an explanatory note.

THE HAULOVER A flat in Dare County, Kennekeet Township at

35°16′15″N 75°31′15″W and located but not shown on the Buxton map. The flat is the remnant of former Chaneandepeco Inlet 1.1 mi. (1.8 km) east of Buxton and 2.3 mi. (3.7 km) north of Cape Hatteras. **Historical note** See Haulover Point for an explanatory note.

The Haulover See Barden Inlet

The Haulover See Chaneandepeco Inlet

The Haven See Trinitie Harbor

THE HIGH HILLS Sand dunes, 22 ft. (6.4 m) high, in Carteret County, Portsmouth Township at 34°53′40″N 76°15′37″W and located but not named on the Atlantic map. The hills are 4.2 mi. (6.7 km) north of Old Drum Inlet (Portsmouth and Atlantic Townships) and 4.6 mi. (7.4 km) east of the mainland town of Atlantic. **Historical note** The name is descriptive and was used especially on Core Banks to indicate dunes that were never awash and could be used as landmarks.

THE HIGH HILLS A marsh, 0.5 mi. (0.8 km) wide, in Carteret County, Portsmouth Township at 35°01′15″N 76°06′42″W and located on the Portsmouth map. The marsh is on Portsmouth Island just northeast of Whalebone Inlet, 4.4 mi. (7 km) southwest of the village of Portsmouth and 10.4 mi. (16.7 km) southwest of the village of Ocracoke. **Historical note** The feature is now usually awash, and the hills indicated by the name are all but gone. See High Hills above for an additional explanatory note.

THE INSIDE A former area. This was a previously popular term, especially on Hatteras and Pea islands, used on the Outer Banks prior to the building of roadways. It referred to any of the pathways or vehicle tracks behind the beach dunes used for transportation. The term fell into disuse in the 1940s and 1950s after the building of State Highway 12.

The Kill Devil Hills See Kill Devil Hills (sand dunes)

THE KNOLL A sand dune, 22 ft. (6.7 m) high, in Hyde County, Ocracoke Township at 35°08′35″N 75°52′53″W and located on the Howard Reef map. The dune is on Ocracoke Island 6.8 mi. (10.9 km) south of Hatteras Inlet and 7.8 mi. (12.5 km) north of the village of Ocracoke.

The Lead See Great Gap (Currituck County, Poplar Branch Township)

The Marshes See Roanoke Marshes

The Nags Head See Nags Head

The Narrows See Croatan Sound

THEOFF POINT A point of land in Dare County, Nags Head Township at 35°49′23″N 75°34′35″W and located on the Oregon Inlet map. It is a marsh point on southeast Bodie Island, 0.3 mi. (0.5 km) north of Cedar Island, 0.8 mi. (1.3 km) northwest of Bodie Island Lighthouse and 3.8 mi. (6.1 km) east southeast of Wanchese. **Historical note** The name is a contraction and reference to a nearby water passage known as The Cutoff. The one-word form is probably a transcribing error.

The Point See Cape Point (Dare County)

The Port of Beacon Island See Beacon Island Roads

THE PLAINS A flat, 1.5 mi. (2.4 km) long, in Hyde County, Ocracoke Township at 35°07′04″N 75°57′00″W and located on the Ocracoke map. The flat sandy area is at the southwest end of Ocracoke Island 2.1 mi. (3.4

km) northeast of the village of Ocracoke. **Historical note** The name is derived from the extreme flatness and the pure white sand found there.

THE RUN A former stream in Dare County, Atlantic or Nags Head Townships and located but not shown on the Manteo map. It was a small stream that formerly connected Fresh Ponds to Roanoke Sound prior to 1900. **Historical note** The former stream's course is not certain, but it is likely to have had its source in the Fresh Ponds and flowed either west or southwest to Roanoke Sound through Nags Head Woods approximately 1 mi. (1.6 km) north of Manns Point or approximately 0.5 mi. (0.8 km) northeast of Manns Point and approximately 3 mi. (4.8 km) northwest of Nags Head.

THE SANDS A beach, 1.5 mi. (2.4 km) long, in Carteret County, Portsmouth Township at 34°54′25″N 76°14′37″W and located on the Wainwright Island map. The beach is on Core Banks just southwest of Old House Beach, 14.7 mi. (23.5 km) southwest of the village of Portsmouth and 20.7 mi. (33.1 km) southwest of the village of Ocracoke.

The Shoals See Diamond Shoals

The Shoehole See Shoehole Bay

THE SLASH A water passage, 1 mi. (1.6 km) wide, in Dare County, Hatteras Township at 35°13′14″N 75°41′02″W and located on the Hatteras map. The water passage is located in Pamlico Sound at the village of Hatteras. **Historical note** The name is descriptive of the appearance of the feature.

THE SLUE A former channel, about 1 mi. (1.6 km) long, in Carteret County, Morehead Township at 34°40′45″N 76°42′15″W and located but not shown on the Beaufort map. The channel separated two unnamed shoals in the Atlantic Ocean, 2.5 mi. (4 km) southwest of Beaufort Inlet and 3.2 mi. (5.1 km) south of the mainland town of Morehead City. **Historical note** The feature had disappeared by the twentieth century. See Shackleford Slue for an additional explanatory note.

The Sound See Core Sound

The Sound See Pamlico Sound

The Spit See Hatteras Shoals

The Spit See Inner Diamond Shoal

THE STRAITS A water passage, 4 mi. (6.4 km) long and 0.5 mi. (0.8 km) wide, in Carteret County, Harkers Island Township at 34°42′50″N 76°31′14″W (east end), 34°43′15″N 76°55′23″W (west end), and 34°43′01″N 76°33′15″W (center) and located on the Harkers Island map. The water passage separates Harkers Island and Browns Island from the mainland and connects Core Sound and North River 1.4 mi. (2.2 km) north of the village of Harkers Island. **Other names** Core Sound

THE SWASH A cove, 0.8 mi. (1.3 km) long and 0.4 mi. (0.6 km) wide, in Carteret County, Smyrna Township at 34°47′14″N 76°23′42″W and located on the Davis map. The cove is in Core Sound between Horse Island and Core Banks 3.8 mi. (6.1 km) east of the mainland town of Davis. **Other names** Horse Island Bay **Historical note** See Daniel Swash for an explanatory note.

THE THOROFARE A water passage, 0.6 mi. (1 km) long, in Currituck County, Poplar Brach Township at 36°19′32″N 75°51′03″W (south end), 36°19′55″N 75°50′53″W (north end), and 36°19′44″N 75°50′59″W (center)

and located on the Mossey Islands map. The water passage is in Currituck Sound between Thorofare Island and Brant Island, 3.5 mi. (5.6 km) south southwest of Corolla and 13.2 mi. (21.1 km) north northwest of Duck. **Other names** Throufare Creek

The Three Dunes See Three Dunes

The Three Hillocks See Styron Hills

The Three Sand Hills See Three Dunes

THE TRENCH A cove, 0.3 mi. (0.5 km) long, in Dare County, Kennekeet Township at 35°43′10″N 75°30′37″W and located on the Pea Island map. The cove is between Goose Island Point and Pea Island Point 4.8 mi. (7.7 km) south of Oregon Inlet and 8.7 mi. (13.9 km) north northeast of Rodanthe.

The Western Ocean See Atlantic Ocean

THOROFARE ISLAND An island, 0.3 mi. (0.5 km) long, in Currituck County, Poplar Branch Township at 36°19′53″N 75°51′05″W and located on the Mossey Islands map. It is in Currituck Sound just north of The Thorofare, 5.3 mi. (8.5 km) south southwest of Corolla and 13.7 mi. (21.9 km) north northwest of Duck. **Other names** Throufare Island

THREE DUNES Sand dunes, 55.8 ft. (17 m) high (north dune), 67.3 ft. (20.5 m) high (center dune), and 45.9 ft. (14 m) high (south dune), in Currituck County, Poplar Branch Township at 36°18′43″N 75°48′44″W (north dune), 36°18′05″N 75°48′23″W (south dune), and 36°18′27″N 75°48′36″W (center dune) and located on Currituck Banks 1 mi. (1.6 km) east of Mossey Islands, 5 mi. (8 km) south southeast of Corolla and 11 mi. (17.6 km) north northwest of Duck. **Other names** The Three Dunes, The Three Sand Hills, and Three Sand Hills

THREE HATS SHOAL A shoal, 1.5 mi. (2.4 km) across in Carteret County, Portsmouth Township at 35°04′30″N 76°08′00″W and located but not shown on the Portsmouth map. The shoal is in Pamlico Sound, 3.5 mi. (5.6 km) west of the village of Portsmouth and 8 mi. (12.4 km) west southwest of the village of Ocracoke. **Historical note** The shape of the feature on early charts bears some resemblance to three hats, otherwise the origin of the name is unknown.

Three Sand Hills See Three Dunes

Throufare Creek See The Thorofare

Throufare Island See Thorofare Island

TILLETS CAMP A former camp in Dare County, Atlantic Township and located but not shown on the Manteo map. The camp was just north of Jockeys Ridge and about 2 mi. (3.2 km) north northwest of Nags Head. **Other names** Tillets Fish Camp **Historical note** See Ira Morris Camp for an explanatory note.

Tillets Fish Camp See Tillets Camp

TILLETT COVE A cove in Dare County, Atlantic Township at 36°03′10″N 75°42′40″W and located but not named on the Kitty Hawk map. The cove is in the north part of Kitty Hawk Bay at Poor Ridge Landing, 1 mi. (1.6 km) southwest of Kitty Hawk and 8.1 mi. (13 km) northwest of Nags Head.

Titepano See Currituck Sound

TOMBSTONE POINT A point of land in Carteret County, Morehead

Township at 34°42′10″N 76°41′20″W and located on the Beaufort map. The point of land is on the east end of Bogue Banks 2.1 mi. (3.3 km) southeast of the mainland town of Morehead City and 2.9 mi. (4.4 km) east of Atlantic Beach.

TOMMY HAMMOCK A hummock, 0.2 mi. (0.3 km) wide and 5 ft. (1.5 m) high, in Dare County, Nags Head Township at 35°51′10″N 75°35′37″W and located on the Oregon Inlet map. This area of high ground is on southwest Bodie Island 2.9 mi. (4.7 km) northwest of Bodie Island Lighthouse and 2.9 mi. (4.7 km) north northeast of Wanchese. **Other names** Tommys Hammock

Tommys Hammock See Tommy Hammock

Topsail Inlet See Beaufort Inlet

Torpedo Junction See Diamond Shoals

Town Creek See Shallowbag Bay

TOWN MARSH A marsh, 0.4 mi. (0.6 km) long and 0.2 mi. (0.3 km) wide, in Carteret County, Beaufort Township at 34°42′45″N 76°40′20″W and located on the Beaufort map. The marsh is just south of the mainland town of Beaufort and 3 mi. (4.8 km) east of the mainland town of Morehead City.

TOWN MARSH CHANNEL A former channel, about 1 mi. (1.6 km) long in Carteret County, Beaufort Township at 34°42′37″N 76°40′20″W and located but not shown on the Beaufort map. The channel separated Town Marsh from Bird Island Shoal, 1.2 mi. (1.9 km) south of the mainland town of Beaufort.

Trent See Frisco

Trent Woods See Frisco

Trent Woods See Frisco Woods

Trinety Harbor See Caffeys Inlet

Trinety Harbor See Trinitie Harbor

TRINITIE HARBOR A former water passage in Dare County, Atlantic Township at 36°12′15″N 75°45′53″W and located on the Jarvisburg map. The former inlet connected Albemarle Sound through Currituck Banks to the Atlantic Ocean about 3 mi. (4.8 km) northwest of Duck and approximately 6.8 mi. (11 km) north northwest of Kitty Hawk. **Other names** New Inlet, The Haven, Trinety Harbor, Trinitie Harbro, Trinity Harbor, Wercester Inlet, and Worcester Inlet **Historical note** The inlet opened prior to 1585 and closed prior to 1660, and is named because it was discovered on one of the Sundays after Trinity. The location of the inlet is very controversial and many different locations for the inlet are given by authors who have written about the Outer Banks. Jeanguite Creek, Caffeys Inlet, and a site approximately 5 mi. (8 km) north of Caffeys Inlet near Poyners Hill are the most frequently cited locations for Trinitie Harbor. The inlet is believed to have been in the vicinity of former Caffeys Inlet, but approximately 1 mi. (1.6 km) south of former Caffeys Inlet. It is likely that this was the inlet first used by Amadas and Barlowe who were among the first to explore the Outer Banks. They were dispatched by Sir Walter Raleigh to locate a suitable site for establishing a colony. Their report of the area was highly favorable and several years of exploring began which culminated in the disappearance of the Lost Colony. Amadas and Barlowe had taken the Indians, Manteo and

Wanchese, to England in 1584 and they returned in 1585. It should also be noted that the use of the generic harbor to refer to an inlet was common until the 18th century and indicates that ships rode at anchor just off the beach near the inlet.

Trinitie Harbor See Caffeys Inlet

Trinitie Harbor See Currituck Inlet

Trinitie Harbro See Trinitie Harbor

Trinity Harbor See Trinitie Harbor

TRY YARD CREEK A water passage, 0.3 mi. (0.5 km) long, in Carteret County, Smyrna Township at 34°41′23″N 76°28′53″W and located on the Horsepen Point map. The water passage is in Core Sound and separates Core Banks from an unnamed marsh island 4.4 mi. (7 km) east of the village of Harkers Island. **Historical note** The origin of the name is not clear to many people today, and some believe it to be a reference to nautical terminology as in "lieing to" or "coming about." However, the term "try yard" really refers to a place where a beached whale was processed as a result of the former Outer Banks method of whaling which relied on the occasional beached whale or later by attacking the whale from longboats launched through the surf. The name was applied historically when a now obsolete meaning of the word "try" meant to render oil from blubber or fat.

TRY YARD CREEK A cove, 0.2 mi. (0.3 km) wide, in Hyde County, Ocracoke Township at 35°08′02″N 75°53′42″W and located on the Howard Reef map. The cove is in Pamlico Sound, 6.1 mi. (9.8 km) northeast of the village of Ocracoke and 7.6 mi. (12.2 km) southwest of Hatteras Inlet. **Historical note** See Try Yard Creek above for an explanatory note.

Two Legged Lump See Legged Lump

U

UNCLE JIMMYS LANDING A landing, in Dare County, Kennekeet Township at 35°36′02″N 75°28′10″W and located on the Rodanthe map. The landing is 0.4 mi. (0.6 km) northeast of Greens Point and 0.5 mi. (0.8 km) northwest of Rodanthe.

Upper End See Manteo

UPPER MIDDLE A shoal, 2.2. mi. (3.5 km) long, in Hyde County, Ocracoke Township at 35°17′25″N 76°20′00″W and located on Chart number 11555. The shoal is on the northwest part of a large shoal named Middle Ground in Pamlico Sound 19.6 mi. (31.2 km) northwest of Ocracoke Inlet and 19.8 mi. (31.5 km) northwest of the village of Ocracoke.

Upper Middle See Middle Ground (35°15′20″N 76°18′00″W)

V

VERA CRUZ SHOAL A shoal, 0.4 mi. (0.6 km) long, in Carteret County, Portsmouth Township at 35°03′57″N 76°01′34″W and located on the Portsmouth map. The shoal is in Ocracoke Inlet 2.1 mi. (3.4 km) east of the village of Portsmouth and 4.2 mi. (6.7 km) southwest of the village of

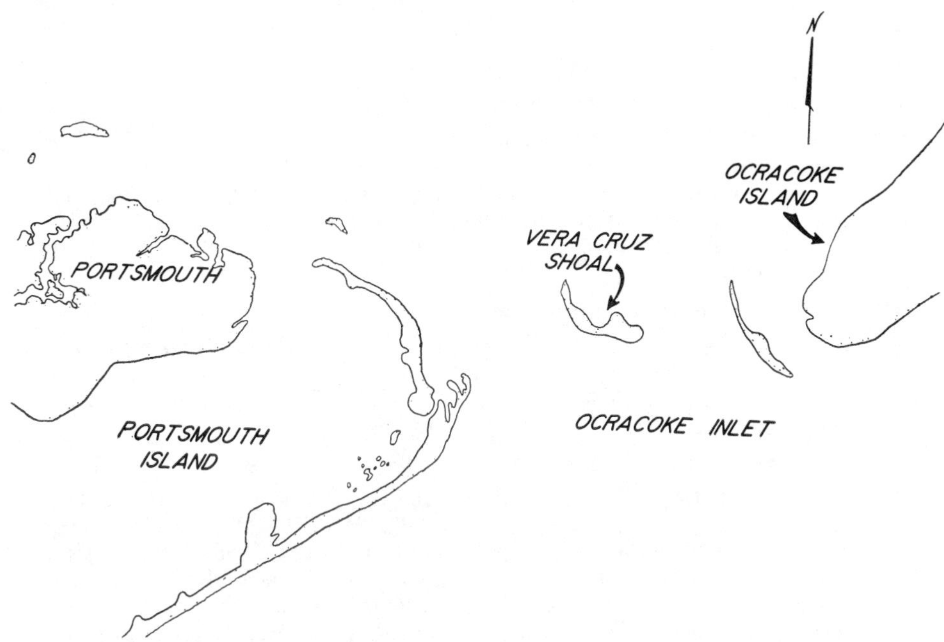

Ocracoke. **Other names** Dry Sand Shoal and Dry Shoal Point **Historical note** The shoal was originally named Dry Sand Shoal in the 18th century because it was only covered with water during storms. The name of the shoal changed in the early twentieth century after the ship Vera Cruz VII was stranded here on May 8 and 9, 1903. All passengers, crew, and cargo were saved; and remnants of the Vera Cruz are still on the shoal.

Verazzano Isthmus See Outer Banks

Verazzanos Sea See Pamlico Sound

Vieu Passage See Gunt Inlet

View Passage See Gunt Inlet

View Passage See Roanoke Inlet

VIRGINIA An historical region. Prior to the settlement of Jamestown, the area in and around Roanoke Island and all English lands in North America were named Virginia in honor of Queen Elizabeth I of England "the virgin queen." Since the Roanoke Island colony failed and the first successful colony was further north at Jamestown, the name Virginia was applied to that colony.

Virginia See Outer Banks

Vokokon See Ocracoke Island

Vokokon See Wococon

Vokokon Inlet See Swash Inlet

W

Wades Hammock See Wades Shore

WADES SHORE A former populated place in Carteret County, Harkers Island Township and located but not shown on the Harkers Island map. It was formerly a small community of about 100 people located on the north or sound side of western Shackleford Banks near Mullet Pond. **Other names** Mullet Pond, Mullet Shore, Shackleford, Shackleford Banks and Wades Hammock

Wades Shore See Shackleford Banks

WADING POINT A point of land in Carteret County, Harkers Island Township at 34°42′43″N 76°32′54″W and located on the Harkers Island map. The point of land is the northwest point of Browns Island 1.3 mi. (2.1 km) northeast of the village of Harkers Island.

Wainwright Channel See Wainwright Slue

WAINWRIGHT ISLAND An island, 0.3 mi. (0.5 km) wide, in Carteret County, Cedar Island Township at 34°59′24″N 76°12′32″W and located on the Wainwright Island map. The island is in Core Sound 3.3 mi. (5.2 km) east of Harbor Island, 10.2 mi. (16.3 km) southwest of the village of Portsmouth and 16.2 mi. (25.9 km) southwest of the village of Ocracoke. **Historical note** The feature is named for James Wainwright who settled in the area.

Wainwright Slough See Wainwright Slue

WAINWRIGHT SLUE A channel, 1 mi. (1.6 km) long, in Carteret County, Cedar Island Township at 34°59′45″N 76°11′45″W and located but not shown on the Wainwright Island map. The channel is in Core Sound at its junction with Pamlico Sound just east of Wainwright Island and 12.7 mi. (20.3 km) south of the village of Ocracoke. **Other names** Wainwright Channel and Wainwright Slough **Historical note** See Wainwright Island and Shackleford Slue for explanatory notes.

Wakokon Inlet See Ocracoke Inlet

Walaces Channel See Wallace Channel

WALKER ISLAND An island, 0.6 mi. (1 km) long and 0.3 mi. (0.5 km) wide, in Dare County, Atlantic Township at 36°00′04″N 75°41′02″W and located but not named on the Kitty Hawk and Manteo maps. The island separates Colington Creek from Deep Ditch and is 1 mi. (1.6 km) southeast of the village of Colington and 4.5 mi. (7.2 km) northwest of Nags Head.

WALLACE CHANNEL A channel in Carteret County, Portsmouth Township at 35°05′15″N 76°02′50″W and located but not shown on the Portsmouth map. The channel is in Ocracoke Inlet just west of Blair Channel 3.7 mi. (5.9 km) southwest of the village of Ocracoke. **Other names** Beacon Island Road, Beacon Island Roads, Walaces Channel, Wallaces Channel, and Walliss Channel **Historical note** The dredging of the channel to keep it open was begun in 1895. There is some confusion as to the origin of the name, and it is either named for John Walace "governor" or part owner of Shell Castle (q.v.) in the late 18th and early 19th centuries or for David Wallace, Jr., whose house on Portsmouth Island was used as a sighting point by pilots using the channel as they entered Ocracoke Inlet from the Atlantic Ocean.

Wallaces Channel See Wallace Channel

Walliss Channel See Wallace Channel

Walter Island See Pond Island

Walter Rawleigh Sound See Roanoke Sound

WALTER SLOUGH A channel, 0.8 mi. (1.3 km) long, in Dare County, Nags Head Township at 35°47′30″N 75°33′30″W (east end), 35°47′32″N 75°34′15″W (west end), and 35°47′30″N 75°33′59″W (center) and located on the Oregon Inlet map. The channel is in Pamlico Sound just north of Old House Slough just northwest of Oregon Inlet and 5.6 mi. (9 km) southeast of Wanchese.

WANCHESE A populated place, 10 ft. (3 m) high with a population of about 950, in Dare County, Nags Head Township at 35°50′34″N 75°38′20″W and located on the Wanchese and Oregon Inlet maps. It is a scattered community located on the southern part of Roanoke Island 5.1 mi. (8.3 km) south of Manteo. **Other names** Lower End **Historical note** The community was named for one of the two Indians taken to England by Amadas and Barlowe in 1584. Wanchese was sometimes referred to as Lower End and Manteo as Upper End because of their relative locations on Roanoke Island, but many felt that this reference was improper and the name Lower End fell into disuse. Wanchese is the commercial fishing center for the Outer Banks.

WARE CREEK A tidal stream, 0.7 mi. (1.1 km) long, in Currituck County, Poplar Branch Township at 36°17′53″N 75°48′47″W and located on the Mossey Islands map. It is in a marshy sound side area of Currituck Banks, 0.7 mi. (1.1 km) south of Three Dunes, 6 mi. (9.6 km) south of Corolla and 10.2 mi. (16.3 km) north northwest of Duck. **Historical note** The spelling of ware is probably a misspelling of weir. See Weir Point for an explanatory note.

WARREN GILGOS CREEK A cove, 0.2 mi. (0.3 km) long, in Carteret County, Portsmouth Township at 35°04′05″N 76°04′10″W and located on the Portsmouth map. The cove is just east of Baymarsh Thorofare 0.4 mi. (0.6 km) west southwest of the village of Portsmouth and 6.8 mi. (11 km) southwest of the village of Ocracoke.

WARRENS ISLAND An island, 0.3 mi. (0.5 km) across, in Dare County, Nags Head Township at 35°53′30″N 75°36′14″W and located but not named on the Roanoke Island NE map. The island is in Roanoke Sound at Bodie Island just north of Headquarters Island, 5 mi. (8 km) south of Nags Head and 5.2 mi. (8.3 km) southeast of Manteo.

WASH WOODS A former woods in Currituck County, Fruitville Township at 36°30′28″N 75°52′00″W and located on the Corolla map. It is an area of stumps, the remnants of a former wooded area, approximately 4 mi. (6.4 km) south of the North Carolina-Virginia boundary and 6.5 mi. (10.4 km) north northwest of Corolla. **Historical note** The feature is so named because of the many tree stumps that are awash at low tide.

Wash Woods See Deals

Water Bush Island See Goose Island (Dare County, Atlantic Township)

WAVES A populated place, 5 ft. (1.5 m) high with a population of about 65, in Dare County, Kennekeet Township, at 35°33′57″N 75°28′10″W and located on the Rodanthe map. It is located on Hatteras Island, 1.9 mi. (3.1 km) south of Rodanthe and 2 mi. (3.2 km) north of Salvo. **Other names**

Chicamacomico, Chickamicomico, South Chicamacomico, Southern Woods, South Rodanthe and Waves P.O. **Historical note** A post office was established here in 1939 and the name Waves was chosen for no apparent reason other than its reference to the environment. The Post Office Department avoided using the original community name of Chicamacomico because it was too difficult to spell and was confusing. Actually, Chicamacomico was a broad reference and Waves was really South Chicamacomico. The variant Waves P.O. (Post Office) is important because its use and cartographic application continued for about 50 years indicating a reluctance to give up using the original name of Chicamacomico. The increased tourist trade completed the transition.

WAVES LANDING A landing in Dare County, Kennekeet Township at 35°34′02″N 75°28′14″W and located on the Rodanthe map. The landing is just west of Waves and 1.9 mi. (3.1 km) north of Salvo. **Historical note** See Waves for an explanatory note.

Waves P.O. See Waves

WEIR POINT A point of land in Dare County, Nags Head Township at 35°55′30″N 75°43′27″W and located on the Manteo map. The point is on the northwest part of Roanoke Island 2.7 mi. (4.3 km) northwest of Manteo and 1.2 mi. (1.9 km) west southwest of Fort Raleigh National Historic Site. **Other names** Weirs Point **Historical note** A weir is a net, stake or some kind of enclosure set in the water for catching fish. The original meaning of the term was simply fishing place, but has evolved to include the many mechanisms employed at "the fishing place." The name is descriptive of the activity near this point.

Weirs Point See Weir Point

WELLS BAY A bay, 1 mi. (1.6 km) wide, in Currituck County, Poplar Branch Township at 36°18′45″N 75°50′43″W and located on the Mossey Islands map. The cove is in Currituck Sound just west of Mossey Islands, 4.5 mi. (7.2 km) south southwest of Corolla, and 11.9 mi. (19 km) north northwest of Duck. **Other names** Wells Creek and Wills Bay

WELLS CREEK A water passage in Currituck County, Poplar Branch Township at 36°17′55″N 75°49′25″W and located on the Mossey Islands map. It is located in Currituck Sound just southeast of Mossey Islands and separated from Sanders Creek by Sedge Island, 1 mi. (1.6 km) southwest of Three Dunes, 5.5 mi. (8.8 km) south of Corolla and 10.6 mi. (16.7 km) north northwest of Duck.

Wells Creek See Wells Bay

Wells Creek See Wells Creek Inlet

WELLS CREEK INLET A former water passage in Hyde County, Ocracoke Township at 35°08′20″N 75°53′30″W and located but not shown on the Green Island map. The inlet was located about 6 mi. (9.6 km) northeast of the village of Ocracoke. **Other names** Wells Creek, Wells Inlet, and West Inlet **Historical note** The inlet was open for only about ten years in the mid-nineteenth century and is shown on only a few maps. There is very little information available for this feature, but evidence and local opinion supports the location near Try Yard Creek.

Wells Inlet See Wells Creek Inlet

WELLS POND A cove, 0.1 mi. (0.2 km) wide, in Currituck County, Poplar Branch Township at 36°19′05″N 75°50′42″W and located on the Mossey

Islands map. The cove is just north of Wells Bay, 4.2 mi. (6.7 km) south of Corolla and 12.4 mi. (19.8 km) northwest of Duck. **Other names** Wills Pond

Wercester Inlet See Trinitie Harbor

West End See Northwest Point

Western Rocks See Oyster Rocks

WEST HILL A hill, 50.9 ft. (15.5 m) high, in Dare County, Atlantic Township at 36°01'00"N 75°40'30"W and located on the Kitty Hawk map. The stabilized dune is on Currituck Banks, 0.4 mi. (0.6 km) west northwest of Kill Devil Hill, 3.9 mi. (6.2 km) southeast of Kitty Hawk and 4.7 mi. (7.5 km) northwest of Nags Head.

West Hill See Kill Devil Hill

West Inlet See Old Hatteras Inlet

West Inlet See Wells Creek Inlet

WEST MOUTH BAY A bay, 1 mi. (1.6 km) wide, in Carteret County, Harkers Island Township at 34°42'17"N 76°33'15"W and located on the Harkers Island map. The bay is located in The Straits and separates the north part of Harkers island from Browns Island, 0.8 mi. (1.3 km) north of the village of Harkers Island. **Other names** Westmouth Bay

Westmouth Bay See West Mouth Bay

West Point of Roanoke Island See Northwest Point

Whalebone See Whalebone Junction

Whale Bone See Whalebone Junction

WHALEBONE INLET A former water passage, 0.7 mi. (1.1 km) long, in Carteret County, Portsmouth Township at 35°01'02"N 76°06'53"W and located on the Portsmouth map. The inlet was in Pamlico Sound and separated The High Hills on Portsmouth Island from Whalebone Island, 4.7 mi. (7.5 km) southwest of the village of Portsmouth and 10.7 mi. (17.1 km) southwest of the village of Ocracoke. **Other names** High Hills Inlet and Wococon Inlet **Historical note** The inlet opened in 1865 and closed in the early 1900s. It reopened in 1940 and closed again in the early 1960s. Some local usage is for the variant name High Hills Inlet, but all map references use the name Whalebone Inlet.

Whalebone Inlet See Swash Inlet

WHALEBONE ISLAND An island, 0.5 mi. (0.8 km) long, in Carteret County, Portsmouth Township at 35°01'10"N 76°07'04"W and located on the Portsmouth map. The island is located in Pamlico Sound just south of Whalebone Inlet, 4.9 mi. (7.8 km) southwest of the village of Portsmouth and 10.9 mi. (17.4 km) southwest of the village of Ocracoke.

WHALEBONE JUNCTION An area in Dare County, Nags Head Township at 35°54'28"N 75°35'53"W and located on the Roanoke Island NE map. It is a small locality that grew around an intersection, but is now part of Nags Head 2.5 mi. (4 km) south of the center of Nags Head. **Other names** Whalebone, Whale Bone, and Whale Bone Junction **Historical note** The name was applied to the junction of U.S. Highways 64 and 158 and State Highway 12 because the owner of a service station at the junction displayed the skeleton of a whale that had washed ashore in the 1930s.

Whale Bone Junction See Whalebone Junction

WHALE CREEK A cove, 0.3 mi. (0.5 km) wide, in Carteret County, Harkers Island Township at 34°40′17″N 76°35′42″W and located on the Harkers Island map. The cove is located in Back Sound just off Shackleford Banks at Cabs Creek, 2.5 mi. (4 km) south southwest of the village of Harkers Island and 4.8 mi. (7.7 km) northwest of Barden Inlet.

WHALE CREEK A former populated place in Carteret County, Harkers Island Township at 34°40′10″N 76°35′47″W and formerly located but not named on the Harkers Island map. The community of several families was located on central Shackleford Banks at Whale Creek 2.5 mi. (4 km) south southwest of the village of Harkers Island.

WHALE HEAD BAY A bay, 1.2 mi. (1.9 km) wide, in Currituck County, Fruitville Township at 36°22′05″N 75°49′55″W and located on the Mossey Islands map. The bay is in Currituck Sound 1 mi. (1.6 km) south of Corolla and 2.7 mi. (4.3 km) north of Mossey Islands.

WHALE HEAD HILL A sand dune, 13 ft. (4 m) high, in Currituck County, Fruitville Township at 36°21′54″N 75°49′35″W and located on the Mossey Islands map. The sand dune is 0.7 mi. (1.1 km) south of Currituck Beach and 1 mi. (1.6 km) south of Corolla. **Other names** Whaleshead, Whales Head, Whales Head Barchane and Whales Head Hill **Historical note** The variant name Whales Head Barchane has been used by some authors because some of the dunes in this area are crescent-shaped and some have suggested that these dunes are known locally as Whales Heads. This is not locally substantiated.

Whaleshead See Whale Head Hill

Whales Head See Corolla

Whales Head See Whale Head Hill

Whales Head Barchane See Whale Head Hill

Whales Head Hill See Whale Head Hill

WHITE ASH SWAMP A swamp, 1 mi. (1.6 km) wide, in Carteret County, Morehead Township at 34°41′50″N 76°49′45″W and located but not named on the Mansfield map. The swamp is just west of Hoop Pole Woods and 5.1 mi. (8.2 km) west of Atlantic Beach. **Historical note** The name is descriptive of the vegetation found here, and the name has been in use since the earliest maps of the area were published.

WHITEHURST ISLAND An island, 0.3 mi. (0.5 km) long, in Carteret County, Harkers Island Township at 34°39′15″N 76°31′09″W and located on the Harkers Island map. It is a marsh island at the junction of Core Sound and Back Sound, 1.6 mi. (2.6 km) north of Barden Inlet and 3.7 mi. (5.9 km) south southeast of the village of Harkers Island.

WHITE POINT A point of land in Carteret County, Harkers Island Township at 34°42′02″N 76°33′09″W and located on the Harkers Island map. It is a marsh point at the north entrance to Henry Jones Creek on Harkers Island 0.5 mi. (0.8 km) north northeast of the village of Harkers Island.

WHITE SHOAL A shoal in Carteret County, Portsmouth Township at 35°05′10″N 76°03′45″W and located but not shown on the Portsmouth map. The shoal is in Pamlico Sound, 0.9 mi. (1.4 km) north of the village of Portsmouth and 5.4 mi. (8.6 km) west southwest of the village of Ocracoke.

WHITE SHOAL MARSH An island, 0.2 mi. (0.3 km) long, in Carteret County, Harkers Island Township at 34°39′57″N 76°33′37″W and located on the Harkers Island map. It is a marsh island 2.1 mi. (3.4 km) south of the village of Harkers Island and 2.9 mi. (4.6 km) northwest of Barden Inlet.

Wilets Hill See Poyners Hill

WILLIAMS POINT A former point of land in Hyde County, Ocracoke Township at 35°04′30″N 76°00′00″W and located but not named on the Ocracoke and Portsmouth maps. The feature was the former terminus of Ocracoke Island, 2.5 mi. (4 km) southwest of the village of Ocracoke. **Historical note** Today, Ocracoke Island extends 1 mi. (1.6 km) beyond the original application of the name Williams Point.

WILLIS CREEK A cove, 0.1 mi. (0.2 km) long, in Carteret County, Portsmouth Township at 35°03′45″N 76°04′23″W and located on the Portsmouth map. The cove joins Bill Salters Creek in southeast Casey Bay 0.8 mi. (1.3 km) southwest of the village of Portsmouth and 7.2 mi. (11.5 km) southwest of the village of Ocracoke.

WILLIS LANDING A landing in Carteret County, Morehead Township at 34°41′45″N 76°47′44″W and located on the Mansfield map. The landing is on Bogue Banks (ocean side) at Hoop Pole Woods 2.2 mi. (4 km) west of Atlantic Beach and 5.1 mi. (8.2 km) southwest of the mainland town of Morehead City.

WILLOW POND A flat, 5 ft. (1.5 m) high, in Carteret County, Harkers Island Township at 34°41′20″N 76°32′04″W and located on the Harkers Island map. The flat is a drained area on the southwest part of Harkers Island 1.7 mi. (2.7 km) east southeast of the village of Harkers Island.

Wills Bay See Wells Bay

Wills Pond See Wells Pond

WIMBLE SHOALS Shoals in Dare County, Kennekeet Township at 35°32′45″N 75°25′45″W and located but not shown on the Rodanthe map. The shoals are in the Atlantic Ocean, 3 mi. (4.2 km) southeast of Rodanthe, 15 mi. (24 km) south of Oregon Inlet and 20 mi. (32 km) north northeast of Cape Hatteras. **Other names** Five Fathoms Bank **Historical note** These shoals are the remnants of Cape Kenrick (q.v.) and named for James Wimble who charted the shoals in the eighteenth century.

Wimble Shoals See Cape Kenrick

WINDMILL POINT A point of land in Hyde County, Ocraocke Township at 35°06′50″N 75°59′25″W and located on the Ocracoke map. The point is on Ocracoke Island at the southern entrance to Silver Lake 0.4 mi. (0.6 km) west of the village of Ocracoke. **Historical note** The feature is so named because a windmill was at one time on this point of land. Windmills were prominent throughout the Outer Banks in the eighteenth and nineteenth centuries, but only a few place name references indicate their previous use.

WINTER MARSH A marsh, 0.5 mi. (0.8 km) across, in Currituck County, Poplar Branch Township at 36°14′08″N 75°46′45″W and located but not named on the Jarvisburg map. The marsh is just west of Currituck Banks, 5.3 mi. (8.5 km) north northwest of Duck and 10.2 mi. (16.3 km) southeast of Corolla.

WISES CREEK A former tidal stream in Dare County, Kennekeet Township at approximately 35°45′35″N 75°31′15″W and located but not shown on the Oregon Inlet map. The tidal stream was located on Pea Island about 1.5 mi. (2.4 km) southeast of Oregon Inlet and about 8 mi. (12 km) southeast of Wanchese. **Historical note** The feature no longer exists in its original form.

Woccock See Ocracoke

Woccock See Ocracoke Island

Woccock Inlet See Ocracoke Inlet

Woccocon See Ocracoke Island

Wococan See Ocracoke

Wococock See Ocracoke Island

Wococock Inlett See Ocracoke Inlet

WOCOCON A former island. The name was applied on early maps to most of present Ocracoke Island from Old Hatteras Inlet (q.v.) southwest to Ocracoke Inlet. **Other names** Gordons Ile, Vokokon, Wocotan, and Wosoton **Historical note** The name was misapplied by early map-makers. The word generally means fort or enclosed place and probably referred to a specific site in the general vicinity of the present village of Ocracoke.

Wococon See Ocracoke

Wococon See Ocracoke Island

Wococon See Portsmouth Island

Wococon Inlet See Ocracoke Inlet

Wococon Inlet See Whalebone Inlet

Wococon Inlett See Ocracoke Inlet

Wococon Island See Core Banks

Wocoken Inlet See Ocracoke Inlet

Wocokon See Ocracoke

Wocokon See Ocracoke Island

Wocotan See Ocracoke Island

Wocotan See Wococon

Wokokon See Ocracoke Island

Wokokon Inlet See Ocracoke Inlet

Wokoton Inlet See Ocracoke Inlet

WOOD ISLAND An island, 0.4 mi. (0.6 km) long, in Carteret County, White Oak Township at 34°41′10″N 76°57′07″W and located on the Salter Path map. The island is in Bogue Sound 0.6 mi. (1 km) north of Emerald Isle and 4.5 mi. (7.2 km) west of Salter path. **Other names** Cat Island

WOODLEIGH A populated place in Currituck County, Fruitville Township at 36°31′32″N 75°55′07″W and located but not named on the Knotts Island map. It is a scattered community on Knotts Island 1.1 mi. (1.8 km) north northeast of the village of Knotts Island.

Worcester Inlet See Trinitie Harbor

Wosoton See Ocracoke Island

Wosoton See Wococon

Wosoton Inlet See Ocracoke Inlet

Woston Inlet See Ocracoke Inlet

WRECK CREEK A cove, 0.7 mi. (1.1 km) long and 0.1 mi. (0.2 km) wide, in Dare County, Kennekeet Township at 35°39′50″N 75°29′14″W and located on the Pea Island map. The cove trends east-west in Pamlico Sound and separates Cedar Hammock from Goulds Lump 4.9 mi. (7.8 km) north northwest of Rodanthe.

WRECK HILL A sand dune in Dare County, Nags Head Township at approximately 35°51′00″N 75°34′40″W and located but not named on the Oregon Inlet map. The dune is located on Bodie Island in the general vicinity east of Tommy Hammock and about 3 mi. (4.8 km) east of Wanchese. **Other names** Hill of the Wreck and Lookout Hill **Historical note** Only remnants of this dune remain today.

WRECK POINT A point of land in Carteret County, Harkers Island Township at 34°37′04″N 76°32′21″W and located on the Cape Lookout map. The point is on a projection of sand into Lookout Bight and partly submerged at times. It is 0.9 mi. (1.4 km) north of the former village of Cape Lookout and 5.2 mi. (8.3 km) south of the village of Harkers Island.

WRIGHT BROTHERS NATIONAL MEMORIAL A monument, 88.6 ft. (27 m) high, in Dare County, Atlantic Township at 36°00′52″N 75°40′10″W and located on the Kitty Hawk map. The monument is on Currituck Banks at the summit of Kill Devil Hill 3.7 mi. (5.9 km) south southeast of Kitty Hawk and 4.3 mi. (6.9 km) north northwest of Nags Head.

Y

Yankee Pond See Little Yankee Pond

YAUPON HAMMOCK GUT A cove, 0.2 mi.(0.3 km) wide, in Carteret County, Portsmouth Township at 34°48′57″N 76°22′23″W and located on the Styron Bay map. The cove is in Core Sound 5 mi. (8 km) south of the mainland town of Atlantic. **Historical note** Yaupon is a member of the Holly family and in the southern United States, especially on the Outer Banks, has been used as a substitute for tea. This yaupon tea is also known as "the black drink" and has quite a strong taste and pungent odor.

YELLOW HILL LANDING A landing in Carteret County, White Oak Township at 35°40′40″N 76°57′30″W and located on the Salter Path map. The landing is on Bogue Banks (sound side) at Emerald Isle 5 mi. (8 km) west of Salter Path.

Z

ZACK CREEK A water passage, 0.6 mi. (1 km) long, in Carteret County, Smyrna Township at 34°42′43″N 76°28′02″W and located on the Horsepen Point map. The water passage is in Core Sound and separates an unnamed marsh island from Cowpen Island 4.9 mi. (7.8 km) east of the village of Harkers Island.

About the Author

Roger L. Payne is a native of Winston-Salem, North Carolina, and now resides in northern Virginia. He is a geographer and a historian who specializes in automated data processing, toponomy, and locational analysis. He holds a bachelors degree in geography and history and a masters degree in geography from East Carolina University, and his professional experience includes automated names processing and extensive field work on the Outer Banks. Mr. Payne is a geographer at the U.S. Geological Survey's National Headquarters and is Chief of the Geographic Names Information Section as well as manager of the Geographic Names Information System. He has written several manuals and books on automated name processing and has presented a number of papers concerning place names and the processing and analysis of place names.

This book was prepared by the author as a private individual without any contribution of government facilities, funds, materials or information which is not readily available or that may be made available to the general public upon request to the U.S. government or the U.S. Geological Survey.